Good Housekeeping Institute has been
caring about good cooking for over
40 years. In the Institute's unique
testing kitchens recipes are devised,
cooked and tasted and then tested
over and over again to guarantee
that you get perfect results.
With Good Housekeeping cookery
books you buy more than a collection
of recipes – you buy a share of the
Institute's long experience and an
open invitation to ask the experts for
advice on your cookery problems.
All you have to do is to write to
Good Housekeeping Institute,
Chestergate House, Vauxhall Bridge
Road, London, S.W.1.
This series of Good Housekeeping
cookery books contains all the best of
the huge collection of recipes which
have been cooked, tested and
photographed in Good Housekeeping
Institute.

GOOD HOUSEKEEPING LIBRARY
OF COOKING
A complete list of titles

Fish and Shellfish

GOOD HOUSEKEEPING LIBRARY OF COOKING

SPHERE BOOKS LTD.
30/32 Grays Inn Road, London W.C.1.

First published in Great Britain in 1969
by Sphere Books

© National Magazine Co. Ltd. 1969

Set in Times New Roman

Four-colour illustrations printed by
Acorn-Typesetting and Litho Services Ltd.
Feltham, Middx.

Text printed and bound by C. Nicholls & Company, Ltd., Manchester.

Contents

List of
Colour Plates

CHAPTER 1

Fish cookery

In this preliminary chapter we give detailed practical guidance on buying and preparing fish and the different methods of cooking it. For sauces, stuffings, accompaniments and garnishes, turn to Chapter 7, page 138; this also contains recipes for the different kinds of pastry needed for certain fish dishes and savouries.

Throughout the book, recipes are for four people unless otherwise indicated. When a whole fish is cooked, the number of servings obviously depends on the size of the fish.

Buying Fish

Use fish when it is in season and at its best. Some kinds can be bought all the year round, others have a close season (usually covering the spawning period). The Dictionary of Fish at the end of the book gives details on seasons, etc. Frozen fish is of course available all the year round.

Buy fish the day you intend to use it. Look for firm flesh, silvery scales, clear markings, red gills and bright eyes; reject any fish that does not have a fresh smell. (Colour picture No. 1).

Most frozen fish and shellfish are of high quality, there is no waste and they are quick to cook. The freezing does not affect the flavour or the food value. Frozen fish can be bought in a variety of ways – whole, filleted, in cutlets, or as fingers or cakes. Use it like fresh fish, but follow the manufacturers' individual instructions concerning storage, thawing and cooking.

Cleaning Fish

Whole Fish: Remove any scales by using a knife and scraping from tail to head, rinse frequently.

To remove the entrails from round-bodied fish such as herrings or trout, make a slit along the abdomen from the gills

7

half-way to the tail, draw out the insides and clean away any blood. Rub with a little salt to remove the black skin.

With flat fish, such as sole and plaice, open the cavity which lies in the upper part of the body under the gills and clean out the entrails in the same way.

Cut off the fins and gills, if the fish is to be served whole. The head and tail may be cut off if you prefer, but if the head is left on, take out the eyes. Rinse the fish in cold water.

Fillets and Cutlets: Wash and then wipe with a paper towel.

Skinning Fish

Whole Flat Fish (e.g. sole): Wash the fish and cut off the fins, using a really sharp, pliable knife. Make an incision across the tail, slip the thumb between the skin and the flesh and loosen the dark skin round the sides of the fish. Hold the fish down firmly with one hand and with the other take hold of the skin and draw it off quickly, upwards towards the head. (Dip your fingers in some salt to get a good grip.) The white skin can be removed in the same way, but unless the fish is particularly large, it is generally left on.

Fillets of Flat Fish (e.g. plaice): Lay the fillet on a board, skin side down, salt the fingers and hold the tail end of the skin firmly with the fingers. Then separate the flesh from the skin by sawing with a sharp knife from side to side, pressing the flat of the blade against the flesh. Keep the edge of the blade close to the skin while cutting, but don't press it down at too sharp an angle or the skin will be cut.

Round Fish (e.g. haddock): These are more usually cooked with the skin on, but if you want them skinned, start from the head.

Cut off a narrow strip of skin along the spine and cut across the skin just below the head; loosen the skin under the head with the point of a sharp knife, dip the fingers in salt and gently pull the skin down towards the tail, working carefully to avoid breaking the flesh. Skin the other side of the fish.

Filleting Fish

Flat Fish (e.g. plaice): Four fillets are taken from one fish, two from each side. Using a small, sharp-pointed knife, make an incision straight down the back of the fish, following the line of the bone. Insert the knife under the flesh and carefully remove it with long, clean strokes. Take the first fillet from the left-hand side of the fish, working from head to tail, then turn the fish round and cut off the second fillet from tail to head. Fillet the other side of the fish in the same way. When this is finished, no flesh should be left on the bone.

8

Round Fish (e.g. haddock): Cut along the centre of the back to the bone, using a sharp knife, and cut along the abdomen of the fish. Remove the flesh cleanly from the bones, working from the head down, pressing the knife against the bones and working with short, sharp strokes. Remove the fillet from the other side in the same way. If the fish is large, cut the fillets into serving-size pieces. Skin the fillets or not, as preferred.

Herring and Mackerel: Cut off the head, tail and fins. Split the fish open along the underside, remove the entrails and rub off the black inner skin, using a little salt on the fingers. Put the fish on a board, cut side down, and press lightly with the fingers down the middle of the back to loosen the bone. Turn the fish over and ease the backbone up with the fingers, removing with it as many of the small bones as possible. If the fish contains roes, remove these before filleting it (to cook and serve with the fish or to use separately, as you prefer).

Methods of Cooking Fish

These are general directions – you must follow individual recipes for any specialised points. A selection of sauces, stuffings and accompaniments is given in a separate chapter.

POACHING
Suitable for:
   Fillets, steaks or small whole fish – halibut, turbot, brill, haddock, flounder, salmon, salmon trout, smoked haddock, kippers.

Although we sometimes speak of "boiling" fish, true boiling spoils it and it should actually be poached – that is, simmered in the liquid. The cooking may be done either in a saucepan on top of the stove or in a shallow covered casserole in a moderate oven (350°F., mark 4).

Whole fish and large pieces are usually cooked on top of the stove, completely covered with the liquid. This may be salted water, flavoured with some of the following: parsley sprigs, a small piece of onion and/or carrot, a few mushroom stalks, a squeeze of lemon juice, ½ a bay leaf or some peppercorns. For the more classic dishes you can cook whole fish such as trout and large pieces such as salmon or turbot in a court-bouillon. (See the recipe given overleaf.)

Heat the liquid until it is simmering, put in the fish, cover and simmer very gently until it is tender, allowing 10–15 minutes per lb., according to the thickness of the cut, or about 20 minutes for a small piece. Drain the fish, place it on a

9

hot dish and serve with a sauce made from the cooking liquid (see p. 140, Sauces chapter). Alternatively, serve the poached fish cold, in aspic or with a mayonnaise dressing.

Fish fillets are often cooked in the oven and they need only be half-covered with cold liquid – whether seasoned milk and water, cider or dry white wine – which is then used as basis for a sauce to accompany the cooked fish.

COURT-BOUILLON FOR POACHED FISH

1 quart water (or dry white wine and water mixed)
1 small carrot, sliced
1 small onion, sliced
1 small stalk of celery, scrubbed and chopped (optional)

1 tbsp. vinegar or lemon juice
A few sprigs of parsley
½ a bay leaf
3–4 peppercorns
2 level tsps. salt

Place all the ingredients in a pan and simmer for ½ hour. Allow to cool and, if preferred, strain the liquid before using it.

STEAMING

Suitable for: Thin fillets of sole, plaice.

Wash and wipe the fish and lay it on a greased plate; dot with a few pieces of butter, add 1 tbsp. milk and a little salt and pepper, cover with another plate and place over a pan of boiling water. Cook for 10–15 minutes. The liquid round the fish plus a little milk can be made into a sauce – for instance, parsley, shrimp, egg or cheese. (See Sauces chapter, p. 138.)

GRILLING

Suitable for:

Small fish, thin fillets and thicker cuts – sole, plaice, halibut, turbot, hake, brill, cod, haddock, flounder, salmon, salmon trout, trout, herring, mackerel, smoked haddock, kippers.

Wash the fish. If it is whole, remove the scales and fins. When it is too plump to allow the heat to penetrate easily (e.g. herring, mackerel) make three or four diagonal cuts in the body on each side. White fish such as plaice, halibut, sole, cod and haddock should be brushed with oil or melted butter to prevent drying, but oily ones like herrings, mackerel and salmon do not need it.

Thin fillets or steaks can be cooked by grilling on one side only, but thicker pieces or whole fish should be turned once (use a fish slice or palette knife) to ensure thorough cooking on both sides.

Cook under a moderate heat, allowing 4–5 minutes for thin fillets, 10–15 minutes for thicker fillets, steaks and small whole fish.

10

Serve with maître d'hôtel or melted butter (see p. 146), lemon wedges and parsley.

FRYING

Most fish can be fried and the method is especially good for those that have little natural flavour or colour. Both shallow and deep-fat frying are used. Wash and dry the fish and coat it well with one of the following:

SEASONED FLOUR. Mix about 2 level tbsps. flour with about 1 level tsp. salt and a good sprinkling of pepper. Either pat it on to the fish or dip the pieces in the flour and shake them gently before cooking.

EGG AND CRUMBS. Have a beaten egg on a plate and some fresh white or dry bread-crumbs on a piece of kitchen paper. Dip the fish in the egg and lift it out, letting it drain for a second or two. Transfer it to the crumbs and tip the paper until the fish is well-covered. Press in the crumbs, then shake the fish to remove any surplus.

COATING BATTER. See under Deep-frying, p. 12.

Chipped potatoes are a very popular accompaniment for most fried fish. Any sauce should be served separately.

SHALLOW FRYING

Suitable for:
  Fillets, steaks and small whole fish – sole, plaice, dabs, bass, bream, cod, haddock, mackerel, herring, trout, perch, pike – also for fish cakes etc.

Coat the fish with seasoned flour or with egg and bread-crumbs. Heat some shallow fat gently until it is fairly hot – if you let it smoke it is too hot. Lard or oil is generally used, but for fish cooked à la meunière (see below), butter is essential. Put in the piece of fish so that the side which you wish to be uppermost when it is served goes down first into the fat or oil. Cook gently and when the first side is browned (about 5 minutes), turn the fish and cook the other side. Allow about 10 minutes in all, according to thickness. Use a slice or palette knife to turn fish and to lift it out of the pan. Drain well on crumpled kitchen paper and serve with lemon and parsley or maître d'hôtel butter.

FRYING À LA MEUNIÈRE

Suitable for:
  Fillets or whole fish – sole, plaice, trout, pike, perch.

Shallow-fry the fish in butter as described above. When it is

11

cooked, transfer it to a hot dish. Lightly brown a little extra butter in the frying-pan, add a squeeze of lemon juice and pour it over the fish. Garnish with chopped parsley.

DEEP FRYING
(See colour picture No. 2)
Suitable for:
Fillets coated with batter or egg and bread-crumbs, small whole fish – cod, haddock, hake, whiting, coley, gurnet, skate, sprats, smelts, fresh sardines, whitebait; also fish cakes, etc.

You need a deep pan with a wire basket (except for batter-coated fish), and enough fat (2–3 lb.) or oil to come about three-quarters up the pan. Clarified dripping, lard and cooking oil are suitable. The fat must be pure and free from moisture.

Heat the fat to 350°–370°F. A simple way to test it is to put in a 1-inch cube of bread, which should brown in 60 seconds. If the fat is too cool, the fish will be soggy; if it is too hot, the outside will brown before the inside is cooked. While the fat is heating coat the fish with batter (see below) or with egg and bread-crumbs.

Lower the fish gently into the fat, using the basket for egg-and-crumbed pieces; cook only a little at a time, to avoid lowering the temperature. As soon as the fish is golden-brown – 5–10 minutes – lift it out and drain it really well on crumpled kitchen paper before serving. The fat may be strained into a clean basin and kept for future use.

COATING BATTER – 1

4 oz. flour
A pinch of salt
1 egg

¼ pint milk or milk and water (approx.)

Mix the flour, salt, egg and sufficient liquid to give a stiff batter which will coat the back of the spoon; beat well until smooth. Dip the fish into the batter, holding the pieces on a skewer or fork, and drain slightly before putting into the hot fat.

COATING BATTER – 2

4 oz. flour
A pinch of salt
1 tbsp. oil

1 egg, separated
2–3 tbsps. water or milk and water

Mix the flour, salt, oil and egg yolk with sufficient water to give a stiff batter which will coat the back of the spoon; beat until smooth. Just before using, whisk the egg-white stiffly and fold it into the batter. Dip the fish pieces into seasoned flour before coating them as above.

This method gives a lighter, crisper batter than the first.

12

BAKING

Suitable for:

Fillets, steaks, cuts from large fish and small whole fish – cod, haddock, hake, whiting, sole, plaice, turbot, halibut, salmon.

Unless otherwise directed in the particular recipe, use a moderate oven (350°F., mark 4).

Wash and wipe the fish and prepare according to type. Put in a stuffing if you wish and place the fish in an ovenproof dish. Add 3–4 tbsps. milk or white or red wine and a bouquet garni (or a small piece of onion and ½ a bay leaf). Cover with a lid or foil and bake in the centre of the oven until tender – allow 10–20 minutes for fillets, 20 minutes for steaks, 25–30 minutes for small, whole fish.

Alternatively, place the prepared fish on buttered foil, add a squeeze of lemon juice and a sprinkling of salt and pepper, wrap loosely and put on a baking tray. Bake in the centre of the oven, allowing about 20 minutes for a steak and 6–10 minutes per lb. plus 6–10 minutes over for large pieces, according to size. This method is particularly suitable for thicker cuts and whole fish.

FLAKED FISH

Almost all made-up fish dishes require cooked flaked fish, which is prepared as follows:

Wash the fish, put it in a pan, cover with cold water, add a little salt and cover with a lid. Bring slowly to the boil, turn off the heat and leave the fish covered for 5 minutes. Drain off the liquid (this can be used with an equal amount of milk for making a sauce – see p. 140). Skin the fish, flake roughly and remove any bones.

Herbs for Flavouring

Many of the recipes for fish casseroles, soups and so on suggest flavouring the liquor or sauce with a bouquet garni – a small bunch of herbs tied together in muslin or with a thread round the stalks. Here are two versions:

TRADITIONAL BOUQUET GARNI

A bay leaf	Tied with a small piece of leek leaf; if peppercorns are included use muslin
A sprig of parsley	
A sprig of thyme	
A few peppercorns (optional)	

You can, of course, choose other herbs, or include some dried ones – mixed or otherwise.

BOUQUET GARNI USING DRIED HERBS

A small bay leaf
A pinch of mixed dried herbs
6 peppercorns

1 clove
A pinch of dried parsley

Tie the herbs together in a small square of muslin with a string or cotton, leaving a long end free to tie the bouquet garni to the handle of the saucepan.

Fish Cookery Hints

1. Fish is sufficiently cooked when it will readily separate from the bone (test with the back of a knife), or when the flesh is white and firm.
2. Frozen fish can be substituted in many of the recipes in this book; canned fish is good in made-up dishes.
3. To minimise the smell of such fish as herrings, cook in a covered container or wrap in greaseproof paper or aluminium foil.
4. Wipe fish pans, dishes and cutlery with soft paper immediately after use and rinse in cold water. A little mustard in the washing-up water will help to kill the smell.

14

CHAPTER 2

Fish "Starters"

A very wide range of fish may be used in the first course of a meal, and this is a particularly good way of serving the more expensive kinds, since only a small amount is required. Fish cocktails are frequently made with shellfish, so a variety of such recipes is included here, together with scallops and mussels served as hors d'oeuvre; for other shellfish recipes, see the special chapter later in this book, page 96.

Thin brown bread and butter is often served with fish hors d'oeuvre.

CRAB OR LOBSTER COCKTAIL

4–6 oz. flaked crab or lobster meat
¼ lettuce, washed and shredded
2 tbsps. mayonnaise or salad cream
2 tbsps. tomato ketchup
2 tbsps. single cream
Salt and pepper
A squeeze of lemon juice or a dash of Worcestershire sauce
Cucumber slices, capers or lemon wedges to garnish

Crabmeat may be either fresh or canned – if fresh, use only the white meat; lobster, too, may be either fresh or canned. Line some small glasses with shredded lettuce. Mix the remaining ingredients to make a dressing. Combine the fish and dressing, pile into the glasses and garnish.

Alternatively, arrange the flaked fish on a lettuce-lined dish as in the colour picture No. 5.

CRAB AND GRAPEFRUIT COCKTAIL

2 grapefruit
8 cooked asparagus tips
2 tbsps. salad oil
1 tsp. lemon juice
Salt and pepper
2 level tbsps. crabmeat
4 tsps. mayonnaise
Chopped parsley

Cut the grapefruit in half, carefully remove the flesh, chop and

15

replace in the grapefruit skins or in glasses. Mix the asparagus with the oil, lemon juice, salt and pepper, pile on the grapefruit and top each with a little crab. To decorate, put 1 tsp. mayonnaise on each portion and garnish with parsley.

DUBLIN BAY PRAWN COCKTAIL

1 doz. Dublin Bay prawns,
 shelled
Lettuce
$\frac{1}{4}$ pint tomato ketchup
2 tsps. vinegar

$\frac{1}{2}$ tsp. Worcestershire
 sauce
$\frac{1}{2}$ tsp. horseradish sauce
Juice of $\frac{1}{2}$ a lemon
A pinch of celery salt

Dice the prawn meat; line some cocktail glasses with lettuce leaves. Mix all the remaining ingredients well together, add the prawn meat and serve in the glasses.

MUSSEL COCKTAIL

$\frac{1}{2}$ pint mussels
Salt and pepper
2 tsps. lemon juice
1 tsp. mayonnaise

$\frac{1}{2}$ tsp. tomato ketchup
A dash of Worcestershire
 sauce

Cook the mussels in a small quantity of water in a covered pan for 5–6 minutes, until the shells gape open. Take out the fish from the shells, reserving some of the liquor, and remove the beard – the small black, weed-like portion. Combine the mussels with the other ingredients, chill and serve in small glasses.

PRAWN COCKTAIL

1 small lettuce, shredded
6–8 oz. prawns (peeled fresh,
 canned, or frozen and
 thawed)
5 tbsps. single cream

2 tbsps. salad cream
2 tbsps. tomato ketchup
Worcestershire sauce
Salt and pepper
Lemon slices

Divide the lettuce between 4 small glasses and top with prawns. Mix the cream, salad cream and ketchup, season with Worcestershire sauce, salt and pepper and spoon over the prawns. Garnish with lemon.

Alternatively, the prawns may be piled into halved tomatoes and coated with the above dressing (or with mayonnaise and tomato ketchup).

SHRIMP COCKTAIL: Make as above.

SHRIMPS AND MELON
(see colour picture No. 5.)
Cut balls from melon flesh with a Parisian cutter and combine

16

with some prepared shrimps. Spoon a little mayonnaise over and garnish with whole shrimps.

AVOCADO SHRIMP COCKTAIL

2 avocado pears
2 oz. potted shrimps or
  frozen prawns, thawed
Salt

Lemon juice or French
  dressing
Lemon butterflies to
  garnish

Halve the pears and lift out the stones. Season the shrimps or prawns with a little salt and mix with the lemon juice or dressing. Fill the centre of each avocado half with shellfish and garnish with a lemon butterfly.

MARINADED SEAFOOD COCKTAIL

4 oz. prawns or shrimps,
  peeled
1–2 tbsps. dry white wine
2 tbsps. tomato ketchup
2 tbsps. salad cream
1 tbsp. single cream

1 tbsp. white wine or medium
  sherry
Salt, pepper and cayenne
  pepper
1 small lettuce, shredded
Lemon wedges

Sprinkle the prawns with wine and leave for ½ hour, turning them from time to time. Make a sauce by combining the ketchup, salad cream, cream and wine or sherry, and seasoning. Divide lettuce between 4 small dishes and place the drained fish on top. Spoon the sauce over just before taking to table. Serve with lemon wedges.

CAVIARE

This is served ice-cold, with freshly made toast and butter. Lemon juice may be sprinkled over it if you wish. Alternatively, spread the caviare on croûtes of fried bread or toast and sprinkle with a few grains of cayenne pepper.

FILLETS OF HERRING PORTUGAIS

1 large herring
1 tsp. olive oil
2 shallots, finely
  chopped
2 tomatoes, skinned

2–3 tbsps. white vinegar
½ pint fish stock or water
2–3 tbsps. tomato paste
Salt and pepper
Cucumber to garnish

Remove the herring head and fillet the fish, then cut each fillet into 2 or 3 pieces. Heat the oil in a small pan and lightly fry the shallots. Cut the tomatoes into even-sized pieces and add to the pan, with the vinegar, stock, tomato paste, salt and pepper. Bring to the boil and simmer for a few minutes until the sauce has thickened. Poach the pieces of herring in the sauce until tender, keeping the lid on. Serve the herring cold, garnished with thin slices of cucumber.

MOULES MARINIÈRE

1 quart fresh mussels
1 pint water
1 onion, skinned and chopped
1 stick of celery, scrubbed and chopped
1 carrot, scraped and chopped
1 clove of garlic, chopped
A bouquet garni (see p. 13)
Salt and pepper
1 oz. butter
3 level tbsps. flour
Chopped parsley to garnish

Wash the mussels, thoroughly scrubbing each shell and scraping the joint to remove the filament; lift the shells out of the water, leaving behind the sediment and filaments. Put the mussels into a large pan with the 1 pint fresh water, the vegetables, garlic, bouquet garni, salt and pepper. Cover, bring to the boil and cook gently for a few minutes, shaking the pan over the heat. As the shells gape, open the mussels, keeping the fish on the half-shell; place in a dish and keep covered to prevent them from drying. Reduce the liquid a little by boiling and remove from the heat. Work together the butter and flour and stir in the liquid. Return the mixture to the pan, stirring well until it thickens. Pour the sauce over the mussels and sprinkle with parsley.

SAVOURY MUSSELS

3 tbsps. olive oil
1 small onion, chopped
2 leeks, prepared
2 tomatoes, skinned and cut up
1 clove of garlic, chopped
A sprig of thyme
Bay leaf
A pinch of saffron
Salt
Coarsely ground pepper
¼ pint dry white wine or water
1 pint mussels, cleaned
Chopped parsley

Heat the oil in a thick-bottomed pan and add the chopped onion and the white part of the leeks, sliced thinly. Cook for a few minutes, then add the tomatoes, garlic, thyme and bay leaf, saffron, salt and pepper and wine, if used. Continue to cook for a few minutes until the mixture is somewhat reduced, then add the mussels. Put on the lid and shake the pan occasionally. The shells will soon open, but keep the pan on the gentle heat for another 5 minutes. Remove the beards from the mussels, then take them out of their shells, place them in the serving dish and pour the strained stock over them. Serve hot or cold, with chopped parsley.

OYSTERS AU NATUREL

Ideally oysters should be eaten as soon as they are opened – and not longer than an hour afterwards. They may be opened by the fishmonger if bought near enough to the serving time, but after a little practice you can learn to open them yourself. Allow 4–6 per person.

Open the oysters, remove the beard from each and loosen the oysters, leaving them in the half-shell. Season lightly and serve with cayenne pepper, thin brown bread and butter, lemon wedges and Tabasco sauce (optional).

SMOKED (CANNED) OYSTERS
Remove from the can and drain well. Serve with thin brown bread and butter, lemon wedges and freshly ground black pepper.

BAKED OYSTERS CAPRICE

12–18 oysters
Streaky bacon

1 green pepper, de-seeded

Oven temperature: moderate (350°F., mark 4)

Leave the oysters in the deep shells, with their liquor, and put them on a baking sheet. On top of each oyster place a neat ½-inch square of bacon and a smaller square of green pepper, then a smaller square of bacon on top again. Bake towards the top of the oven for 10–15 minutes, according to size. Serve at once.

OYSTERS AU GRATIN

12 oysters
4 tbsps. single cream

4 level tbsps. grated
Parmesan cheese

Open the oysters, remove the beard and loosen the oysters, but leave them in the half-shell. Pour the cream over, sprinkle with the cheese and cook for 3–4 minutes under a hot grill, until golden and bubbling.

PRAWN AND CUCUMBER CUPS
Cut 1-inch lengths of cucumber and strip off the peel at ¼-inch intervals, to give a striped effect. Scoop out a spoonful of the soft centre part of each chunk and replace it by mayonnaise. Pile a few peeled prawns on top and decorate with a prawn's head. Garnish with crisp lettuce heart.

PRAWN KEBABS
(see colour picture No. 4)

1½–2 doz. Dublin Bay prawns, shelled
Mayonnaise
A pinch of curry powder
Turmeric

Tomato sauce
Chopped parsley
A little finely grated cheese
A small lettuce

Stick the prawns on skewers or cocktail sticks. Mix the mayonnaise with a little curry powder and turmeric, using just

19

enough to flavour it. Dip some of the prawns into the flavoured mayonnaise, some into the tomato sauce and some into chopped parsley; dip the rest into the cheese and then grill them. Put the lettuce into an attractive dish or bowl and fix the skewers of prawns into this. Any extra curry mayonnaise or tomato sauce can be arranged in shells or small basins round the base.

POACHED SCALLOPS
Wash and beard 4–8 scallops and remove any black parts; rinse and dry them. Place in a pan, cover with milk, add about 1 oz. butter and some seasoning and poach them gently for 8–10 minutes, until they are quite cooked. Remove the scallops from the pan and replace them in 4 of the shells, allowing 1–2 per shell, according to size. Make a Béchamel sauce of coating consistency (see recipe on p. 139), using some of the milk in which the scallops were cooked; pour this over the scallops and sprinkle with chopped parsley.

GRILLED SCALLOPS

8 scallops, prepared	1 clove of garlic, skinned and
Olive oil	finely chopped
Salt and pepper	Chopped parsley
2 oz. butter	Lemon

Brush the scallops with oil and sprinkle with salt and pepper. Place under a medium grill and grill for 3–4 minutes on each side, then put on to a very hot dish. Heat 3 tbsps. olive oil with the butter and garlic and pour over the scallops. Garnish with parsley and lemon wedges.

SCALLOPS AU GRATIN

8 scallops, prepared	4 oz. cheese, grated
¾ pint milk	Salt and pepper
1½ oz. butter	Browned crumbs
1½ oz. flour	

Grease 4 individual dishes or deep scallop shells. Cut each scallop into 2–3 pieces and simmer in a little of the milk until tender – about 10 minutes. Drain, reserving the milk, and make this up to ¾ pint.

Melt the butter in the pan, stir in the flour and cook for 2–3 minutes. Remove the pan from the heat and gradually stir in the milk. Bring to the boil and continue to stir until it thickens. Add 3 oz. of the cheese and some salt and pepper. Divide the fish between the dishes or shells and pour the sauce over. Mix the crumbs with the rest of the cheese and sprinkle over the top; brown under a hot grill. Garnish with olives and sliced tomato, or as desired.

BAKED SCALLOPS

Oven temperature: moderate (350°F., mark 4)

Allow 1–2 scallops per person. Clean them and grease one half-shell for each scallop. Coat with bread-crumbs, place the scallop on top and sprinkle with seasoning and a small knob of fat. Cover with fresh white bread-crumbs, add a squeeze of lemon juice and bake for about 30 minutes. Serve with thin bread and butter.

SCALLOPS IN CREAM

6–8 scallops, prepared	1 shallot, skinned and
2 tbsps. olive oil	finely chopped
Lemon juice	2–3 tbsps. white wine
Seasoned flour	¼ pint single cream
2 oz. butter	Salt and cayenne pepper
2 oz. button	2 level tbsps. Parmesan
mushrooms, sliced	cheese, grated

Cut up the scallops. Mix the oil and 1 tsp. lemon juice and marinade the scallops for 1 hour; drain well, then toss in flour and fry gently in the butter. Place the scallops in 4 shells, then fry the mushrooms and shallot lightly in the butter. Add the wine and reduce well, then stir in the cream. Heat gently, season and add a few drops of lemon juice. Pour over the scallops, sprinkle with cheese and brown under the grill.

CHINESE FRIED SCALLOPS

8 scallops, prepared	A little sesame oil
Oil for frying	1 level tsp. salt
A piece of fresh ginger,	Pepper
finely cut	2 level tsps. flour
6 spring onions, finely cut	1 level tsp. monosodium
½ a cucumber, chopped	glutamate
Wine or oyster sauce	

Slice the scallops. Heat the oil, fry the scallops for 5–6 minutes and remove from the pan. Fry the ginger, spring onions and cucumber, put in the scallops and add a few drops of wine or oyster sauce. Add the remaining ingredients, mix well and pour the mixture into 4 of the scallop shells.

SCALLOPS WITH MUSHROOMS

Fry 1 small chopped onion. Prepare and wash 4–8 scallops and poach them in salted water. When they are tender, chop the red and the white part and add to the onion, together with tomato, some parsley, a few cooked mushrooms, salt and pepper. Cook for a few minutes, bind the mixture with a little creamy white sauce, fill the deep shells with it and brown under the grill or in the oven.

SCALLOPS FLORENTINE

Make ½ pint Mornay sauce and keep it hot. Prepare, cook and chop 1 lb. of spinach. Poach 4 prepared scallops in water for 5 minutes. Put the spinach at the base of a flameproof serving dish, place the scallops over this bed of spinach and pour the sauce over. Sprinkle with a little grated cheese and place under a hot grill until browned on top.

CREAMED SHRIMPS

¼ pint peeled shrimps	Salt and pepper
½ pint white sauce	Fresh white bread-crumbs
1 oz. cheese, grated	

Add the shrimps to the white sauce, together with half of the cheese. Season to taste and simmer for 5 minutes. Put the mixture into individual ramekin dishes and sprinkle the top with remaining cheese and a few bread-crumbs. Re-heat under the grill or in a hot oven (425°F., mark 7) for 10 minutes.

FRIED SHRIMPS IN BATTER

Shell ¼ lb. shrimps but leave the tails on; split them, taking care not to cut right through. Make a batter of 2 egg whites and 4 level tbsps. flour. Heat some oil for deep fat frying, dip the shrimps into the batter then drop one by one into the oil. When they are brown and float on the surface, they are ready. Serve hot.

SHRIMPS IN WINE SAUCE

8 oz. shrimps (weight after peeling)	2 tbsps. warm water
1 oz. flour	Salt and pepper
2 tbsps. olive oil	A pinch of cayenne pepper
3 tbsps. white wine	Sliced lemon and chopped
2 tsps. tomato paste	parsley to garnish

Coat the shrimps with flour and fry them in the oil until golden-brown. Add the wine to the shrimps and cook for about 3 minutes. Add the tomato paste, water, salt, pepper and cayenne pepper and cook gently for about 2 minutes. Garnish and serve hot.

SHRIMP BALLS (CHINESE)

1 lb. shrimps, peeled	Deep fat for frying
6 large water chestnuts, peeled and finely chopped	2 medium-sized mushrooms
	1 oz. bamboo shoots
2 tbsps. ginger wine	2 level tbsps. butter
1 level tsp. salt	1 lettuce, finely shredded
1 oz. cornflour	1 tbsp. soy sauce
1 egg, beaten	

Chop the shrimps finely and add to chestnuts. Combine the

ginger wine, salt and cornflour. Add half this mixture to the shrimps and chestnuts and stir in the egg. Drop spoonfuls into deep hot fat, fry until golden-brown, then drain. Slice the mushrooms and bamboo shoots and fry them in the butter with the lettuce; add the remainder of the flavouring mixture and all the soy sauce. Put in the fried shrimp balls and serve very hot.

SHRIMPS IN ASPIC

1 pint liquid aspic jelly
¼ pint peeled shrimps

2 tbsps. white sauce
2 tbsps. mayonnaise

Pour a little aspic jelly into each of 6 dariole moulds and leave to set. Dip some of the shrimps in liquid jelly and arrange them in a pattern on the jelly in the moulds; leave to set, then cover the shrimps with more jelly. Mix together the rest of the shrimps, the sauce, mayonnaise and remaining aspic jelly and fill up the moulds; leave to set firmly and turn out on to a bed of salad.

Prawns may also be served in this way.

POTTED SHRIMPS
(see colour picture No. 8)

1 pint shrimps, picked
4 oz. butter, melted
A pinch of ground mace

A pinch of cayenne pepper
A pinch of ground nutmeg
Clarified butter

Heat the shrimps very slowly in the butter, but without allowing them to come to the boil. Add the seasonings, then pour the shrimps into small pots or glasses. Leave them to become quite cold and cover each pot with a little clarified butter; use within a few days.

Unless the pots are really attractive, turn the shrimps out on to individual plates lined with a few lettuce leaves, but try to retain the shape of the pot. Serve with lemon wedges. brown bread or Melba toast and butter and freshly ground pepper.

FRIED WHITEBAIT
(see colour picture No. 3)

Wash the fish and dry in a cloth. Put 2–3 level tbsps. flour in a dry cloth and toss the whitebait in it a few at a time. Place them in a frying basket. Heat some deep fat until it will brown a 1-inch cube of bread in 1 minute. Fry the whitebait for 2–3 minutes, until lightly browned, then drain them on crumpled kitchen paper. Sprinkle with salt, garnish with lemon and parsley and serve with brown bread and butter.

WHITEBAIT AND BREAD-CRUMB FRITTERS (NEW ZEALAND)

4–6 oz. whitebait
2 eggs
½ level tsp. salt
Pepper

2 large tbsps. fine soft
white bread-crumbs
Butter for frying

Wash the whitebait and dry them in a cloth. Beat the eggs, add the seasoning, crumbs and whitebait and mix. Heat a knob of butter in a frying pan, drop tablespoonfuls of mixture into the fat and fry on both sides. Serve hot, with lemon slices.

SAVOURY COCKLES

1 quart cockles
2 oz. butter
1 tsp. mushroom ketchup

2 tbsps. chopped parsley
Red pepper

Wash the cockles thoroughly. Put them into a pan of cold salted water, bring to the boil and boil for 5 minutes. Drain, then remove all the shells. Melt the butter in a pan and toss the cockles in it, adding the mushroom ketchup. Just before serving, add the chopped parsley. Put the cockles in individual dishes and sprinkle with red pepper.

SNAILS À LA BOURGUIGNONNE

A can of snails, plus empty shells
½ pint dry white wine
Salt and pepper
A bouquet garni

1 small onion, skinned and
chopped
6 cloves
¼ pint brandy (optional)

For the Snail Butter

4 oz. butter
1 shallot, skinned and
chopped
1–2 tsps. chopped parsley

1 clove of garlic, skinned
and crushed
A pinch of mixed spice
Salt and pepper

Put the snails into a large saucepan with the remaining ingredients, cover and cook gently for 1 hour. Allow to cool in the cooking liquid, then drain and push the snails into the shells. To make the dressing, cream the butter with the shallot and other ingredients. Fill up the stuffed snail shells with this butter, place the snails in a shallow ovenproof dish and heat through in a hot oven (425°F., mark 7) for about 10 minutes.

BIRD'S NEST SALAD (Swedish)

4–5 anchovy fillets, chopped
1–2 tbsps. diced pickled
beetroot
1 tbsp. chopped onion

1 tbsp. chopped chives
1 tbsp. capers
1 tbsp. diced cooked potato
2 raw egg yolks

24

Use a small oblong or oval dish. In the middle put 2 small mounds of anchovy, with a little beetroot between them. Arrange concentric rings of the other ingredients around the 2 heaps, pinching in the rings a little at the middle of each long side, to give a figure-of-eight effect. Make a slight depression in the centre of each of the two original mounds and put a raw egg in each "nest". Serve chilled. (2 servings.)

The first person to help himself to this classic Smörgåsbord dish stirs all the ingredients well together to blend them completely.

OTHER FISH HORS D'OEUVRE

ANCHOVIES. Drain and serve on a bed of lettuce, garnished with the chopped white and sieved yolk of a hard-boiled egg.

SARDINES. Drain and serve on a bed of lettuce, garnished with strips of pimiento and chopped parsley. They can be coated with a French dressing or mayonnaise, if not canned in a sauce.

ROLLMOP OR SOUSED HERRINGS. Serve with the liquor in which they were cooked; garnish with chopped parsley or thin onion rings.

BUCKLING. Serve with lemon and bread and butter.

SMOKED COD'S ROE. If bought whole, skin, slice and serve on small leaves of lettuce; if a jar of cod's roe is used, spoon it out on to the individual plates. Serve with thin brown bread and butter, lemon wedges and freshly ground black pepper.

SMOKED EEL. Arrange on a bed of lettuce and serve with thin brown bread and butter, lemon wedges and freshly ground black pepper.

SMOKED HADDOCK Poach and skin the haddock and serve coated with mayonnaise, on a bed of lettuce; garnish with sliced cucumber or cucumber cones.

SMOKED TROUT. Remove the skin from the body of the fish, but leave the head and tail intact. Serve with lemon wedges and horseradish sauce. Alternatively, skin the fish, remove the fillets from the bone and serve on lettuce leaves, with lemon and brown bread.

SMOKED SALMON. Serve thinly sliced with thin brown bread and butter, lemon wedges and paprika pepper. (Allow 1–2 oz. per portion.)

FRESH SALMON. Cold poached salmon can be divided into small portions, dressed with mayonnaise and served on a bed of lettuce. Garnish with cucumber slices or cones.

CHAPTER 3

Everyday recipes for the main course

In general, the recipes in this chapter are arranged in alphabetical order according to the name of the fish used. There follow a number of recipes for dishes in which several kinds of fish could be used equally well; next comes a group of made-up fish dishes, and finally a few fish soup recipes.

Where the method for a sauce or stuffing is not given in the actual recipe, it will be found in Chapter 7, page 138.

SAVOURY COD CUTLETS

4 cod cutlets	2 tsps. lemon juice
2 oz. shrimps	Flour
4 oz. fresh white	2 eggs, beaten
bread-crumbs	Bread-crumbs to coat
Salt and pepper	Deep fat for frying

Dry the cutlets thoroughly. Mix the shrimps, bread-crumbs, seasoning and lemon juice and bind with egg. Spread the mixture on one side of the cutlets only, dip each cutlet in flour. then in egg and bread-crumbs. Place the fish in a frying basket and fry in very hot deep fat for 4–5 minutes, till the cutlets are golden-brown and cooked through. Serve with an anchovy or shrimp sauce, tomatoes and slices of lemon.

COD AU GRATIN

1–1½ lb. cod fillet	3 oz. cheese, grated
A little milk	1 tbsp. chutney
½ oz. butter	2 oz. sultanas
½ oz. flour	Salt and pepper

Oven temperature: moderate (350°F., mark 4)

Skin the fish, place in a buttered dish with some milk, cover with buttered paper and bake in the centre of the oven for 20 minutes. Strain off the liquor and make it up to ½ pint with milk. Melt the butter and add the flour, gradually work in the milk and cook for 3–4 minutes, then add cheese, chutney and sultanas and season to taste. Pour over the flaked fish and return it to the oven for 10 minutes to heat through.

COD À LA HOLLANDAISE

1 lb. cod, cooked	Salt and pepper
1 lb. potatoes, sliced	1 egg yolk, beaten
2 medium-sized onions, skinned and sliced	Chopped parsley
1 oz. butter	1–2 tbsps. browned bread-crumbs
½ oz. flour	A little grated cheese
¾ pint milk	

Flake the cod and boil the potatoes and the onions. Melt the butter, add the flour and cook gently for 2 minutes; add the milk, season and cook for a few minutes, stirring. Pour the sauce on to the egg yolk, stir, return the mixture to the pan and re-heat, but don't boil; add the parsley. Place the potatoes in a greased pie-dish, then lay the onions over them. Add the cod, pour the sauce over and sprinkle with bread-crumbs, then the grated cheese; re-heat under the grill and garnish as desired.

DEVILLED FILLETS OF COD

4 small fillets of cod	1 tsp. vinegar
1 tbsp. olive oil	2 tbsps. browned bread-crumbs
2 level tsps. dry mustard	
Cayenne pepper and salt	1 oz. butter
1 tbsp. chutney	

Oven temperature: moderate (350°F., mark 4)

Wash and dry the fillets and brush them over with olive oil. Mix the mustard, seasonings, chutney and vinegar, spread this mixture on the fillets and place them on a well-greased oven-proof dish. Sprinkle with bread-crumbs and place a dab of butter on top of each. Cover with greaseproof paper and bake in the centre of the oven for 25–30 minutes.

STUFFED COD STEAKS
(see colour picture No. 6)

4 cod steaks (or cutlets)	2 tomatoes, skinned and chopped
½ an onion, skinned and finely chopped	2 oz. fresh white bread-crumbs
4 oz. streaky bacon, rinded and chopped	Salt and pepper
½ oz. butter	¼ pint milk (approx.)

Oven temperature: moderate (350°F., mark 4)

27

Wash and wipe the fish, trim off the fins and remove the central bone with a sharp-pointed knife; place the fish in a greased ovenproof dish. Fry the onion and bacon gently in the butter for about 5 minutes, until soft; stir in the tomatoes and bread-crumbs. Season well and add enough milk to bind the mixture. Fill the centre of each steak with this stuffing, pour 2–3 tbsps. milk round the fish, cover with a lid or foil and bake in the centre of the oven for about 20 minutes. Serve with carrots and peas, or other vegetables.

As an alternative filling use fish forcemeat (made with 2 oz. bread-crumbs) or one of the other stuffings in the Sauces and Stuffings chapter, p. 138.

DEVONSHIRE COD WITH MUSHROOMS

1 lb. cod fillet	Butter
Salt and pepper	¾ oz. flour
1 tomato, skinned and	Creamed potatoes
sliced	1–2 oz. grated cheese
2 oz. mushrooms, chopped	Sliced tomato and parsley
A small bottle of cider	to garnish

Oven temperature: fairly hot (375°F., mark 5)

Cut the cod into small pieces and put it into an ovenproof dish, with a sprinkling of salt and pepper, the tomato and the mushrooms. Almost cover the fish with cider and dot the top with shavings of butter. Cover with a piece of greaseproof paper and bake in the centre of the oven for about 30 minutes. Strain off the liquor and use it to make a sauce, with ¾ oz. butter and the flour; season to taste and pour over the fish. Pipe creamed potatoes around the edge of the dish and sprinkle the fish with grated cheese. Garnish with slices of tomato and return to the oven for 10–15 minutes to brown. Decorate with parsley before serving.

TIPSY COD

2 onions, skinned and	Parsley
finely chopped	Peppercorns
1 oz. butter	Salt and pepper
1½ lb. cod fillet	1 small bottle of brown ale
1 bay leaf	½ oz. cornflour
Thyme	

Oven temperature: moderate (350°F., mark 4)

Fry the onions in the butter till faintly coloured, then spread in the bottom of an ovenproof dish. Put the pieces of cod fillets on this mixture, add the herbs and seasonings, then just cover with ale. Cook in the centre of the oven for about 25 minutes. Strain the liquid from the fillets and thicken it with the cornflour, blended with a little water. Bring to the boil, stirring all the time, and pour over the fish.

28

COD SALAD

¾ lb. cod, cooked
1 lettuce
1 small cooked beetroot, cubed
3 tomatoes, halved

2–3 cooked potatoes, sliced
Spring onions, prepared
Mayonnaise
Chopped parsley

Flake the cold fish and place it in the centre of a dish. Surround it with lettuce and decorate with the other vegetable ingredients. Top the cod with some mayonnaise and sprinkle the potatoes with chopped parsley.

SALT COD-FISH IN SAUCE

1 lb. salt cod
2 large onions, skinned and finely chopped
2 cloves of garlic, crushed
2 tbsps. olive oil
Cayenne pepper

2 tomatoes, skinned and chopped
1 tsp. chopped parsley
1 stick of celery, chopped
2 egg yolks, beaten

Soak the fish in cold water for 24 hours, changing the water 2–3 times. Poach it gently in water for 10–15 minutes and cut it into convenient-sized pieces, removing the bones. Fry the onions and garlic in the oil until brown and tender. Add some cayenne pepper, tomatoes, parsley and celery; pour in ¾ pint boiling water and simmer for a few minutes. Add the pieces of fish, baste with the mixture, then simmer gently. When the fish is tender, take it off the heat and add the beaten egg yolks, pouring them in at several different places; shake the pan gently to mix the contents, then slide the fish and sauce carefully into a shallow casserole dish to serve.

CASSEROLLED CONGER EEL (Chile)

2½ lb. conger eel
Salt and pepper
Olive oil
2 tbsps. butter
2 tbsps. lard
2 onions, skinned and chopped
2 cloves of garlic, crushed

A little marjoram
A little ground cumin seed
4 tomatoes, skinned and sliced
4 potatoes, peeled and sliced
8 oz. corn kernels
Croûtons and hard-boiled egg to garnish

Oven temperature: warm (325°F., mark 3)

Cut the conger eel into individual portions, season and brown lightly in the oil. Heat the butter and lard in a saucepan and add the onions, garlic, marjoram and cumin. When the onions are soft, add the tomatoes, potatoes and corn kernels. Cover and cook until the potatoes are done, then season to taste. Put half this vegetable mixture in a casserole, lay the fish on top and add the remaining vegetables. Cover and cook in the centre of the oven for about 1 hour, until the fish is done. Garnish with croûtons and sliced egg. (Serves 4–6.)

29

CASSEROLE OF DABS

1 onion, skinned and sliced
2 carrots, peeled and diced
3 sticks of celery,
   roughly chopped

Salt and pepper
A little fish stock or milk
1½–2 lb. dabs, prepared
A little lemon juice

Oven temperature: moderate (350°F., mark 4)

Mix together the onion, carrots and celery; season and place at the bottom of a greased casserole. Add a little fish stock or milk, cover the dish and cook in the centre of the oven for 20 minutes. Lay the dabs on the vegetables, sprinkle with lemon juice and continue to cook for a further 20 minutes. Serve with the vegetables.

Dabs are also excellent baked in a little milk or stock, or fried in either deep or shallow fat.

STEWED EELS

1½–2 lb. eels, prepared
Salt and pepper
A squeeze of lemon juice
A few sprigs of parsley

1½ oz. butter
1½ oz. flour
½ pint milk
2–3 tbsps. chopped parsley

First skin the eels (or ask the fishmonger to do this for you). Cut off the head, turn back the skin at the head end and peel it off with a sharp pull. Split open the body and remove the backbone. Clean well and wash the eels in salted water.

Cut the eels into 2-inch pieces, cover with water and add the seasoning, lemon juice and sprigs of parsley. Simmer for about ¾ hour, until tender. Drain and retain ½ pint of the cooking liquid and keep the fish warm. Melt the fat, stir in the flour and cook for 2–3 minutes. Remove the pan from the heat and gradually stir in the cooking liquid from the fish, with the milk. Bring to the boil and continue to stir until the sauce thickens. Remove from the heat, stir in the parsley, add seasoning to taste and serve the eels coated with this sauce.

CASSEROLE OF EEL

1½–2 lb. eels, skinned
2 onions, skinned and cut
   in rings
1 clove of garlic, skinned
A bunch of herbs
Salt
A few peppercorns
1 liqueur glass of Cognac

Red wine
½ lb. mushrooms, cooked
1½ oz. butter
1½ oz. flour
Gravy browning
Fried croûtons and peeled
   prawns to garnish

Clean the fish thoroughly and wash them in salted water, then cut them in pieces 2–3 inches long. Put the onions with the garlic, herbs, salt and peppercorns into a flameproof casserole; place the pieces of eel on top. Put over the heat, add the Cognac, light it with a taper and allow to burn for about a minute, to "flame" the eel. Add enough red wine to cover the fish and cook for 20 minutes. Remove the pieces of eel, place in a deep dish and add the mushrooms. Reduce the liquid and then thicken it with the butter blended with a little flour – this sauce should be creamy but not too thick; darken it with a little gravy browning, as the wine gives an unpleasant violet colour. Simmer for a moment, then pour the sauce over the eel and mushrooms. Garnish with fried croûtons and prawns.

BAKED EELS

1½–2 lb. eels	Ground nutmeg
4 oz. butter, melted	Salt and pepper
Fresh white bread-crumbs	2 tsps. vinegar

Oven temperature: cool (300°F., mark 1–2)

Clean the fish and cut into 2-inch lengths. Put in an oven-proof dish with the butter. Sprinkle with bread-crumbs and season with nutmeg, salt, pepper and vinegar. Cook in the centre of the oven for 2–2½ hours.

EEL PIE

1½ lb. eels	A squeeze of lemon juice
Salt and pepper	1 hard-boiled egg, sliced
1 tsp. chopped parsley	A little fish stock
A pinch of mixed herbs	½ lb. rough puff pastry

Oven temperature: hot (425°F., mark 7)

Clean the eels, removing the head, tail and skin, and cut the fish into small pieces. (The skin may be used for the stock.) Put the eels into a pie dish with the seasoning, herbs, lemon juice and egg. Add a little fish stock and cover the pie with the pastry. Bake towards the top of the oven until the pastry is cooked, then cover with greaseproof paper, lower the temperature to moderate (350°F., mark 4) and continue to bake for about 1 hour in all, until the fish is cooked. Fill up the pie with fish stock and serve it either hot or cold.

BAKED GRAYLING

2–3 grayling	2 oz. butter
A little milk	Juice of 1 lemon
Seasoned flour	Chopped parsley

Oven temperature: fairly hot (400°F., mark 6)

Clean the fish, wash thoroughly and leave in salted water for at least an hour before cooking. Dry them well and make 2 incisions down each side. Dip the fish in milk and then in seasoned flour, shaking off any surplus. Heat the butter in a pan and brown the fish on both sides, then lay them in an ovenproof dish, pour any remaining butter over them and sprinkle with lemon juice. Cover and bake for 10–15 minutes, in the centre of the oven. Serve sprinkled with freshly chopped parsley.

CHEESY GRILLED HADDOCK

1½ lb. haddock fillet	⅔ pint milk
A little oil	4 oz. cheese, grated
1½ oz. butter	Salt and pepper
3 level tbsps. flour	

Skin the fish and cut into 4 portions. Place on the grill rack, brush with oil and cook for 7–10 minutes on each side. Meanwhile, melt the butter in a pan, add the flour, stir well and remove from the heat. Pour in the milk gradually, stirring all the time, return the mixture to the heat and bring to the boil. Still stirring, add 3 oz. of the cheese and season to taste. Place the fish in a serving dish and cover with the cheese sauce. Sprinkle with the remaining cheese and brown under the grill.

POACHED HADDOCK AND SHRIMP SAUCE

1 haddock (about 2 lb.)	A few peppercorns
½ level tsp. salt	1 oz. flour
2 tbsps. chopped celery	1 oz. butter
1 tbsp. chopped onion	2 tbsps. shelled
A sprig of parsley	shrimps

Fillet the haddock, then cut each fillet in half lengthwise. Cover the bones, head and trimmings with cold water, add the salt and bring slowly to the boil; skim and add the celery, onion, parsley and peppercorns. Simmer for about ½ hour, then strain into a shallow pan and add the fish fillets, folded in three; bring to the boil and simmer for about 10 minutes. Remove the fish and keep hot on a dish. Thicken the liquor by stirring in the flour and butter worked together, add the shrimps and pour the sauce over the fish.

HADDOCK WITH LOBSTER SAUCE

2 lb. haddock fillet	¼ level tsp. pepper
Juice of ½ a lemon	A small can of lobster
2 oz. butter, melted	bisque
A good pinch of	3 tbsps. sour cream
marjoram	A pkt. of frozen mixed
½ level tsp. salt	vegetables (optional)

Oven temperature: moderate (350°F., mark 4)

Wash the fish and cut into 4 portions. Place in a shallow fireproof casserole, sprinkle with the lemon juice and allow to soak for 5 minutes, then discard the juice. Pour the melted butter over the fish and sprinkle with the marjoram and seasonings. Grill for about 10 minutes, basting once. Mix the bisque and sour cream together, pour over the fish and cook for 30 minutes in the centre of the oven. Serve garnished with the cooked vegetables.

HADDOCK WITH BEETROOT SAUCE

1½ lb. haddock fillet	A few peppercorns
Salt and pepper	Milk or water to cover
Juice of 1 lemon	Parsley to garnish
1 bay leaf	

For the Beetroot Sauce

½ pint white sauce (see page 138)	1 medium-sized beetroot, cooked and diced
1 egg yolk	

Oven temperature: moderate (350°F., mark 4)

Wash and skin the fillet and cut into 4 portions. Sprinkle with salt, pepper and lemon juice, lay them in a greased ovenproof dish with the bay leaf and peppercorns and pour on just enough liquid to cover. Bake in the centre of the oven until tender – about 20 minutes. (Alternatively, poach slowly on the top of the stove for 20–30 minutes). Drain the fish, reserving the liquor, and keep hot while making the sauce (see below). Place the fish on a dish, pour the sauce over and garnish with parsley.

Beetroot Sauce

Make ½ pint of white sauce, using the fish stock, and add the egg yolk and diced beetroot.

HADDOCK BAKED IN CREAM

1½ lb. fresh haddock fillet	1 tsp. Worcestershire sauce
1 onion, skinned and finely chopped	Salt and pepper
Juice of ½ a lemon	¼ pint single cream

Oven temperature: moderate (350°F., mark 4)

Wash and wipe the fish, place it in a greased ovenproof dish and sprinkle with the onion. Mix the lemon juice, Worcestershire sauce, seasoning and cream and pour over the fish. Cover with a lid or foil and bake in the centre of the oven for 20–30 minutes, or until the fish and onions are cooked. (Don't worry if the cream curdles.)

STUFFED HADDOCK

Mushroom stuffing (see page 153)	Dripping
1 haddock (about 2 lb.)	Anchovy (or white) sauce (see pages 140 and 138)
Egg and bread-crumbs	Creamed potato

Oven temperature: moderate (350°F., mark 4)

Begin by making the stuffing. Clean the haddock, without removing the head, and stuff with the mixture. Join the flaps, using a fine skewer, then shape the fish into an "S" curve. Egg and crumb the fish and place in a small baking tin, with the dripping over it. Bake in the centre of the oven for 20–30 minutes, according to size, basting frequently. Remove the skewers, place the fish on a hot dish and pour the sauce round it. Garnish with piped creamed potato, or as desired.

FRIED HADDOCK, WEST INDIAN STYLE

2 medium-sized fresh haddock fillets (about 1½ lb.)
1 canned red pimiento, chopped
¾ oz. salt
Juice of 1 large lemon
Oil for frying

Wash and dry the fish fillets. Mix the chopped pimiento with the salt and spread this mixture on both sides of the fillets. Place them in a bowl and sprinkle with half the lemon juice. leave for 2 hours, then drain off the liquor and sprinkle the fish with the remaining lemon juice. Heat the oil and brown the fillets, top side first. Cover the pan and fry gently until the fish is cooked. Drain on kitchen paper and cut into serving-size portions.

CIDERED HADDOCK CASSEROLE

1–1½ lb. haddock or cod fillet, skinned
½ lb. tomatoes, skinned and sliced
2 oz. button mushrooms, sliced
1 tbsp. chopped parsley
Salt and pepper
¼ pint cider
2 tbsps. fresh white bread-crumbs
2 tbsps. grated cheese

Oven temperature: moderate (350°F., mark 4)

Wash the haddock (or cod) fillet, cut into cubes and lay these in an ovenproof dish. Cover with the sliced tomatoes and mushrooms, the parsley and seasonings and pour the cider over. Cover with foil and bake in the centre of the oven for 20–25 minutes. Sprinkle with the bread-crumbs and cheese and brown in a hot oven (425°F., mark 7) or under a hot grill.

HADDOCK AND MUSHROOM CASSEROLE

1½ lb. fresh haddock fillet, cut up
2 small onions, skinned and chopped
2 oz. mushrooms, sliced
A knob of butter
2 level tsps. flour
A medium-sized can of tomato juice
A pinch of mixed herbs
Salt and pepper
2 level tsps. sugar

Oven temperature: moderate (350°F., mark 4)

Wash the fish, cut into pieces and put in a greased ovenproof dish. Fry the onions and mushrooms in the butter, adding the

34

flour when they begin to colour. Add the tomato juice and bring to the boil; add the herbs, seasoning and sugar and pour over the fish. Cover with greased greaseproof paper and cook in the centre of the oven for 30 minutes.

HADDOCK AND VEGETABLE HOTPOT

1 lb. fresh haddock	Salt and pepper
1 onion, skinned and chopped	A small can of tomatoes
4 oz. French beans, prepared	2–3 large potatoes, peeled
4 oz. cheese, grated	and sliced

Oven temperature: moderate (350°F., mark 4)

Skin the fish and cut into cubes. Cover with onion, beans, half the cheese and some seasoning. Add the tomatoes, cover with the sliced potatoes and season again. Bake in the centre of the oven for 1 hour. Take from the oven, cover with the remaining cheese and brown under the grill.

BAKED HAKE

4 medium-sized steaks	1 tsp. chopped parsley
of hake (about 2 lb.)	1 tsp. chopped onion
Flour	1 oz. butter
Salt and pepper	

Oven temperature: moderate (350°F., mark 4)

Wash and dry the fish and place the slices side by side in a greased baking dish. Dredge well with flour, season, spread the parsley and onion over, and add the butter, in small pieces. Bake gently in the centre of the oven for about ½ hour, basting occasionally, then place the fish on a hot dish and strain the liquor over it.

GRILLED HALIBUT OR TURBOT

Allow 6 oz. fish per person. Wash and trim the fish, wipe and place on a greased grill grid. Brush with melted butter and sprinkle with salt and pepper. Grill gently for about 15 minutes altogether, turning the pieces once, brushing the second side with butter and sprinkling with salt and pepper. Serve with grilled mushrooms and a tomato or other well-flavoured sauce.

HERRINGS IN OATMEAL

Have the herrings boned and the heads and tails removed. Clean the flesh by rubbing with a little salt, rinse and dry well. Sprinkle with salt and pepper and coat with fine oatmeal, pressing it well into the fish on both sides. Fry in a small amount of lard or butter in a frying pan, turning the fish once, until brown on both sides. Drain well on crumpled kitchen paper and serve with lemon and parsley.

35

GRILLED HERRINGS

Have the heads cut off and the fish cleaned but left whole. Wash and wipe, make 2–3 diagonal cuts in the flesh on both sides of the fish and sprinkle with salt and pepper. Brush with oil or melted butter and cook on a greased grill grid for 10–15 minutes under a moderate heat, turning the fish once, until thoroughly cooked on both sides. Serve at once, garnished with lemon. Mustard sauce is good with grilled herrings (see Sauces chapter, p. 138).

DEVILLED HERRINGS

Clean the herrings, removing the heads, and score each one across on both sides. Place some French mustard in each of the score marks. Brush with melted butter and cook under a hot grill. Serve with sauté potatoes and a mixed green salad.

SAVOURY HERRINGS

4 herrings	2 medium-sized onions,
Seasoned flour	thinly sliced
3 oz. lard or dripping	1–2 tbsps. vinegar

Clean the fish and remove the backbone and roes; wash and dry carefully. Score the fish 2–3 times on each side and dip into seasoned flour. Heat the fat in a frying pan and arrange the fish side by side in the fat; cook for 3 minutes till golden-brown, turn, add the onions and fry for a further 3 minutes. Remove the fish and drain well, then put it in a serving dish. Continue to cook the onions for a further few minutes. Arrange them on or around the fish. Add the vinegar to the drippings in the pan and heat slightly, then pour over the herrings.

CIDERED HERRINGS

2 small onions, 1 chopped and 1 sliced	4 herrings, boned
	2 level tsps. cornflour
2 tomatoes, skinned and chopped	A bunch of watercress
	Chopped parsley
5 peppercorns	1 apple, chopped and tossed
1 bay leaf	in lemon juice
Salt and pepper	3 sticks of celery, chopped
½ pint cider	

Put the chopped onion and the tomatoes, peppercorns, bay leaf and seasoning into a frying-pan with the cider and bring to the boil. Wash, trim and dry the herrings and put them into the boiling cider; cook on each side for 4 minutes, then put on a plate and keep hot. Strain the liquor and return it to the pan. Mix 2 tbsps. of the liquor with the cornflour and add to the remainder in the pan. Bring to the boil, stirring all the time, and boil for 2 minutes until the sauce thickens. Pour it over the herrings and decorate with the sliced onion, divided into rings, a few sprigs of watercress and some chopped parsley. Serve with a salad made from the remaining watercress, the apple, celery and a little chopped parsley.

SCALLOPED HERRINGS

2–3 fresh herrings, cooked
1 egg yolk
¼ pint thick white sauce
1 tbsp. vinegar
2 tbsps. lemon juice
Salt and pepper

Browned bread-crumbs
½ lb. potatoes, cooked and mashed
Tomatoes or mushrooms to garnish

Oven temperature: hot (425°F., mark 7)

Remove the bones and skin from the herrings and flake the fish. Beat the egg yolk into the white sauce, add the vinegar and lemon juice and season to taste. Grease some scallop shells and sprinkle with bread-crumbs. Mix the fish with the sauce and put into the shells. Sprinkle with more bread-crumbs and scallop mashed potato around the edge. Bake in the top of the oven for a few minutes or grill until golden-brown. Serve garnished with baked or grilled sliced tomatoes and small mushrooms.

SOUSED HERRINGS

4 large or 6–8 small herrings, cleaned and boned
Salt and pepper
1 small onion, skinned and sliced into rings

6 peppercorns
1-2 bay leaves
A few parsley stalks
¼ pint malt vinegar
¼ pint water

Oven temperature: moderate (350°F., mark 4)

Trim off the heads, tails and fins, sprinkle the fish with salt and pepper and roll up from the head end. Pack into a fairly shallow ovenproof dish and add the onion, peppercorns and herbs. Pour in the vinegar and enough water to almost cover the fish. Cover with greaseproof paper or foil and bake in the centre of the oven for about ¾ hour, or until tender. Leave to cool in the cooking liquid before serving with salad.

Note: For a decorative effect leave the tails on the fish; when the rolled fish are put in the dish, arrange the tails pointing upwards. Herrings can also be soused whole.

FINNISH HERRING AND POTATO CASSEROLE

2 large salt herrings
1 lb. boiled potatoes, sliced
1 tbsp. chopped onion or spring onion

2 tbsps. melted butter
1 pint milk
3 eggs, beaten
½ level tsp. pepper
1 oz. dried bread-crumbs

Oven temperature: moderate (350°F., mark 4)

Soak the fish for 6 hours, skin and bone them and cut in long strips. Butter a baking dish and put in a layer of potato, then one of herring, with a little onion; repeat, finishing with a potato layer, and pour melted butter over the top. Add the milk to the eggs with the pepper, pour into the baking dish and sprinkle with bread-crumbs. Bake in the centre of the oven for 30–40 minutes, or until browned.

Canned salmon may be used instead of salt herring.

HERRING SALAD

3 soused herrings (see recipe p. 37)
3–4 potatoes, cooked
1 pickled cucumber
1–2 dessert apples
2 tbsps. olive oil
2 tbsps. vinegar
Salt and pepper
2–3 eggs, hard-boiled and sliced
1 beetroot, cooked and sliced

Cut the fish into small pieces. Dice the potatoes and cucumber; core the apples and cut up without peeling. Blend the oil, vinegar and seasoning in a good-sized bowl and add the salad ingredients. Mix thoroughly and serve garnished with the sliced eggs and beetroot.

SALT HERRING FRICASSEE

1 onion, skinned and sliced
Fat for frying
3 salt herrings, boned
2 apples
1 gherkin
1 oz. ham
About 6 tbsps. brown or white sauce
Salt and pepper
Vinegar
Chopped parsley

Fry the onion in the fat until it is golden-brown. Mince the herrings, apples, gherkin and ham and add to the onion, with sufficient sauce to moisten. Season as required and add a little vinegar to sharpen the flavour. Place the mixture in a dish, sprinkle with chopped parsley and serve with floury baked potatoes.

JOHN DORY PROVENÇALE

1 small John Dory
2–3 oz. fat for frying
1 small onion, skinned and finely chopped
½ oz. flour
Salt and pepper
4 tbsps. fish stock or white wine
1 tomato. skinned and chopped
1 tsp. chopped parsley

Remove the head, trim the fins and tail of the fish and score across. Fry in the hot fat, allowing about 6 minutes on each side, then remove the fish and keep hot. Add the onion and flour to the fat and stir round, without browning. Add the seasoning, the fish stock or wine, tomato and parsley. Simmer very gently for 5–10 minutes, then strain over the fish.

GRILLED MACKEREL
(see colour picture No. 7)

Clean and score the fish, dip in seasoned flour and dab with melted fat, then cook on both sides under a hot grill for 15–20 minutes. Serve on a hot dish, with grilled tomatoes, lemon and parsley, maître d'hôtel butter or chutney.

FRIED FILLETS OF MACKEREL

2 mackerel, filleted
Oil for frying
A few mushrooms, washed
1 onion, skinned and thinly
  sliced

1 clove of garlic, skinned and
  crushed
A little vinegar
Grilled tomatoes
Chopped parsley

See Chapter 1, p. 8, for notes on method of filleting fish.

Cook the fillets in very hot oil, then arrange them on a dish. Cook the mushrooms, onion and crushed garlic in the hot oil, browning them well, and put over the fillets. Heat the vinegar until very hot, pour over the fillets and surround with grilled tomatoes; sprinkle with chopped parsley.

STUFFED MACKEREL

2–4 mackerel (according to
  size)
1 oz. butter
1 onion, skinned and chopped
2 oz. mushrooms, chopped

1 tbsp. chopped parsley
2 oz. boiled rice or fresh
  white bread-crumbs
Salt and pepper

Oven temperature: fairly hot (400°F., mark 6)

Have the fish gutted, but ask the fishmonger to give you the roes. Clean the fish inside with salt and water and trim off the fins with scissors.

Make the stuffing by melting the butter in a frying pan and adding the remaining ingredients and chopped roes, frying them together for 5 minutes. Stuff the fish with this mixture and wrap each one in buttered foil. Bake in a shallow dish or on a baking sheet in the middle of the oven for about ½ hour.

BRETON MACKEREL

Allow one fish for each person; clean the fish well, cut each into 2 pieces and open out flat. Dry the pieces, roll them in a little flour and sprinkle with salt and pepper. Melt some butter in an ovenproof dish and put in the mackerel pieces, skin side uppermost. Cook quickly for a few minutes, turn and cook more slowly for 15 minutes, with a lid on the dish. Serve in the dish, squeezing some lemon juice over them at the last minute. (If the fat has become too dark, drain it off and add a little more melted butter.)

SOUSED MACKEREL: see Soused Herrings, page 37.

MACKEREL SALAD

1 lettuce, washed and trimmed	2 cupfuls sliced cooked potatoes
1 tbsp. chopped chives	1–2 mackerel, cooked and flaked
2 tbsps. anchovy essence	
4 tbsps. French dressing	2 cupfuls cooked French beans

Use most of the lettuce to line a salad bowl. Mix the chives and anchovy essence with the French dressing and toss the potatoes in half of this mixture. Drain them and arrange in a thick layer in the bowl. Toss the mackerel and French beans in the remaining dressing and arrange on top of the potatoes. Garnish with crisp lettuce leaves and chill before serving.

BAKED RED MULLET

Oven temperature: moderate (350°F., mark 4)

Clean 1 mullet for each person and put into a well-buttered ovenproof dish. Add some salt and pepper, put a little butter on each fish, cover with greased greaseproof paper and cook for about 20 minutes in the centre of the oven.

GRILLED MULLET

4 mullet, whole and cleaned	A few peppercorns
3–4 tbsps. oil	½ a bay leaf or a few parsley stalks
3–4 tbsps. vinegar	
A piece of onion, finely chopped	Tomato sauce (see Sauces chapter, p. 138)

Wash the fish and wipe them well. Put in a dish with the oil, vinegar and flavourings and leave to marinade for about 1 hour, turning them several times. Drain the fish and put on a greased grill grid. Cook under a medium heat for about 10 minutes, basting with some of the marinade and turning them once. Serve with tomato sauce.

BAKED PIKE

Oven temperature: moderate (350°F., mark 4)

Scale, clean and wash the fish, stuff with veal forcemeat (see Sauces and Stuffings chapter, p. 138) and put in a greased ovenproof dish. Brush the fish with melted butter and sprinkle with salt, pepper, a little chopped parsley and a few fresh white bread-crumbs. Cover with a lid of foil and bake in the centre of the oven for about 1 hour (depending on the size of the fish) until tender. Serve with anchovy sauce (see Sauces chapter, p. 138).

Note: The foil can be removed for the last ¼ hour to brown the crumbs, if you wish.

STEWED PIKE (Switzerland)

A pike weighing 2–3 lb.	1 onion, spiked with 2
Salt and pepper	cloves
3½ oz. fat bacon	1 tsp. anchovy or lobster
1 carrot	paste
¼ pint stock	2 oz. butter
¼ pint dry white wine	1 tbsp. cream
3–4 sage leaves	Lemon juice

Oven temperature: moderate (350°F., mark 4)

Scale, clean and wash the fish; wipe it dry and put some salt inside, then pull off the skin on either side of the dorsal fin and insert tiny strips of bacon in the flesh. Wash and peel the carrot and put it in the abdominal slit. Butter an ovenproof dish and put in the fish, back uppermost. Pour in the stock and wine, add the sage leaves, onion, fish paste, some pepper and a little salt, cover the fish with knobs of butter and bake in the centre of the oven, covering the dish for the first 15 minutes, then uncovering it for the next 30 minutes, till the fish turns a light gold colour and is well cooked; baste it 2–3 times with the stock and wine. Dilute the cooking juices with a little water and strain. Add the cream and a few drops of lemon juice and serve with the fish – which should be left whole. (Serves 4–6.)

BAKED STUFFED PILCHARDS

4 fresh pilchards	Fish forcemeat (see Sauces
Fine oatmeal	and Stuffings chapter, p. 138)
Salt and pepper	Shavings of butter

Oven temperature: fairly hot (400°F., mark 6)

Remove the heads from the pilchards, slit the fish open and remove the backbones. Dip into fine oatmeal seasoned with salt and pepper. Spread with the fish forcemeat and put flat on to a greased baking tin. Dot with shavings of butter, cover with greaseproof paper and bake in the centre of the oven for 15–20 minutes, removing the paper for the last 5 minutes, to allow the stuffing to brown.

Baked tomatoes make a good accompaniment.

FRIED FILLETS OF PLAICE

Allow 2 fillets per person. Wash and wipe them and dip into seasoned flour; shake off any excess and dip the fish into beaten egg and then in dry bread-crumbs. (See notes in Chapter 1, p. 11). Put into hot butter or lard, skin side uppermost, and fry for 3–5 minutes; turn them once and fry for a further 2–3 minutes, until crisp and golden. Drain on crump-

41

led kitchen paper and serve with wedges of lemon and Tartare sauce, or with maître d'hôtel butter and accompanied by chipped potatoes.

BAKED PLAICE WITH BLACK BUTTER

8 fillets of plaice	Black butter sauce (see
Juice of 1 lemon	Sauces chapter, p. 138)
Salt and pepper	2–3 gherkins, chopped

Put the fillets of fish on to a board and sprinkle with lemon juice and seasoning; fold each in three and put in a buttered dish. Pour the rest of the lemon juice over the fish, cover with a well-buttered paper and cook in the centre of the oven for 10–15 minutes. Pour the black butter over the fish and sprinkle with chopped gherkins.

BAKED PLAICE WITH MUSHROOM SAUCE

8 fillets of plaice	2 oz. mushrooms, sliced
A squeeze of lemon juice	¼ pint milk
Salt and pepper	1 level tbsp. cornflour
1 medium-sized onion, skinned and finely chopped	Parsley to garnish

Oven temperature: fairly hot (375° F., mark 5)

Fold each fillet with the ends underneath and put them into a greased ovenproof dish. Squeeze a little lemon juice over, sprinkle with salt and pepper and scatter the onion and mushrooms over them; add the milk. Cover with a lid or foil and bake at the bottom of the oven for 10–15 minutes. Transfer the fillets to a serving dish. Blend the cornflour with the remaining fish liquor and put into a saucepan; bring to the boil, stirring, and cook for 2–3 minutes. Pour this sauce over the fillets and garnish with sprigs of parsley.

STUFFED ROLLED PLAICE FILLETS

2 hard-boiled eggs, shelled and chopped	2 oz. butter, melted
2 oz. cheese, grated	Salt and pepper
1 tbsp. chopped parsley	2 plaice, filleted and skinned
3 oz. fresh white bread-crumbs	White or parsley sauce

Oven temperature: moderate (350°F., mark 4)

Mix the eggs with the cheese, parsley and 2 oz. of the bread-crumbs. Bind with the butter and add some seasoning. Spread this mixture over the skinned side of the fillets and roll them up, starting from the tail end; secure them if necessary with a wooden cocktail stick. Place in a buttered shallow ovenproof dish, sprinkle with the remaining bread-crumbs and bake in the centre of the oven for about 20 minutes, until the fish is tender and the bread-crumbs crisp on top. The liquid that comes from the fish as it cooks can be strained off and used with milk to make a white or parsley sauce to serve with the fish. (See Sauces chapter, p. 138).

PLAICE AU GRATIN

Cooking oil
¼ lb. mushrooms, peeled and chopped
1 large plaice, filleted
Salt and pepper
Juice of 1 lemon

1 oz. white bread-crumbs
2 oz. Gruyére cheese, grated
Sliced lemon, sliced stuffed olives and grilled mushrooms to garnish (optional)

Oven temperature: moderate (350°F., mark 4)

Grease a baking tin or ovenproof dish with a little oil, sprinkle with half the chopped mushrooms, then lay the fillets on top, folding them in half. Season, pour the lemon juice over and add the remaining mushrooms. Cover with a layer of crumbs and lastly the cheese. Pour 1 tbsp. oil over and cover the dish with greaseproof paper. Bake in the centre of the oven for ½ hour. Garnish with lemons, olives and mushrooms.

PORTUGUESE PLAICE

1 tbsp. chopped chives
3 tomatoes, skinned and sliced
1 oz. butter

8 fillets of plaice, skinned
A little white wine
Salt and pepper

Oven temperature: moderate (350°F., mark 4)

Fry the chives and tomatoes in the butter for a few minutes, then pour into an ovenproof dish. Fold each plaice fillet in three and lay them on the tomatoes; cover the tomatoes and fish with wine. Season and bake in the centre of the oven for 25 minutes.

STUFFED WHOLE PLAICE

2 plaice, whole but cleaned
2 oz. fresh bread-crumbs
1 oz. suet
1 tbsp. chopped parsley
½ level tsp. dried thyme

Grated rind of ½ a lemon
Salt and pepper
Milk or egg to bind
1 oz. butter
¼ pint dry white wine
Parsley and lemon garnish

Oven temperature: moderate (350°F., mark 4)

Get the fishmonger to make a slit down the backbone of the fish and lift the top fillets slightly to form 2 pockets. Mix together the bread-crumbs, suet, herbs, lemon rind and seasoning and bind with milk or egg. Divide this mixture between the 2 fish, stuffing it into the pockets. Place the fish in a large, shallow ovenproof dish and dot with the butter. Pour the wine over, cover the dish with foil and bake in the centre of

43

the oven for about 20 minutes, or until tender. Spoon the cooking liquid over the fish and serve garnished with parsley and lemon wedges.

Alternatively, make a stuffing with 3–4 oz. boiled rice, mixed with 4 chopped tomatoes, 1 chopped onion, a large pinch of mixed herbs and salt and pepper, bound with beaten egg.

PLAICE AND BACON ROLLS

8 rashers of back bacon, rinded
8 small fillets of plaice
Salt and pepper

Juice of 1 lemon
Gravy (see recipe)
Sprigs of parsley

Oven temperature: fairly hot (375°F., mark 5)
Flatten out the bacon rashers with the back of a knife on a board. Put a plaice fillet on each rasher and add salt, pepper and a squeeze of lemon juice. Roll up the stuffed rashers and bake in the centre of the oven for about 25 minutes. Serve with a gravy made from dripping and vegetable stock or from yeast extract, thickened with flour. Garnish with parsley sprigs.

PLAICE AND MUSHROOM HOTPOT

2 medium-sized plaice
1 oz. butter
1 oz. flour
¾ pint milk and fish liquor

Salt and pepper
½ lb. mushrooms, peeled
1 lb. parboiled potatoes, sliced

Oven temperature: moderate (350°F., mark 4)
Fillet and skin the fish and wash the fillets. Cover the fish-bones with water and cook for 15 minutes. Melt the butter, add the flour, cook for 1–2 minutes, then stir in the liquid gradually. Bring to the boil and boil for 5 minutes, then season. Cut the fillets in half and put a layer of fish at the bottom of a casserole, next the mushrooms, then the rest of the fish. Pour the sauce over and cover with the sliced potatoes. Put the lid on and cook in the centre of the oven for ¾–1 hour. When the hotpot is half-cooked, remove the lid to allow the potatoes to brown.

SARDINE AND POTATO SALAD

3 large new potatoes, peeled
1 small onion, skinned
Salt and pepper
French dressing
2 small cans of sardines

Juice of 1 lemon
Chopped parsley
Carrot balls and lettuce or watercress for garnish

Cook the potatoes and when cold cut into cubes; chop the onion finely and mix the two ingredients together. Add some seasoning and toss the mixture in the French dressing. Pile in a pyramid shape in the centre of a dish, arrange the sardines round and sprinkle with lemon juice and parsley. Garnish with carrot balls and lettuce leaves or sprigs of watercress.

FRIED SKATE

1½–2 lb. prepared skate   Dry bread-crumbs
Seasoned flour   Fat for frying
Beaten egg

Preparation of Skate: The "wings" of young small skate are often sold whole, but those of larger fish are usually sold cut in slices. Pieces of small skate can be cooked without any preparation, but larger skate, which tend to be rather tough and flavourless, are better if first simmered in salted water or court-bouillon until just tender, skinned and cut into pieces measuring about 2–3 inches. They can then be fried or cooked in any way you wish.

Frying: Drain the skate well, coat with seasoned flour, egg and crumbs and fry it gently for 5 minutes on each side in shallow fat (or for 5 minutes in all, in deep fat), until the pieces are tender and golden. Serve with cut lemon and a sharp-flavoured sauce such as Tartare (see Sauces chapter, p. 138).

SKATE IN BATTER

1½–2 lb. skate   Deep fat for frying
Coating batter

Prepare the skate as described in the recipe above and dip it in the coating batter (see Chapter 1, p. 12). Fry in deep fat for about 5 minutes, until crisp and golden. Drain on crumpled kitchen paper and serve with Tartare or any sharp sauce.

If preferred, the raw skate can be marinaded before being coated with the batter. Make the marinade (see below), allow the fish to stand in it for 2–3 hours, drain the pieces well and continue cooking as above.

Marinade: Combine 2 tbsps. olive oil, 1 tbsp. lemon juice, a little chopped onion and a little chopped parsley, with salt and pepper to taste.

POACHED SKATE WITH BLACK BUTTER

1 lb. skate wing (approx.)   1 tbsp. vinegar
1 pint court-bouillon   Chopped parsley
1½ oz. butter

Cut the skate into convenient portions for serving and poach it in the court-bouillon for 10–15 minutes. Remove the pieces of fish carefully, drain and place on a hot dish. Make the black butter (see Sauces chapter, p. 138), pour over the fish, sprinkle with a little chopped parsley and serve at once.

FRIED AND BAKED SMELTS

Cook smelts just before they are to be served, so that they retain their crispness. Clean the fish but leave on the head. Dip them in milk, then in flour, put a few at a time into very hot fat and cook for about 4 minutes on each side, till golden. Pile on a plate and garnish as desired.

Alternatively, smelts may be baked. Sprinkle the bottom of a well-greased pie dish thickly with fresh white bread-crumbs, mixed with salt, pepper and chopped parsley. Put in the cleaned and dried fish, cover with more seasoned crumbs and pour over 1 tbsp. lemon juice and 1 glass of sherry. Put little pieces of butter on top, and bake in a moderate oven (350°F., mark 4) for about ½ hour.

GRILLED SOLE

2 medium-sized sole
Juice of 1 lemon
Salt and pepper
1 oz. butter, melted

Maître d'hôtel butter
  (see Sauces chapter p. 138)
Lemon to garnish

Remove the dark skin from the sole and sprinkle the fish with lemon juice, salt and pepper. Brush the fish all over with some of the butter. Heat the grill and brush the grid with the remaining melted fat. Cook the sole for 7–10 minutes, lowering the heat if necessary when both sides are brown. Garnish with pats of maître d'hôtel butter on top and lemon wedges. Serve with fried straw potatoes and buttered carrots, etc.

TUNA CURRY CASSEROLE

4 oz. quick-cooking macaroni
A large can tuna (7-oz.)
A medium-sized can of
  condensed mushroom soup
¼ pint milk

1 level tbsp. dried onion
  flakes
1 level tsp. curry powder
½ level tsp. dried herbs
1 oz. potato crisps

Oven temperature: moderate (350°F., mark 4)
Cook the macaroni in boiling salted water for 7 minutes and drain well. Combine with all the other ingredients (except the crisps) and put into a 2-pint casserole. Top with the crumbled crisps and cook in the centre of the oven for 30–35 minutes.

TUNA RISOTTO

8 oz. long-grain rice
½ level tsp. salt
A large can of mushroom
  soup (15-oz.)
2 large cans tuna (7-oz.)

A small pkt. of frozen
  peas, thawed
½ a red pepper, chopped
2 oz. button mushrooms,
  washed

Place the rice in salted water, bring to the boil and simmer for 5 minutes; drain and replace in the saucepan. Add the mush-

46

room soup and bring to the boil. Meanwhile open the cans of tuna, drain off the oil and flake the fish with a fork. When the rice mixture is boiling add the tuna, peas, pepper and mushrooms. Simmer, stirring from time to time, until the liquid is all absorbed and the rice is cooked but not mushy. Serve immediately.

CHIP-TUNA CASSEROLE

2 large cans tuna (7-oz.)
2 level tbsps. plain flour
½ level tsp. salt
Pepper
2 cups milk

⅓ cup sherry or 2 tbsps. Worcestershire sauce
1 cup crumbled potato crisps

Oven temperature: fairly hot (375°F., mark 5)
Put into a double saucepan 2 tbsps. of the oil from the tuna; gradually stir in the flour, salt, pepper and milk and cook, stirring, until smooth and thickened, then add the sherry or the Worcestershire sauce. Cover the bottom of a greased 1½-quart casserole with a quarter of the potato crisps. Add one-third of the tuna, in chunks, then one-third of the sauce. Repeat, making 3 layers; top with the rest of the crisps, cover and bake in the centre of the oven for 20 minutes, then take off the lid and bake the casserole for a further 10 minutes, or until brown.

TUNA AND CELERY CASSEROLE

1 oz. butter
1 oz. flour
½ pint milk
Salt and pepper
6 oz. cheese, grated

2 large cans tuna (7-oz.)
4 eggs, hard-boiled and sliced
6 sticks of celery
Toasted bread-crumbs

Oven temperature: moderate (350°F., mark 4)
Melt the butter in a small saucepan, add the flour and cook, stirring, for 1 minute. Add the milk gradually, stirring constantly. Bring to the boil and cook until smooth. Remove from the heat and stir in the seasoning and 4 oz. of the grated cheese. Drain the oil from the tuna fish, place the flesh in a basin and chop slightly. Slice the hard-boiled eggs and celery and arrange in layers in a casserole with the tuna fish and cheese sauce. Top with the remaining grated cheese and the bread-crumbs and cook in the centre of the oven for about 30 minutes, until crisp and golden-brown.

BAKED TURBOT
Oven temperature: moderate (350°F., mark 4)
Choose 4 turbot steaks about 1 inch thick. Put them in a greased ovenproof dish, add enough milk to come half-way up the fish, season and put a knob of butter on each steak. Bake in

47

the centre of the oven for 20–25 minutes and serve with shrimp sauce poured over.

FRIED CURLED WHITING

Clean, wash and skin the whiting, removing the eyes but not the heads of the fish; dry well in a cloth. A few minutes before the whiting are to be fried, remove them from the cloth and put the tail of each fish into its mouth. Brush the fish over with beaten egg, roll them in bread-crumbs, shaking off any loose crumbs. Heat some deep fat until it will brown a 1-inch cube of bread in 1 minute; fry the whiting for 5–10 minutes, handling them carefully, as they break easily. Drain well on crumpled kitchen paper, garnish with fried parsley and serve with anchovy or other suitable sauce.

BAKED WHITING

4 medium-sized whiting	Browned bread-crumbs
Fat	Baked tomatoes, parsley and
Salt and pepper	lemon to garnish

Oven temperature: moderate (350°F., mark 4)

Clean, scale and trim the fish and remove the eyes. Curl each whiting round with the tail in the mouth or through the eye sockets. Brush with melted fat and sprinkle with seasoning and fine bread-crumbs. Put into a greased tin and dot with fat. Bake in the centre of the oven for about 30 minutes. Garnish with baked tomatoes, parsley and lemon, and serve with tomato sauce (see Sauces chapter, p. 138).

STUFFED WHITING

4 medium-sized whiting	1–2 tsps. chopped onion
6 tbsps. fresh white bread-crumbs	Anchovy essence
	Beaten egg
$\frac{1}{2}$ level tsp. mixed herbs	Egg and bread-crumbs
2 tsps. chopped parsley	for coating
Salt and pepper	Dripping

Oven temperature: fairly hot (400°F., mark 6)

Trim the fins and tails of the fish and remove the eyes. Clean the inside and wash thoroughly. Make a stuffing in the usual way with the bread-crumbs, herbs, seasonings and flavourings, binding it with egg. Stuff each fish and close by sewing with thin string and a trussing needle, stitching so that the string can easily be withdrawn when desired. Put the fish in an ovenproof dish or baking tin, brush with beaten egg and sprinkle with bread-crumbs. Put a few dabs of fat on each fish, cover with greaseproof paper and bake in the centre of the oven for 20–30 minutes. Any stuffing that is left over can be used to stuff mushrooms or tomatoes as a garnish for the fish.

48

FRIED FISH IN BATTER

1½ lb. fillets of plaice,
  haddock or cod
4 oz. flour
A pinch of salt

1 egg
¼ pint milk and water
Seasoned flour
Deep fat for frying

Wash the fish and dry it thoroughly in a cloth. Put the flour and salt in a basin, make a well in the centre and drop in the egg. Gradually add the liquid, using enough to give a coating consistency. Beat the batter well and leave it for a few minutes. Heat the fat until it will brown a 1-inch cube of bread in 60 seconds. Meanwhile dip the fish into the flour and then in the batter, put into the hot fat immediately and fry golden-brown – it should take 3–5 minutes, according to thickness. Drain very well, garnish with sprigs of parsley and lemon slices and serve with potato chips.

CHEESE GRILLED FISH

4 fish steaks (e.g. cod,
  haddock) weighing about
  1½ lb.
½ a small onion, grated
4 oz. cheese, grated

2 oz. butter
1 level tsp. dry mustard
Salt and pepper
A little melted butter
2 tomatoes, sliced

Wash, wipe and trim the fish steaks and remove the centre bone with a sharp-pointed knife. Mix the remaining ingredients (except tomatoes). Brush the fish with melted butter, place on the grill rack and grill under a medium heat for about 5 minutes, turn them and grill for a further 3 minutes. Spread the cheese mixture over the fish and lay 1–2 slices of tomato on each steak. Grill for a final 3–5 minutes, until the cheese topping is golden and the tomatoes are cooked.

SAVOURY BAKED FISH

4 oz. white fish fillets
4 oz. streaky bacon,
  rinded and chopped
2 onions, skinned and sliced
1½ oz. butter
1 level tsp. mixed herbs or
  1 tbsp. chopped parsley

1 oz. flour
½ pint milk
3 oz. cheese, grated
Salt and pepper
1 oz. fresh white
  bread-crumbs
1 tomato, sliced

Oven temperature: moderate (350°F., mark 4)

Wash and wipe the fish. Sauté the bacon and onions in ½ oz. butter for 5 minutes, drain and place in an ovenproof dish. Sprinkle with herbs and cover with the fish. Melt the remaining butter in a saucepan, stir in the flour and cook for 2–3 minutes, remove from the heat and gradually add the milk. Return the pan to the heat, bring to the boil and cook, stirring, until the sauce thickens; add the cheese, season well and

49

pour over the fish. Sprinkle with bread-crumbs and bake in the middle of the oven for ½ hour; after ¼ hour, add a border of tomato slices and complete the cooking.

BAKED FISH, SPANISH STYLE

4 cod steaks	4 anchovy fillets
1¼ level tsps. salt	4 tomatoes, peeled and
¼ level tsp. pepper	cut in thick slices
¼ level tsp. cayenne pepper	3 tbsps. chopped chives
¼ level tsp. grated nutmeg	¼ lb. mushrooms, thinly
1 tbsp. olive oil	sliced
1 large onion, skinned and	¼ cup white wine
thinly sliced	2 oz. butter, melted
1½ tbsps. chopped pimiento	4 oz. fresh white bread-crumbs

Oven temperature: fairly hot (400°F., mark 6)

Wash the fish and dry it. Sprinkle with a mixture of salt, pepper, cayenne and nutmeg. Put the oil into a large ovenproof dish and add the onion and pimiento. Arrange the seasoned fish slices side by side on top of the onion, and place an anchovy fillet on each. Cover the fish with tomato and sprinkle with chives. Scatter the mushroom over all, and pour on the wine. Cover and bake for 30 minutes in the centre of the oven. Meanwhile, mix the melted butter and bread-crumbs. Sprinkle this mixture on top of the fish and continue baking, uncovered, until well browned – about 5–10 minutes.

SOUTH SEAS FISH BAKE

4 portions of any white	Juice of 1 lemon
fish – ½–¾ lb. each	½ level tsp. ground ginger
6 tbsps. melted butter	½ lb. fresh spinach leaves,
2 tsps. soy sauce	washed

Oven temperature: moderate (350°F., mark 4)

Cut 4 squares of aluminium foil each large enough to wrap one portion of fish. Clean and wash the fish. Stir the melted butter, soy sauce and lemon juice together and brush on to the fish, inside and out. Sprinkle the inside and outside of the fish generously with the ginger. Place a few spinach leaves on each piece of foil and cover with a piece of fish. Place a few more spinach leaves on top and wrap up, turning the ends of the foil in and folding securely. Place on a shallow baking tray and cook in the centre of the oven for 30–40 minutes. Serve in the foil. (If you prefer, you can wrap several pieces of spinach-covered fish in one large piece of foil and remove from the foil to a hot plate for serving.)

Note: The foil is used as substitute for the large leaves of various tropical plants. The leaves or husks of sweet corn could also be used.

50

STEAMED FISH CUTLETS

Put the cutlets on to a greased plate; using about 1 oz. butter, add a small piece to each cutlet. Put the plate of cutlets on top of a saucepan of boiling water, cover with another plate and steam for about 20 minutes. Meanwhile, melt 1 oz. butter and add 1 oz. flour to make a roux; gradually add ½ pint milk, bring to the boil, season well and add 1 tbsp. chopped parsley. Serve the fish partially covered with the sauce and garnished with lemon slices or wedges.

The sauce may have anchovy essence, chopped hard-boiled egg or grated cheese added to it instead of the parsley.

CHINESE STEAMED FISH SLICES

1 lb. filleted fish
1 level tsp. salt
2 scallions or spring
   onions, chopped
2 slices of fresh ginger,
   chopped

1 tbsp. soy sauce
1 tbsp. vinegar
1½ tbsps. sherry
½ level tsp. sugar
2 slices of ham
6 mushrooms, sliced

Cut the fish into 2-inch slices, rub with salt and put on a plate. Mix the scallions, ginger, soy sauce, vinegar, sherry and sugar. Place some sliced ham and sliced mushrooms on each piece of fish, pour the sauce over, place another plate on top and steam for 20 minutes.

SIMPLE FISH CURRY

1 large onion, skinned and
   chopped
2 oz. butter
3 tomatoes, skinned and
   quartered

1½ lb. fillet of cod, skinned
2 level tsps. curry powder
Salt
A pinch of sugar
Boiled rice

Fry the onion in the butter and add the tomatoes. Cut the fish into pieces and coat with curry powder. Fry until brown, then add the salt and sugar; cover and simmer for 10 minutes. Serve with boiled rice.

CURRIED FISH

1½ lb. fish (e.g. cod,
   haddock), skinned
1 large onion, skinned
   and chopped
1 oz. butter
3 level tsps. curry powder
4 level tbsps. flour
½ pint chicken stock (made
   from a cube)

½ pint milk
1 small apple, peeled,
   cored and chopped
2 tomatoes, skinned
   and chopped
1–2 sultanas
Salt and pepper
Boiled rice
Lemon to garnish

Cut the fish into 1-inch cubes. Fry the onion gently in the

51

butter for 5 minutes without browning. Stir in the curry powder, fry for 2–3 minutes, add the flour and cook for a further 2–3 minutes. Remove the pan from the heat, stir in the stock and milk gradually and bring to the boil, stirring until the sauce thickens. Add the apple, tomatoes, sultanas and a good sprinkling of salt, cover and simmer for 15 minutes. Add the fish, stir and simmer for a further 10 minutes, or until the fish is tender. Add more salt and some pepper if necessary and serve with boiled rice and lemon wedges.

FISH PILAU

2 oz. butter	1½ pints stock
1 onion, skinned and	Salt
chopped	1½ lb. white fish fillets, skinned
6 oz. long-grain rice	Parsley to garnish

Melt the butter and fry the onion till pale golden; add the rice and brown a little. Add the stock, then some salt, and simmer for 10 minutes. Cut the fish into pieces, lay these on the rice and simmer until the fish is cooked and the stock absorbed. Arrange on a hot dish and garnish with parsley sprigs or chopped parsley.

FISH AND TOMATO CASSEROLE

1½ lb. fresh haddock, steamed	1 wineglass of wine
2 shallots, finely chopped	1 lb. tomatoes, skinned and
1 tsp. finely chopped parsley	sliced
A small can of anchovies,	2–3 tbsps. fresh white
finely chopped	bread-crumbs
Pepper and salt	A little butter
Juice of 1 lemon	

Oven temperature: moderate (350°F., mark 4)
Skin, bone and flake the fish, put it in a deep greased casserole and press down. Mix the shallots, parsley, anchovies, seasoning and lemon juice; add sufficient wine to make a paste and spread over fish. Cover with sliced tomatoes, sprinkle with bread-crumbs and dot with butter. Cover and cook in the centre of the oven for 20–30 minutes.

FISH AND BACON CASSEROLE

4 oz. bacon, rinded and cut up	Salt and cayenne pepper
3 onions, skinned and chopped	1 tsp. Worcestershire sauce
½ oz. butter	¼ pint tomato sauce
1½ lb. white fish, free of	¼ pint water
skin and bones	

Oven temperature: moderate (350°F., mark 4)
Fry the bacon and onion in the butter. Put alternate layers of

bacon and onion and the fish into an ovenproof casserole, sprinkling each layer with salt and cayenne pepper. Mix the sauces with the water and pour over the fish. Cover and cook in the centre of the oven for 45 minutes.

FISH AND MACARONI CASSEROLE

2 oz. macaroni (weight before cooking)
1½ lb. filleted cod
Salt and pepper
2 tsps. chopped parsley

2 oz. fresh white bread-crumbs
½ pint milk
1 egg, beaten
Butter

Oven temperature: fairly hot (375°F., mark 5)
Boil the macaroni in salted water until just tender – about 15 minutes. Put the cod in a greased ovenproof casserole, season well and add the parsley. Arrange the macaroni and bread-crumbs in layers round the cod. Heat the milk, add the egg and pour over the macaroni. Put a knob of butter on top, cover and bake in the centre of the oven for 1 hour, removing the lid before the end to let the top brown.

CIDER FISH CASSEROLE

1½ lb. fillet of cod or haddock
2 onions, skinned and finely chopped
½ lb. tomatoes, skinned and sliced
¼ pint dry cider

1 level tsp. dried sage or mixed herbs
Salt and pepper
2–3 tbsps. fresh white bread-crumbs
1 oz. cheese, grated (optional)

Oven temperature: warm (325°F., mark 3)
Wash the fish, cut into 4 pieces and place in an ovenproof casserole. Sprinkle the onion and tomatoes over and pour the cider round the fish. Sprinkle with the herbs and seasoning, cover with a lid or foil and bake in the centre of the oven for 20–30 minutes, until tender. Remove the lid, sprinkle the fish with the crumbs and cheese (if used) and brown under a hot grill before serving.

JELLIED TOMATO AND FISH SALAD

½ oz. gelatine
2 level tsps. sugar
1 tsp. Worcestershire sauce
Salt and pepper
1 pint tomato juice
Cooked peas

1½ lb. cooked white fish
¼ pint well-seasoned white sauce
Chopped chives, shelled shrimps and watercress sprigs to garnish

Dissolve the gelatine in a little hot water. Mix the sugar, Worcestershire sauce, seasoning and tomato juice and add the gelatine. Pour a little of this mixture into a wetted ring mould,

53

add the peas, then the rest of the liquid, and allow to set. Turn out on to a dish and fill the centre of the mould with the fish, bound together with white sauce. Garnish with chives, shrimps and watercress.

FISH SALAD

1 lettuce	1 tbsp. chopped gherkins
½ lb. cooked cod or	2 tomatoes, chopped
other fish	Mayonnaise
1 tbsp. cooked peas	Watercress, cooked peas
1 tbsp. chopped cooked	and cauliflower sprigs
cauliflower	to garnish

Arrange the lettuce round the edge of the dish, mix the fish, peas, cauliflower, gherkins, tomatoes and mayonnaise and place in the centre, then garnish.

FISH AND EGG SALAD PLATTER

Flake some cooked fish, mix with salad cream and seasoning and arrange down the middle of a long dish. Place some sliced peeled tomatoes, cooked peas and watercress round the dish and garnish the fish with slices of egg, sprinkled with red pepper.

Made-up Fish dishes

For the method of preparing flaked fish, which is required for most made-up dishes, see Chapter 1, p. 13.

FISH PIE

1 lb. cod fillet or any other	3 level tbsps. flour
white fish	2 tbsps. chopped parsley
1½–2 lb. potatoes	Salt and pepper
1½ oz. butter	2–4 oz. cheese, grated
¼ pint milk, plus 2–3 tbsps.	(optional)

Oven temperature: fairly hot (400°F., mark 6)

Cook and flake the fish, retaining ¼ pint of the cooking liquid. Boil and mash the potatoes in the usual way, add ½ oz. butter and 2–3 tbsps. milk and beat with a wooden spoon until creamy. Melt the remaining butter, stir in the flour and cook for 2–3 minutes. Remove the pan from the heat and gradually stir in the fish liquid and ¼ pint milk; bring to the boil. When the sauce has thickened, remove it from the heat and stir in the flaked fish, the parsley and seasoning to taste. Pour into an ovenproof dish and cover with the creamed potatoes, sprinkle with the cheese and bake near the top of the oven for about 30 minutes, until the pie is well heated through and the cheese golden.

The parsley sauce can be replaced by a white sauce to which one of the following has been added:

4 oz. mushrooms, chopped and lightly fried
4 oz. shrimps, peeled
2–4 oz. cheese, grated

FISH AND MUSHROOM PIE

1 lb. white fish
½ an onion, skinned and
  chopped
2 oz. mushrooms, sliced
1 oz. butter
A small can of condensed
  mushroom soup

2 tbsps. chopped parsley
Salt and pepper
1½–2 lb. hot creamed
  potatoes
1 tomato, sliced, to
  garnish

Bring the fish to the boil in a covered pan, turn off the heat and leave for 5 minutes. Sauté the onion and the mushrooms in the butter, then add the soup. Drain, skin and flake the fish and add it to the sauce, with the parsley and seasoning. When the mixture is hot, pour it into an ovenproof dish. Pile the hot potato over the fish. Arrange the tomato on the top. Re-heat and brown the pie under the grill or in the oven before serving.

FISH AND RICE PIE

1 lb. white fish
Milk
1 bay leaf
6 oz. long-grain rice
1 tbsp. chopped parsley
Juice and grated rind of
  ½ a lemon
1 small onion, skinned
  and chopped

½ a green pepper, chopped
1 oz. butter
1 egg, beaten
A little Worcestershire sauce
Salt and pepper
2 tbsps. fresh white
  bread-crumbs
Tomato or cheese sauce (see
  Sauces chapter, page 138)

Oven temperature: fairly hot (375°F., mark 5)
Poach or bake the fish in a little milk with a bay leaf until tender; drain and flake, removing all bones. Meanwhile cook the rice (see Sauces and Accompaniments chapter, p. 155). When it is cooked mix with the fish, parsley, lemon juice and rind, onion, green pepper, butter and egg; season with Worcestershire sauce, salt and pepper. Turn the mixture into a buttered casserole, top with the crumbs and bake in the centre of the oven for 30–40 minutes. Serve with a tomato or cheese-flavoured sauce.

FISH CAKES

½ lb. white fish (cod, haddock)
¾ lb. potatoes, peeled and
  quartered
1 oz. butter
1–2 tbsps. chopped parsley

Salt and pepper
Milk or beaten egg to bind
1 egg, beaten, to coat
Dry bread-crumbs
Fat for frying

Cook and flake the fish. Boil and drain the potatoes and mash with the butter. (Alternatively, use ½ lb. left-over mashed potatoes.) Mix the fish with the potatoes, parsley and salt and pepper to taste, binding if necessary with a little milk or egg. Form the mixture into a roll on a floured board, cut into 8 slices and shape into cakes. Coat with egg and bread-crumbs, fry in hot fat (deep or shallow) until crisp and golden; drain well on kitchen paper. As fish cakes tend to be dry, serve with a sauce such as tomato or parsley.

Vary the flavour of the cakes by using smoked haddock, herrings, canned tuna or salmon instead of white fish.

Cold fish sauce, if available, may be used instead of milk or egg to bind the mixture.

SALMON FISH CAKES

½ a pkt. of instant potato	2 tbsps. chopped parsley
1 oz. butter	Salt and pepper
1 oz. flour	1 small egg, beaten
¼ pint milk	Dry crumbs to coat
A medium-sized can of salmon	1½ oz. lard or cooking fat
(approx. 7½ oz.), drained	Parsley sauce (see p. 147)

Make up the potato as directed and leave to cool. Melt the butter in a saucepan, add the flour and cook for 2 minutes without browning, stirring continuously. Gradually stir in the milk and boil for 1 minute. Flake the salmon into a bowl, removing any bones. Add the potato, sauce and parsley, with salt and pepper to taste; cover and cool in a refrigerator. Divide the mixture into eight and form each piece into a flat round. Coat the cakes with egg followed by bread-crumbs and fry in the hot lard or fat for about 2 minutes on either side, until golden-brown. Drain them on crumpled kitchen paper and serve with parsley sauce.

FISH TIMBALE

¾ lb. hot cooked potatoes	½ lb. white fish, cooked
1 oz. butter	and flaked
2 oz. cheese, grated	Grated rind of ½ a lemon
Salt and pepper	1 tbsp. chopped parsley
Browned bread-crumbs	1 egg, beaten

Oven temperature: fairly hot (375°F., mark 5)

Mash the potatoes, add the butter, cheese and seasoning and beat until smooth. Grease a 6-inch cake tin, sprinkle with the bread-crumbs and line with most of the potato. Mix the fish. lemon rind and parsley, bind with the beaten egg, season well and place in the tin. Cover with the remaining potato mixture. Cover with greaseproof paper and bake at the top of the oven for 30 minutes. Turn out before serving.

56

CREAMED FISH AU GRATIN

¾–1 lb. white fish
¼ pint milk and water
1 small onion, sliced
A bouquet garni
Salt and pepper
1 lb. boiled potatoes,
  sliced

2 tomatoes, skinned and
  sliced
1 oz. butter
1 oz. flour
2–3 oz. cheese, grated
Chopped parsley to
  garnish

Oven temperature: moderate (350°F., mark 4)

Place the fish in a saucepan with the liquid, onion, herbs (tied in muslin) and seasoning and simmer gently for 10–15 minutes, or until the fish is cooked. Lift it out, remove any bones and thick skin and place in flakes in an ovenproof dish lined with a layer of the sliced potatoes. Arrange the tomatoes in a layer on the fish and sprinkle with salt and pepper.

Melt the butter and add the flour to make a roux. Slowly add the liquor in which the fish was cooked (making up to ¼ pint if necessary) and bring to the boil, stirring continuously. Boil for 2–3 minutes, then add half the cheese, season with salt and pepper and pour over the fish. Sprinkle with the remainder of the cheese and place in the top of the oven to heat through and brown the top. Before serving, garnish with chopped parsley.

FISH SOUFFLÉ

1 oz. butter
1 oz. flour
¼ pint fish stock and
  milk
3–4 oz. fish (fresh or
  smoked), cooked and
  flaked

1 tsp. anchovy
  essence
1 tsp. lemon juice
Salt and pepper
3 eggs, separated
1 tbsp. top of milk

Oven temperature: fairly hot (400°F., mark 6)

Melt the butter and stir in the flour; cook for a minute, then slowly stir in the liquid, cook well and cool. Add the fish, essence, lemon juice and seasoning and stir in the egg yolks and top of the milk. Fold in the stiffly beaten egg whites and put into a greased 6-inch soufflé dish. (See note below.) Bake towards the top of the oven for 30–40 minutes, until well risen and firm.

Note: It is traditional to use a special dish for a hot soufflé – fairly shallow in depth, smooth inside and fluted outside, and usually of plain white china, but dishes are also obtainable in coloured chinaware and in fireproof glass.

It used to be the fashion to tie a paper band round the dish, arranging it to come 3 inches above the top and greasing the inside. When you peeled the paper off after cooking the soufflé, it was then much higher than the dish. This looks nice, but the process is rather tedious and can quite well be omitted. The dish should always be greased inside.

FISH POTATO SOUFFLÉ

½ lb. white fish, cooked	2–3 tbsps. milk
¼ lb. cold cooked	Salt and pepper
potatoes	1 egg yolk
1 oz. butter	2 egg whites
1 oz. cheese, grated	Watercress to garnish

Oven temperature: fairly hot (400°F., mark 6)

Flake the fish and mash the potatoes. Melt the butter in a saucepan, add the potatoes and cheese and keep over a gentle heat until the cheese is melted. Beat thoroughly, and add enough milk to give a soft, creamy mixture. Add the fish, season and mix thoroughly. Cool slightly, then add the lightly beaten egg yolk. Whip the egg whites stiffly and fold in lightly. Put into a greased 6-inch soufflé dish (see note in previous recipe), and bake towards the top of the oven for about ¼ hour. Serve immediately, garnished with watercress.

SALMON RICE SOUFFLÉ

4 oz. long-grain rice	1 oz. flour
A 7½-oz. can of red or pink	¼ pint milk
salmon	3 eggs, separated
1 oz. butter	Salt and pepper

Oven temperature: moderate (350°F., mark 4)

Cook the rice, using the 1–2–1 method (see p. 155). Flake the salmon, removing any dark skin and bones. Melt the butter and stir in the flour to make a roux. Add the milk gradually, stirring all the time. Bring the sauce to the boil and allow to cook for 3–4 minutes. Cool slightly and add the flaked salmon, egg yolks, rice and seasoning. Whip the egg whites and fold into the salmon mixture. Pour into a greased soufflé dish (see note on Fish Soufflé) and bake towards the top of the oven for 30–40 minutes. Serve immediately.

HADDOCK KEDGEREE

12 oz. smoked haddock	3 oz. butter or margarine
6 oz. long-grain rice	Salt and cayenne pepper
2 hard-boiled eggs	Chopped parsley to garnish

Cook and flake the fish (see Chapter 1, p. 13). Cook the rice in the usual way and drain if necessary. Shell the eggs, chop one and slice the other into rings. Melt the butter or margarine in a saucepan, add the fish, rice, chopped egg, seasoning and stir over a moderate heat for about 5 minutes, until hot. Pile on a hot dish and garnish with lines of chopped parsley and the sliced egg.

KEDGEREE OF SALMON

3 oz. long-grain rice
A 3½-oz. can of salmon
½ pint white sauce
Cayenne pepper

Salt and pepper
A pinch of allspice
A little grated lemon rind
1 egg, hard-boiled

Boil the rice in salted water until tender, drain well and keep hot. Remove the skin and bones from the salmon and heat it in the white sauce. Mix together the rice, fish, sauce, seasonings, allspice, lemon rind and chopped white of egg. Serve at once, garnished with sieved egg yolk. (2 servings.)

FISH MOUSSE

8 oz. white fish, cooked
Pepper
3 tbsps. lemon juice
¼ pint mayonnaise or salad
  dressing

½ level tsp. celery salt
¼ pint fish stock
¾ oz. gelatine
¼ pint unsweetened evaporated
  milk

Mix the fish, pepper, lemon juice, mayonnaise or salad dressing and celery salt together. Heat the stock, dissolve the gelatine in it and allow to cool before adding it to the fish. When the fish and gelatine mixture is almost setting, whisk the evaporated milk and fold into the fish. When set, turn out and serve with salad.

FISH MOULDS

A little butter
½ a small onion, skinned
  and chopped
2 tsps. chopped parsley
6 oz. white fish, cooked and
  flaked
½ oz. gelatine
2 tbsps. hot water

½ pint fish stock
Salt and pepper
Tomato, cooked peas and
  radishes for garnish
Lettuce
4 oz. prawns or shrimps,
  shelled

Melt the butter in a pan and lightly fry the chopped onion. Remove from the heat and add the parsley and the fish. Meanwhile dissolve the gelatine in the hot water, add the fish stock and season well. Place a little of this at the bottom of 4 small moulds with a round of tomato, some peas and a slice of radish to garnish each; allow to set. Add the fish mixture to the remainder of the jelly and fill up the moulds. When set turn on to a dish and garnish with lettuce and prawns or shrimps.

SALMON CREAM RING

A 7½-oz. can of salmon
½ pint white sauce
2 tbsps. cream

Salt and pepper
Creamed potato
Hard-boiled egg to garnish

Flake the fish, mix with the white sauce and cream and season well. Serve in a border of creamed potato and surround the salmon with slices of hard-boiled egg.

SALMON MOUSSE

2 medium-sized cans of salmon (approx. 7½-oz.)
½ pint milk (approx.)
1 oz. butter
3 level tbsps. flour
2 eggs, separated
¼ pint double cream, lightly whipped

2 tbsps. tomato ketchup
1 tsp. anchovy essence
1 tsp. lemon juice
Salt and pepper
½ oz. gelatine
4 tbsps. warm water
Slices of cucumber to garnish

Drain the juice from the salmon and make up to ½ pint with milk. Remove the skin and bones from the fish and mash the flesh until smooth. Melt the butter, stir in the flour and cook for 2–3 minutes. Remove the pan from the heat and gradually stir in the salmon liquid and milk. Bring to the boil and continue to stir until the sauce thickens. Remove from the heat and add the egg yolks. Allow to cool slightly and stir in the cream, ketchup, essence, lemon juice and seasoning to taste and add to the salmon. Dissolve the gelatine in the warm water and stir into the salmon mixture. Whisk the egg whites stiffly and fold into the mixture. Pour into a 7-inch soufflé dish and leave to set in a cool place. Garnish with slices of cucumber before serving. (Serves 4–6.)

SALMON LOAF

2½ oz. butter
A 7½-oz. can of red salmon
1 medium-sized onion, skinned and grated
2 sticks of celery, grated

A pinch of salt
A pinch of pepper
1 egg, hard-boiled and sliced
Cucumber, watercress or hard-boiled egg to garnish

Butter a 1-lb. loaf tin. Drain the salmon and break up with a fork; add 2 oz. butter and beat the mixture until it is light-coloured and smooth in texture. Add the onion and celery to the salmon, with the seasonings. Put alternate layers of salmon and sliced egg into the loaf tin and chill for 4–5 hours. Turn out and garnish with cucumber, watercress or hard-boiled egg. (6 servings.)

SALMON NESTS

1½ lb. potatoes, peeled
Salt and pepper
A medium-sized can of salmon, (approx. 7½-oz.), drained
1½ oz. butter

1 oz. flour
½ pint milk
¼ lb. button mushrooms, sliced
2–3 tbsps. top of the milk

Cook the potatoes in boiling salted water until soft. Meanwhile flake the salmon, removing any bones and skin. Melt 1 oz. of the butter, add the flour and cook for 1–2 minutes. Stir in the milk, bring to the boil, stirring, and cook until the sauce thickens. Add the salmon and the mushrooms and simmer for 10 minutes. Drain the cooked potatoes and mash with the remaining butter, the top of the milk, salt and pepper. Pipe or spoon rings of this potato mixture on to an ovenproof plate and re-heat under a hot grill until brown. Divide the salmon mixture between the potato rings.

SALMON À LA KING

A large can of salmon (approx. 15½-oz.)	1 level tsp. garlic salt (optional)
2 oz. butter	Milk
3 sticks of celery, chopped	4 oz. button mushrooms, sliced
1 green pepper, seeded and chopped	1 canned red pimiento, chopped
1 oz. flour	Rice or croûtons
½ level tsp. salt	

Drain the salmon, reserving the liquid, and break the fish into chunks, removing any bone and skin. Heat the butter and fry the celery and green pepper for 3–4 minutes. Add the flour, salt and garlic salt (if used) and cook gently for 2–3 minutes. Make the salmon liquid up to ½ pint with milk and gradually add to the vegetable mixture, stirring well. Bring to the boil and simmer for 2–3 minutes. Add the salmon, mushrooms and pimiento and cook for 5 minutes. Serve with rice or croûtons.

Fish Soups

In this country "fish soup" tends to suggest Lobster Bisque and little else, but there are some good inexpensive soups and thick chowders which are well worth a place in the family menu. We give a small selection here, and other fish soups will be found in the next chapter, p. 94, and in the chapter on Shellfish, p. 112.

WHITE FISH SOUP – 1

¾–1 lb. white fish	1½ oz. butter
1 quart water	1½ oz. flour
1 onion or leek	¼ pint milk
Salt and pepper	Chopped parsley
A bouquet garni	Grated cheese (optional)

Wash and clean the fish and place in a pan with the water, sliced onion or leek and a little seasoning. Cook slowly for about 10–15 minutes, then remove the fish and flake it. Add the bouquet garni to the stock and simmer for a further 20 minutes, then strain it. Melt the butter, stir in the flour, cook without colouring. Gradually add the stock and milk. Add the flaked fish and seasoning to taste. Before serving, sprinkle with some freshly chopped parsley and, if desired, a little grated cheese.

WHITE FISH SOUP – 2

2 large onions	Salt
2 oz. butter	1 small white fish, filleted
1 oz. flour	1 roll
1 quart fish stock	Chopped parsley

Skin and slice the onions, fry in the butter until golden, add the flour and stock and stir until boiling. Strain through a sieve, return to the pan and season to taste. Cut the fish fillets into shreds and add to the soup, then simmer until the fish is cooked. Cut the roll into slices and crisp them in the oven, put in the tureen and pour soup over. Sprinkle with parsley.

FISH CHOWDER

1 onion, skinned and sliced	A large can of tomatoes
2 rashers of bacon, chopped	(approx. 15-oz.)
½ oz. butter	1 pint fish stock
3 potatoes, peeled and	Salt and pepper
sliced	1 bay leaf
1 lb. fresh haddock, skinned	2 cloves
and cubed	Chopped parsley to garnish

Lightly fry the onion and bacon in the butter for about 5 minutes, until soft but not coloured. Add the potatoes and the fish. Beat the tomatoes to a thick purée, add to the fish stock, combine with the fish mixture and add the seasoning and flavourings. Simmer for about ½ hour, until all the fish is soft but still in shape. Remove the bay leaf and cloves and sprinkle with parsley before serving.

FISH AND BACON CHOWDER

1 lb. white fish	1 lb. potatoes, peeled
6 rashers of bacon,	and sliced
rinded and chopped	Salt and pepper
1 large onion, skinned	Milk
and sliced	

Oven temperature: fairly hot (375°F., mark 5)
Wash and cut up the fish. Lightly fry the bacon. Put a layer of bacon in a casserole, next a layer of fish, then a layer of onion and potatoes. Season well and continue until the ingredients are used up. Add milk to cover by about 1 inch and bake in the centre of the oven for about 1 hour, or until cooked.

CHAPTER 4

Fish for special occasions

As the title suggests, we include here some recipes which are more elaborate and others which are based on the more expensive kinds of fish. The general arrangement is much the same as in the previous chapter, with the recipes in alphabetical order according to the name of the fish that is used; there follows a group of recipes in which various fish may be used, some made-up dishes, and some fish soups and chowders, including Bouillabaisse.

ANCHOVY RICE RING

2 hard-boiled eggs, sliced
A can of anchovies, drained
8 oz. long-grain rice, cooked

1 tsp. capers
1 tbsp. mayonnaise
Salt and pepper

Arrange the eggs round the base of a ring mould. Chop most of the anchovies and, with the remaining ingredients, add to the rice. Turn the mixture into the mould, press down lightly and chill thoroughly. Turn out and decorate with the remaining anchovies. Serve with salad.

BAKED BREAM
Oven temperature: moderate (350°F., mark 4)
Choose a large fresh-water bream of about 3–4 lb. Wash it, without removing the head, and wrap it in thin slices of bacon. Put in a tin and bake in the centre of the oven till tender (about 40 minutes), basting frequently; when it is cooked, the bacon fat melts and the fish is an attractive golden colour. Put it in a dish, remove the bacon, add a knob of butter and ½ cup cream and sprinkle with pepper.

If desired, the fish may be stuffed with a rice and olive stuffing; bake in a hot oven (425°F., mark 7) for 10 minutes, then in a moderate one as above for 30–40 minutes, or until it is done (i.e. allow about 10 minutes per lb.). Serve with horseradish sauce (see p. 145). (Sufficient for 6–7 people.)

POACHED BRILL

Oven temperature: fairly hot (375°F., mark 5)

Buy a fish weighing about 3–3½ lb., scale it, put into a tin with fish stock or 1 pint white wine or dry cider. Baste lightly and salt it, then cover with greased greaseproof paper; bake near the centre of the oven – a 3-lb. fish takes about 20–30 minutes. Serve it with a border of parsley and garnish with lemon wedges and grilled mushrooms filled with prawn sauce (see p. 148). Reduce and thicken the liquor, and pour over the fish. (Sufficient for 6 people.)

BAKED CARP AND MUSHROOMS

4 cross-cut pieces of carp (about 1½ lb.)	Salt and pepper
4 oz. button mushrooms, sliced	¼ pint red wine
1 tbsp. chopped parsley	¼ pint water
½ a small onion, skinned and finely chopped	1 level tbsp. cornflour or flour

Oven temperature: moderate (350°F., mark 4)

Soak the fish in salted water for 3–4 hours, rinse and wipe well. Put it in a greased ovenproof dish and add the mushrooms, parsley, onion, seasoning, wine and water. Cover with a lid or foil and bake in the centre of the oven for about 30 minutes, or until tender. Remove the fish, spoon the mushroom mixture over it and keep warm. Strain and retain ½ pint of the cooking liquid. Blend the cornflour with a little cold water and stir into the cooking liquid; put into a pan and bring the mixture to the boil, stirring all the time until it thickens. Cook for a further 1–2 minutes and adjust the seasoning if necessary. Serve the fish coated with this sauce.

STUFFED CARP

A whole carp (about 4 lb.), cleaned	1 bay leaf
	2–3 slices of lemon
Veal forcemeat (see Sauces and Stuffings chapter, p. 138)	Salt and pepper
	2–3 tbsps. port or red wine
1 small onion, skinned and finely chopped	1–2 oz. slivered blanched almonds (optional)

Oven temperature: moderate (350°F., mark 4)

Soak the fish in salted water for 3–4 hours, rinse and dry. Stuff the body cavity with veal forcemeat. Sprinkle with the onion, add the bay leaf, lemon, seasoning, about ¼ pint water and the port or red wine. Cover with a lid or aluminium foil and bake in the centre of the oven for about ¾ hour, or until the fish is tender. Put the fish on to a serving dish and keep it

(Cont'd page 65)

warm. Strain the cooking liquid into a pan and reduce slightly by rapid boiling. Serve the fish coated with the cooking liquid and sprinkled with the almonds, lightly browned under the grill. (Serves 6–7 people.)

SPANISH COD WITH RED PEPPER SAUCE

2 lb. fresh cod fillet	1 tbsp. vinegar
2 red peppers	¼ pint olive oil
1 clove of garlic, skinned and chopped	Salt
	Chopped parsley
½ pint fish stock or water	

Skin the fish and cut it into pieces. Halve the peppers, scoop out the seeds and cook the cases in boiling salted water for 5 minutes, then drain them and chop finely. Mix the red peppers and garlic together; crush them well, using the back of a wooden spoon. Choose a suitable-sized pan and add the pepper mixture, stock, vinegar, oil and salt to taste. Bring this liquid to boiling point, add the fish and cook very gently until it is tender. Drain the fish and keep it hot in a serving dish. Boil the liquid until it is reduced by half, pour over the fish and sprinkle with chopped parsley.

ITALIAN COD

1 lb. fresh cod fillet	1 lb. tomatoes
1 egg	2–3 oz. cheese, grated
Browned bread-crumbs	Ripe olives, lemons and
A little butter	parsley to garnish

Oven temperature: fairly hot (375°F., mark 5)

Cut the fillet into convenient-sized portions for serving, coat with egg and bread-crumbs and put on a greased baking tin. Dot with shavings of butter and bake in the centre of the oven for 20–25 minutes. Cut the tomatoes in half crossways and sprinkle with grated cheese. Bake these with the fish until golden-brown, or cook them under a hot grill. Put the fish and tomatoes on to a hot dish and garnish with ripe olives, slices of lemon and sprigs of parsley.

COD VÉRONIQUE

4 cod cutlets	1 oz. butter
1 shallot, skinned and sliced	1 oz. flour
2 oz. button mushrooms	¼ pint milk
Fish stock	1 cupful white grapes,
A little white wine (optional)	(peeled, halved and
Salt and pepper	seeded)

Oven temperature: fairly hot (375°F., mark 5)

Wash the fish and put into an ovenproof dish. Add the shallot and mushrooms and cover with fish stock and the wine, if used. Season and bake near the centre of the oven for 20 minutes. Drain off ¼ pint of the liquid and arrange the fish on a dish. To make a sauce, melt the butter, add the flour and gradually stir in ¼ pint stock and the milk. Season the sauce and boil till it thickens, then add most of the grapes. Pour this sauce over the fish and garnish with the remaining grapes and the mushrooms.

GURNET WITH WHITE WINE

2–3 gurnet	¼ of a Spanish onion, skinned
Salt and pepper	A little butter
1 tomato, skinned	¼ pint white wine
½ a lemon	Potato to garnish (see recipe)

Oven temperature: fairly hot (400°F., mark 6)
Wash and clean the fish, removing the head and fins. Score the skin across 3 times on each side, lay the gurnet in a well-greased shallow ovenproof dish and sprinkle with salt and pepper. Slice the tomato, lemon and onion very thinly and lay the slices over the fish. Sprinkle again with seasoning and put a few pieces of butter on top. Pour the wine round and cook in the centre of the oven for about 20 minutes, basting occasionally with the liquid. Meanwhile peel 3–4 potatoes, cut them into small pieces and boil in salted water until nearly tender; drain, add a small piece of butter and finish cooking on a very low heat. Use these potatoes to garnish the fish on its serving dish, and serve at once.

HADDOCK STROGANOFF
Oven temperature: fairly hot (400°F., mark 6)
Cover the bottom of a shallow baking dish with sliced lemon and arrange on this 1½ lb. skinned haddock fillet. Season lightly, cover, then bake in the centre of the oven for 20–30 minutes, or until the fish can easily be flaked with a fork but is still moist. Uncover, spread lightly with 1 carton of sour cream and sprinkle with salt and paprika; grill until lightly browned. Garnish with watercress.

HADDOCK SOUFFLÉ

½ lb. smoked haddock (or white fish such as cod, haddock)	A knob of butter
	2–3 oz. cheese, grated
2 level tbsps. cornflour	1–2 eggs, separated
½ pint milk	Salt and pepper

Oven temperature: fairly hot (400°F., mark 6)
Cook and flake the fish (see Chapter 1, p. 13). Blend the cornflour with 2 tbsps. of the cold milk and boil the remainder

with the butter; pour on to the blended cornflour, stirring well. Return the mixture to the pan and heat until boiling, stirring until the sauce thickens. Remove from the heat, add the cheese, fish and egg yolks and season well. Whisk the egg whites stiffly and fold into the fish mixture. Pour into a greased 6-in. soufflé dish and bake near the top of the oven for about 20 minutes, until well risen and golden. Serve immediately, for the mixture sinks as it cools.

Variation
Pour the mixture into a deep pie plate lined with shortcrust or flaky pastry and bake as above, allowing about ½ hour.

SALERNO FRIED HAKE

1 oz. butter	2–3 tbsps. stock
1 clove of garlic, skinned and finely chopped	¼ pint white wine
	Salt and pepper
1 tsp. chopped chives	4 fillets of hake or cutlets,
6 mushrooms, sliced	prepared
1 tbsp. chopped parsley	Olive oil
1 level tsp. flour	Parsley to garnish

Melt the butter in a saucepan, add the garlic, chives, mushrooms and parsley and cook for a few minutes. Stir in the flour and cook for a further 3 minutes. Gradually add the stock and wine, season and bring to the boil; cover and simmer gently for 10 minutes. Meanwhile, fry the fillets in oil. Drain, put into a hot dish and cover with the sauce. Garnish with parsley.

Note: Cod may be used in the same way.

MARINADED HAKE
To make the marinade, mix together sufficient white wine and Madeira or cooking sherry to make a tumblerful, season with salt and pepper and add sprigs of thyme and parsley, a bay leaf, and 1–2 chopped shallots.

Fillet the fish, seeing that no bones are left, and slash it at intervals, then leave to marinade for a day. The following day arrange the fillets of fish in a greased ovenproof dish and garnish with sliced mushroom. Strain the liquor over and cook for about 20 minutes in a moderate oven (350°F., mark 4), basting frequently. Before serving, re-season if necessary and add a few small nuts of butter and 2 tbsps. of cream or top of milk to the sauce, stirring well, so that it is evenly bound and thickened.

This method of cooking can be used for cod and for any fish of moderate size with rather dry flesh; it is also good for fresh-water fish such as carp and pike.

HALIBUT MORNAY

4 pieces of halibut	Salt and pepper
(about 1½ lb.)	½ pint milk (approx.)
2–3 slices of lemon	1 oz. butter
2–3 sprigs of parsley	3 level tbsps. flour
½ a bay leaf	4 oz. cheese, grated

Oven temperature: moderate (350°F., mark 4)

Wash and trim the fish, place in a shallow ovenproof dish and add the lemon, parsley, bay leaf, seasoning and half the milk. Cover with foil or a lid and bake in the centre of the oven for about 20 minutes, or until the fish is tender. Drain off, retaining the liquid, and keep the fish warm. Melt the butter, stir in the flour and cook for 2–3 minutes. Remove the pan from the heat and gradually stir in the cooking liquid, made up to ½ pint with more milk. Bring to the boil and continue to stir until the sauce thickens; remove from the heat and stir in 3 oz. of the cheese, with extra seasoning if necessary. Pour the sauce over the fish, sprinkle with the remaining cheese and brown in the oven or under a hot grill.

As a variant, the fish can be baked as above and placed on a bed of chopped spinach (cooked in the usual way) before being coated with the sauce.

Turbot may be used in place of halibut in this recipe.

BRAISED HALIBUT

4 steaks of halibut	2 egg yolks, beaten
2 tsps. chopped capers	1 glass white wine
2 tsps. chopped shallot	Salt and pepper
½ pint Béchamel sauce	Chopped capers and
2 tsps. anchovy essence	parsley to garnish

Oven temperature: moderate (350°F., mark 4)

Place the fish steaks in a greased ovenproof dish and sprinkle with the capers and shallot. Pour the sauce over, cover with greaseproof paper and bake in the centre of the oven for 10–15 minutes. When the fish is tender, lift it out on a hot serving dish. Re-heat the sauce, stir in the anchovy essence and gradually add the beaten egg yolks; don't boil the sauce after adding these, or it may curdle. Lastly, add the white wine, season to taste and strain the sauce over the fish. Serve garnished with chopped capers and parsley.

BAKED HALIBUT WITH ORANGES

4 slices of halibut	2 oranges
Salt and pepper	¼ pint milk
Butter	½ oz. flour

Oven temperature: moderate (350°F., mark 4)

Arrange the halibut in a greased ovenproof dish, season

and place a knob of butter on each piece. Peel the oranges and skin the sections, then put these on the fish and round the edge. Pour the milk over, cover with greased greaseproof paper and bake in the centre of the oven for ½ hour. Make a sauce with ½ oz. butter, the ½ oz. flour and the liquor from the fish. Place the fish in a dish, pour the sauce over it and arrange the orange slices round the edge.

HALIBUT AND CUCUMBER IN CHEESE SAUCE

4 steaks of halibut	½ a cucumber, peeled and
Salt and pepper	diced
6 peppercorns	1 oz. flour
A few parsley stalks	Milk
¼ pint dry cider	2 oz. cheese, grated
2 oz. butter	

Oven temperature: moderate (350°F., mark 4)

Wash and trim the halibut steaks, place in an ovenproof dish with the seasoning and flavourings and pour the cider over. Cover with foil and bake in the centre of the oven for about 20 minutes, until tender. Using 1 oz. butter, simmer the cucumber with some seasoning for about 10 minutes in a covered pan, until tender. When the fish is cooked, remove the peppercorns and parsley and drain off the cooking liquid. Make a sauce from the remaining butter, the flour and the cooking liquid from the fish, made up to ½ pint with milk. When it has thickened, remove from the heat, stir in half the cheese and season to taste. Pour over the fish, sprinkle with the remaining cheese and brown under a hot grill. Serve garnished with the cooked cucumber.

HALIBUT SALAD

1 lb. cooked halibut	Chopped pickles
1–2 hard-boiled eggs,	Mayonnaise
chopped	Watercress and cucumber
A few shrimps, shelled	to garnish
A few capers, chopped	

Remove the bones and skin from the fish and then flake it. Add the chopped egg, shrimps, capers and pickles, and mix all together with a little mayonnaise. Garnish before serving.

JOHN DORY À LA PORTUGAISE

1 small John Dory	⅓–½ pint fish stock or
2–3 oz. clarified fat	white wine
1 onion, skinned and	1 tomato, skinned and
finely chopped	chopped
½ oz. flour	1 tsp. chopped parsley
Salt and pepper	

Remove the head of the fish, trim the fins and tail and score across. Fry in hot fat, allowing about 7 minutes on each side, then remove the fish and keep hot. Add the onion and flour to the fat and stir round without browning. Add the seasoning, liquid, tomato and parsley, simmer very gently for 5–10 minutes, then strain the sauce over the fish.

John Dory is delicious cooked in any way suitable for sole, and may also be served in salads.

STUFFED MACKEREL

4 mackerel	Butter to baste
Fish forcemeat (see p. 152)	

Oven temperature: moderate (350°F., mark 4)

Cut off the heads and tails of the fish, clean them, remove the roes and take out the backbones. Stuff the fish, lay them in a greased ovenproof dish, and cook in the centre of the oven for 40 minutes, basting well with butter during the cooking.

MACKEREL IN CREAM SAUCE

4 mackerel	Fat for frying
A bunch of parsley, chopped	Salt
A little butter	¼ pint water
2 level tbsps. flour	¼ pint sour cream

Wash the fish, fillet them and sprinkle with parsley and a few flakes of butter. Roll up the fillets and tie them with fine string, toss them in flour and fry in a saucepan until brown. Add salt to taste, the water and the sour cream and let them simmer gently in the covered pan for 10 minutes. Remove the string and serve the fillets with the liquor poured over.

BAKED MACKEREL WITH ORANGE AND LEMON STUFFING

4 mackerel, cleaned	Green or orange salad

For the Stuffing

1 large orange, peeled	2 oz. fresh white
¼ an onion, skinned and	bread-crumbs
finely chopped	Juice of 1 lemon
1 tbsp. chopped parsley	Salt and pepper to taste

Oven temperature: moderate (350°F., mark 4)

Trim off the heads and tails from the mackerel and wash and wipe the fish. Chop the flesh of the orange (do this on a plate to retain the juice) and mix with the onion, parsley, bread-crumbs, lemon juice and seasoning. Fill the fish with stuffing and place in a greased ovenproof dish, add 2–3 tbsps. water and cover with a lid or foil. Bake in the centre of the oven for 20–30 minutes, until the fish is tender. Drain well and serve with a green or orange salad.

MACKEREL CALAISIENNE

4 mackerel   Tomato sauce (see p. 150)

For the Stuffing

½ an onion, skinned   1 tbsp. chopped parsley
  and chopped   Grated rind of ½ a lemon
1 hard-boiled egg,   (optional)
  chopped   Salt and pepper
2 oz. fresh white   Milk to mix
  bread-crumbs

Oven temperature: moderate (350°F., mark 4)

Clean and bone the fish and trim off the heads, tails and fins.
Mix the rest of the ingredients to make a stuffing and fill the
fish with it; place in an ovenproof dish with 2–3 tbsps. water,
cover and bake in the centre of the oven for 20–30 minutes.
Serve with tomato sauce.

If the fish have soft roes, these can be chopped and mixed
with the stuffing.

Herrings may, of course, be served in the same way.

RED MULLET EN PAPILLOTES

Oven temperature: moderate (350°F., mark 4)

As this is a thin-skinned fish which easily breaks up, it is often
cooked in a paper case. Clean the mullets, but leave in the
entrails, or at any rate the liver, which is considered a delicacy. Wrap each fish in a piece of strong greased greaseproof
paper, and place the fish in a greased ovenproof dish. Cover
the whole with another piece of greased greaseproof paper and
bake in the centre of the oven for 15–20 minutes. Collect the
liquor from the fish (still leaving each in its paper case), make
it up to ½ pint with stock and use it to make a sauce as follows:
put the liquor in a pan, cream together 1 oz. butter and 1 oz.
flour, add to the liquid and heat gently to boiling point, whisk-
ing all the time; add 4 tbsps. sherry and 1 tsp. anchovy essence, boil for a few minutes and serve separately. Dish the fish
up in the paper cases.

RED MULLET IN TOMATO SAUCE

4 red mullet, whole and   Oil or butter for frying
  cleaned   1–2 tbsps. fresh white
2 level tbsps. seasoned   bread-crumbs
  flour   1 tbsp. chopped parsley

For the Sauce

½ an onion, skinned and   1 lb. tomatoes, skinned
  finely chopped   and quartered
1 clove of garlic, skinned   Salt and pepper
  and crushed (optional)   2 level tsps. sugar
1 oz. butter   ½–1 bay leaf

71

First make the sauce. Fry the onion and the garlic (if used) in the butter for about 5 minutes, until soft. Add the tomatoes, seasoning, sugar and bay leaf, cover with a lid and simmer gently until soft and pulped – about ½ hour; remove the bay leaf. Wash the fish and wipe well. Dip in seasoned flour and fry in shallow fat until tender, turning them once and allowing 6–8 minutes in all. Place half the tomato sauce in a shallow ovenproof dish, lay the fish on top, then cover with the rest of the sauce; sprinkle with the bread-crumbs and brown under a hot grill. Sprinkle with parsley and serve at once.

BAKED PERCH

1 small perch per person	2 tsps. finely chopped parsley
Butter	Fried croûtons, lemon
About ½ pint white wine and fish stock, mixed	wedges and parsley to garnish

Oven temperature: fairly hot (400°F., mark 6)

Plunge the fish into boiling water for 2 minutes to make it easier to remove the scales. Trim, clean and wipe the fish, place in a well-greased ovenproof dish and dot with small pats of butter. Pour the white wine and stock over it, cover with foil or with greased greaseproof paper and bake in the centre of the oven for 20–30 minutes. Drain off the liquid and reduce by boiling. Gradually add 2 oz. butter, stirring constantly, then add the parsley. Serve the fish with this sauce poured over it; garnish with the fried croûtons, lemon and parsley.

GLAZED FILLETS OF PLAICE
(see colour picture No. 8)

8 plaice fillets	Radishes and cucumber skin
2 tbsps. mayonnaise	Tomatoes, lettuce and
1 tbsp. tomato ketchup	radish roses to
⅛ pint liquid aspic jelly	garnish

Skin the fillets, roll them up and steam or poach for 10–15 minutes, then leave on a rack to cool. Mix the mayonnaise, ketchup and aspic jelly and when on the point of setting, coat the cold fish fillets with the mixture. Garnish each fillet with sliced radish and pieces of cucumber skin as seen in the colour picture, and garnish the serving dish with tomatoes (preferably cut into water-lily shapes), radish roses and lettuce leaves.

CHAUDFROID OF PLAICE

Grill, bake or steam the fish, keeping it whole. While it is still hot, remove any skin, taking care not to break the fish. Now mix an aspic dressing (see Sauces chapter, p. 138) and coat the cold fish completely; garnish as desired, with sliced radish-

72

es, tomatoes, lemon butterflies or anchovy fillets, and piped savoury butter. (Soften some butter and mix it with seasoning to taste.)

Alternatively, use plaice fillets, allowing 2 per person. Skin them, roll them up, steam or poach for 10–15 minutes, then leave to cool on a rack. Glaze as above with aspic dressing (include if desired 1 tbsp. tomato ketchup in the dressing).

Salmon, turbot, brill and many other fish, used either whole or in steaks or fillets, may also be served in this way and make excellent summer buffet fare.

POACHED SALMON

In Large Pieces or Whole: If you have a large enough saucepan or a fish kettle you can cook the fish whole; otherwise it is better to cut it into 2–3 smaller pieces, scale, clean and wipe, weigh to calculate the cooking time, then wrap loosely in muslin, so that the pieces are easier to lift in and out of the pan.

Cover with court-bouillon (see the recipe on p. 10) and simmer gently until the fish is tender, allowing about 10 minutes per lb., depending on the thickness of the fish. When it is cooked, the flesh should come easily away from the bone. Serve with parsley sauce, new potatoes and peas. If the fish is to be served cold, let it cool in the cooking liquid before removing it from the pan.

Salmon Steaks or Slices: These tend to break unless very carefully cooked, so wrap them in muslin or buttered greaseproof paper and poach very gently for 10 minutes per lb. in court-bouillon, or more simply in salted water with a squeeze of lemon juice added. It is often easier to cook the pieces in a large frying-pan covered with a lid or large plate rather than in a saucepan, as it is then easier to remove the cooked fish. If it is to be eaten cold, let it cool in the cooking liquid before removing it.

GRILLED SALMON CUTLETS

The cutlets should be about 1 inch thick. Wipe them dry and brush with salad oil or melted butter. Grease the grill pan and cook the fish under a fairly hot grill, allowing about 10 minutes to each side and adding, if necessary, a little more fat as it cooks. Serve garnished with lemon and watercress, accompanied by melted butter, maître d'hôtel butter, or poached cucumber.

Here is an alternative method, which is particularly suitable for salmon that is not of the finest flavour:

Season the required number of slices of fish with salt and pepper, then marinade them for ¾ hour in a mixture of olive

73

oil, chopped parsley and chopped onion. Drain well, brush both sides of each slice with melted butter and grill, allowing about 10 minutes for each side. As soon as the slices have been turned over, place 4 anchovy fillets across the uncooked side before continuing to grill them.

BAKED SALMON STEAKS
Oven temperature: moderate (350°F., mark 4)
Wash and wipe the fish steaks and sprinkle with salt and pepper. Wrap each in greased foil or greaseproof paper, adding 1–2 sprigs of parsley and a squeeze of lemon if you like. Place on a baking sheet or shallow dish and bake in the centre of the oven for 20–30 minutes (according to the thickness of the fish), until tender. Serve hot with Hollandaise sauce or melted butter and lemon.

Traditional vegetable accompaniments are poached diced cucumber, green peas or asparagus and new potatoes.

Alternatively, skin the steaks, remove the central bone and serve the fish cold, with a mixed salad and mayonnaise.

GRILLED WHOLE SALMON
Wash and wipe the fish, sprinkle with salt and pepper and brush well with melted butter. Cook on a greased grill grid under a medium heat. When the top side is cooked, turn the fish, sprinkle the second side with salt and pepper, brush with butter and continue cooking until the fish is tender – about 15–20 minutes altogether, depending on the thickness of the fish. Serve hot, with the same vegetables and accompaniments as for baked salmon steaks.

BAKED WHOLE SALMON
Oven temperature: cool (300°F., mark 1–2)
Wash and wipe the fish. (If it is particularly large, cut it into several pieces, each weighing about 2 lb.). Wrap the fish in greased foil, put it on a baking sheet and bake in the centre of the oven for 30–35 minutes per lb., or until the flesh is just beginning to show signs of coming away from the bone.

STEAMED SALMON CUTLETS
This method of cooking and serving retains the full flavour of a prime cut of fish. Choose cutlets taken from the middle cut of salmon, scrape the skin free of scales and wash the fish carefully, or wipe it with a damp cloth. Steam in the usual way, allowing 12–15 minutes to the lb. and 12–15 minutes over; when the fish is cooked, the flesh should come away from the bone easily. Serve topped with a little melted butter and garnished with lemon butterflies and parsley. Boiled potatoes, peas and cucumber salad are the traditional accompaniments.

SALMON MAYONNAISE
Poach or bake a salmon (or a piece of one) as already described. Leave to cool and remove the skin. Coat the fish evenly
with mayonnaise, surround it with lettuce and garnish with
cucumber, tomato, radish or gherkins.

POACHED SALMON WITH GREEN MAYONNAISE SAUCE
Make ½ pint fish stock, flavouring it with an onion, a sliced
carrot and a bouquet garni. Poach a piece of salmon (see
recipe already given, p. 73) and when it is cooked, skin
carefully. Meanwhile make some mayonnaise and also boil a
handful of spinach leaves in a little water; sieve the spinach
and use this purée to tint the mayonnaise an appetising green
(not too deep a shade). Serve the salmon either hot or cold,
accompanied by the green sauce, which makes a pleasing
colour contrast.

DRESSED SALMON

A salmon	Parsley
Lemons	Watercress
Stuffed olives	Stuffed tomatoes or stuffed
Anchovy fillets	eggs to garnish (optional)
A lettuce	½ pint prawns, shelled

Poach the salmon whole, as already described, remove it from
the pan and leave to cool. Put it on a large dish. Remove part
of the skin on top and decorate this portion with cut lemon
rings, sliced stuffed olives and anchovy fillets; surround the
fish with lettuce leaves, parsley and watercress and garnish
with stuffed tomatoes or eggs. Place some prawns in the flesh
at the back edge of the fish. Serve with Tartare sauce.

SALMON IN ASPIC

1 small salmon	Radishes, cucumber, etc.,
¾ pint aspic jelly	to garnish

Have the fish cleaned but left whole. Poach or bake it in the
usual way (see separate recipes). Remove the skin from the
body, leaving on the head and tail. Make up the aspic according to the instructions and when it is just beginning to thicken,
coat the fish thinly. Decorate the fish, using thin rings of
radish, strips of cucumber skin or thin cucumber slices, diamonds or strips of tomato skin, rings of olive, sprigs of parsley, picked shrimps, etc. Cover with further layers of aspic
until the decoration is held in place.

Note: Probably the easiest way to carry out this process is on
a cooling tray, with a large plate underneath to catch the drips
of aspic as they fall through. When the aspic has set, transfer

75

the fish carefully to a large dish. Leave any remaining aspic to set, chop it on damp greaseproof paper with a sharp knife and use as a garnish. Serve the fish with a mixed salad and mayonnaise.

CHAUDFROID OF SALMON

1 medium-sized cut of cooked salmon (about 1½ lb.)
½ pint mayonnaise
½ pint aspic jelly

Olives, etc., to decorate
Lettuce, cooked carrots, hard-boiled eggs, etc., to garnish dish

Coat the salmon entirely with the mayonnaise sauce, then pour over it some aspic jelly which is just beginning to set. When this is set, decorate the top of the fish with small pieces of black and green olives, cooked carrot, tomato (or other suitable garnishings, as available); make a conventional design, or sprays of flowers, etc. Set the decoration with a little more aspic and put the fish aside until it is quite firm, then wipe the edges of the dish and garnish with lettuce, etc.

SALMON HOLLANDAISE

Butter
1½ lb. middle cut of fresh salmon
Lemon wedges to garnish

Hollandaise sauce (see Sauces and Stuffings chapter, p. 138)

Oven temperature: cool (300°F, mark 1–2)
Butter well a piece of foil or thick greaseproof paper. Lay the prepared fish in the centre of the paper and join the edges in such a way as to enclose the fish completely. Place on an ovenproof dish and bake in the centre of the oven for ¾–1 hour – the bone should just show signs of coming through the flesh. Unwrap while still warm and carefully remove the skin; leave to cool. When cold cut in half through to the bone, carefully lift on to a serving dish, lift the bone away and cut the lower portion in half. Reassemble and garnish with the lemon wedges. Serve the Hollandaise sauce separately.

FRESH SALMON AND CUCUMBER MOUSSE

1 cucumber
2 tbsps. French dressing
1 oz. gelatine
4 tbsps. water
½ lb. cooked salmon, mashed

1 tbsp. mayonnaise
Salt and pepper
¼ pint unsweetened evaporated milk

Cut some very thin slices of cucumber and marinade them in the French dressing for 2 hours or so. Cut the rest of the cucumber in half, discard the seeds and peel the pieces, then boil them for 5 minutes in salted water, drain well and sieve.

Dissolve the gelatine in the water and add to the sieved cucumber, with the salmon, mayonnaise and seasoning. Whip the evaporated milk and add it to the mixture, then pour into a wetted mould or 6-inch cake tin. When the mousse is set, turn it out on to a dish and garnish with the marinaded cucumber slices, which can be overlapped around the top and sides of the mould. Serve with a green or tomato salad.

BAKED SALMON TROUT
Cook as for Salmon; serve with a shrimp or other sauce.

SALMON TROUT IN ASPIC: Cook as for Salmon.

CHELSEA SOLE

2 shallots, skinned and finely chopped	Lemon juice
Salt and pepper	4 button mushrooms
4 fillets of sole	¼ pint white wine and water
Chopped parsley	2 egg yolks

Oven temperature: moderate (350°F., mark 4)
Butter an ovenproof dish and sprinkle in the shallots and seasoning. Wash the sole fillets, fold in half, skin side inwards, then arrange in the dish. Sprinkle with parsley and lemon juice and place slices of mushroom down each fish. Season, pour the liquid over, cover with a buttered paper and bake in the centre of the oven for 20 minutes. Remove the mushroom-covered fillets carefully on to a hot dish and keep hot. Add the egg yolks to the fish liquor, place over a very low heat and stir until the mixture thickens; pour over the fillets and garnish with parsley.

CURLED FILLETS OF SOLE

6 fillets of sole	Fish forcemeat (see Sauces and Stuffings chapter, p. 138)
1 pint prawns	

For the Sauce

¼ pint water	1 oz. flour
1 tbsp. vinegar	¼ pint milk
1 blade of mace	Salt and pepper
1 bay leaf	Anchovy essence
1 oz. butter	Cochineal

Oven temperature: fairly hot (375°F., mark 5)
Trim the fillets neatly; pick the prawns, reserving a few whole ones for garnish and keeping the shells and heads for stock. Make the stuffing and spread some of it on each fillet, then roll up, put in an ovenproof dish, cover with greased greaseproof paper and bake in the centre of the oven for 10 minutes. Meanwhile make the sauce: put the prawn shells, water,

vinegar, mace and bay leaf in a pan, boil for 10 minutes and strain. Melt the butter, mix in the flour, gradually add the stock and milk and cook for 2–3 minutes. Add 3 oz. of the prawns, season to taste and add a few drops of anchovy essence and 1–2 drops of cochineal, to give an attractive colour to the sauce. Cook for a further 2 minutes, pour round the stuffed fillets and garnish with the remaining prawns.

SOLE WITH ORANGE

4 sole, skinned	1 tbsp. sherry
Seasoned flour	$\frac{1}{2}$ tbsp. tarragon vinegar
2 oz. butter	Chopped parsley
1 small orange	

Cut off the fins and wash and wipe the fish. Coat with seasoned flour and fry gently, one at a time, in $1\frac{1}{2}$ oz. of the butter, turning them once to brown and cook the second side; keep them warm. Meanwhile skin and slice the orange. Combine the orange slices and any juice, the sherry and vinegar and heat very gently. When all the fish are cooked, arrange them on a heated serving dish and keep hot. Clean out the pan and lightly brown the remaining butter. Place the orange slices in a line down the centre of the fish, add the liquid in which they were heated to the browned butter in the pan and pour over the fish. Serve at once, garnished with chopped parsley.

Note: Plaice may be cooked in the same way.

SOLE BONNE FEMME

2 soles, filleted	1 tbsp. water
2 shallots (or 2–3 slices of onion), skinned and finely chopped	Salt and pepper
	1 bay leaf
	$1\frac{1}{2}$ oz. butter
4 oz. button mushrooms	2 level tbsps. flour
3 tbsps. dry white wine (e.g. Graves, Chablis)	$\frac{1}{2}$ pint milk (approx.)
	2–3 tbsps. cream

Oven temperature: moderate (350°F., mark 4)
Trim off the fins, wash and wipe the fillets and fold each in three. Put the shallot or onion in the bottom of an ovenproof dish, with the stalks from the mushrooms, finely chopped. Cover with the fish fillets, pour round them the wine and water, sprinkle with salt and pepper and add the bay leaf. Cover with foil or a lid and bake in the centre of the oven for about 15 minutes, until tender. Strain off the cooking liquid and keep the fish warm.

Fry the mushroom caps lightly in half the butter. Melt the remaining butter, stir in the flour and cook for 2–3 minutes. Remove the pan from the heat and gradually stir in the cooking liquid from the fish, made up to $\frac{1}{2}$ pint with milk. Bring to the boil and continue to stir until the sauce thickens, remove from the heat and stir in the cream. Pour the sauce over the fish and serve garnished with the mushroom caps.

Notes: In the classic version of Sole Bonne Femme, the fish is next coated with Hollandaise sauce and is browned under a hot grill before being served, but the recipe given here is the one more usually followed.

Plaice and other white fish can also be cooked in this way.

SOLE COLBERT
(see colour picture No. 10)

1 small sole per person
Seasoned flour
Beaten egg
Dry bread-crumbs
Deep fat for frying

Maître d'hôtel butter
 (see Sauces and Stuffings
 chapter, p. 138)
Lemon and parsley to garnish

Have the heads cut off the fish and the black skin removed. Wash and wipe the soles, make a slit down the backbone and loosen the fillets from the bone on one side, using a sharp knife and taking care to keep the fish whole. Break the backbone at each end, so that it may be more easily removed after the fish is cooked. Dip the soles in seasoned flour and coat with beaten egg and bread-crumbs. Heat the fat until it will brown a 1-inch cube of bread in 1 minute; fry the fish for about 10 minutes and drain on crumpled kitchen paper. Using scissors or a knife, cut the backbone and ease it from the cooked fish. Fill the centre cavity of each fish with maître d'hôtel butter, garnish with lemon and parsley and serve at once.

TOMATO-GLAZED PAUPIETTES OF SOLE

Salt and pepper
8 sole fillets
Anchovy paste
Fish stock or water
$\frac{1}{2}$ pint stiff aspic jelly

$\frac{1}{4}$ pint tomato sauce (see p. 150)
8 rounds of tomato
1 head of lettuce
4 stoned olives

Oven temperature: moderate (350°F., mark 4)
Season the fillets, spread with anchovy paste, roll up neatly and place on a greased tin. Pour on sufficient fish stock or water to come half-way up the fish, cover with greaseproof paper and bake in the centre of the oven for 10–15 minutes. Lift on to a rack and leave to cool. Mix the aspic jelly with the tomato sauce; when cold and on the point of setting, glaze the fish with the mixture. Place each fillet on a round of tomato and garnish with crisp lettuce leaves and any remaining aspic jelly, chopped and placed round the dish. Lay half a stoned olive on top of each paupiette.

79

PAUPIETTES OF SOLE WITH MUSHROOM SAUCE

8 fillets of sole
A small pkt. of frozen
   shrimps
1½ oz. butter

2 oz. button mushrooms
½ pint milk
Salt and pepper
1 oz. flour

Oven temperature: moderate (350°F., mark 4)

Roll the fillets with 2 or 3 shrimps inside each one and stand them upright in a greased ovenproof dish. Put a very small knob of butter on each and cover with paper. Bake in the centre of the oven for 20 minutes. Meanwhile wash the mushrooms and stew them gently in the milk with seasoning for 10–15 minutes. Drain off the liquid, melt 1 oz. of the butter and add the flour, then gradually add the milk and fish liquor. Bring to the boil, add the mushrooms and pour over the fish.

SOLE FILLETS IN ASPIC

8 fillets of sole
Court-bouillon
16 green grapes, peeled
1 large carrot, cooked

½ pint aspic jelly (to which
   2 extra tsps. of sherry have
   been added)

Roll each sole fillet up and secure with a cocktail stick. Poach gently in the court-bouillon, then remove them, chill and take out the cocktail sticks. Place them in a circle on a small dish, so that they touch each other. Place 2 grapes on the top of each roll. Slice the carrot into match-like strips and lay these in the central hollow. Mask both fish and carrots with a coat of aspic – which should be syrupy and almost setting – allow to set and give a second coat. (This dish may be made the day before it is needed, provided it is kept in a refrigerator.)

FILLETS OF SOLE DUGLÉRÉ

2 sole, filleted
1–2 shallots, chopped
½ a bay leaf
A few sprigs of parsley
¼ pint white wine
¼ pint water
Salt and pepper

1 oz. butter
3 level tbsps. flour
3 tbsps. single cream
2 tomatoes, skinned and
   diced, with seeds removed
2 tsps. chopped parsley

Oven temperature: moderate (350°F., mark 4)

Wash and wipe the fish and put in an ovenproof dish with the shallots, herbs, wine, water, salt and pepper. Cover with foil or a lid and bake in the centre of the oven for about 15 minutes, or until tender. Strain off the cooking liquid and keep the fish warm. Melt the butter, stir in the flour and cook for 2–3 minutes. Remove the pan from the heat and gradually stir in the cooking liquid from the fish. Bring to the boil and continue to stir until the sauce thickens. Remove from the heat and stir in the cream, tomatoes and parsley. Adjust the seasoning if necessary and pour over the fish.

Note: You can cook most white fish in Dugléré style.

SOLE MEUNIÈRE

4 small soles, skinned	½–1 tbsp. chopped parsley
Seasoned flour	The juice of 1 lemon
3 oz. butter	Lemon slices to garnish

Cut off the fins from the soles and wipe the fish; coat them with seasoned flour. Heat 2 oz. butter in the frying-pan, put the fish in upper side first and fry gently for about 5 minutes, until brown. Turn them over carefully and continue frying for a further 5 minutes, or until they are tender and golden. Drain on crumpled kitchen paper and place on a hot serving dish. Wipe the pan clean, melt the remaining butter and heat until lightly browned. Add the parsley and lemon juice and pour immediately over the fish. Garnish with lemon.

Note: Although it is more traditional to cook the fish on the bone, fillets of sole can be used. Plaice and other white fish can also be cooked à la meunière.

SOLE VÉRONIQUE

2 sole, filleted	¼ pint dry white wine, (e.g.
2 shallots (or 2–3 slices	Graves, Chablis)
of onion), skinned and	4 oz. white grapes
chopped	¾ oz. butter
2–3 button mushrooms, sliced	2 level tbsps. flour
A few sprigs of parsley	¼ pint milk, approx.
½ a bay leaf	A squeeze of lemon juice
Salt and pepper	1–2 tbsps. single cream
¼ pint water	

Oven temperature: moderate (350°F., mark 4)

Trim off the fins, wash and wipe the fillets and lay them in a shallow ovenproof dish with the shallots, the mushrooms, herbs, seasoning, wine and water. Cover with foil or a lid and bake in the centre of the oven for about 15 minutes or until tender. Simmer the grapes for a few minutes in a little water or extra white wine, peel them and remove the pips.

Meanwhile, strain the liquor from the fish and reduce it slightly by boiling rapidly; keep the fish warm. Melt the butter, stir in the flour and cook for 2–3 minutes. Remove the pan from the heat and gradually stir in the reduced fish liquor, made up to ½ pint with milk. Bring to the boil and continue to stir until the sauce thickens. Remove from the heat and stir in most of the grapes, the lemon juice and the cream. Pour over the fish and serve decorated with the remaining grapes.

Note: You can cook plaice fillets in the same way.

SOLE MORNAY

6–8 fillets of sole
Salt and pepper
Lemon juice
Nutmeg
2 tbsps. white wine
 (or milk)
1 oz. butter

1 oz. flour
Milk
2 oz. cheese, grated
Sprigs of parsley and
 lemon slices or butter-
 flies to garnish

Oven temperature: moderate (350°F., mark 4)

Remove the dark skin from the fillets, season and add the lemon juice; roll up neatly and put into a greased dish. Sprinkle with a little grated nutmeg and add the wine or milk. Cover and bake in the centre of the oven for about 15 minutes, until the fish is cooked. Strain off the liquor, make up to ½ pint with milk. Use this to make a white sauce (see Sauces and Stuffings chapter, p. 138), add lemon juice to taste and stir in most of the grated cheese. Put some of this sauce into the hot serving dish, add the fish and pour the rest of the Mornay sauce over. Sprinkle with the rest of the cheese and brown under the grill if desired. Garnish with parsley and lemon.

Plaice may be cooked in the same way.

SOLE AU VIN BLANC – 1

4 small sole (whole)
2 shallots, skinned and
 finely chopped
½ oz. butter
¼ pint white wine

½ oz. flour
A few button mushrooms,
 washed
Salt and pepper

Oven temperature: moderate (350°F., mark 4)

Wash the fish and put into an ovenproof dish. Fry the shallots in the hot butter for 3–4 minutes. Add the wine and pour over the soles. Cover with greased greaseproof paper and bake in the centre of the oven for 7 minutes. Drain off the liquid and add the flour, blended with a little water; bring to the boil, add the mushrooms and boil gently for 2–3 minutes; season well and pour over the sole.

SOLE AU VIN BLANC – 2

2 soles, filleted
2 oz. butter
Salt and pepper
½ pint dry white wine
½ oz. flour

¼ pint water
2 egg yolks
Shrimps and parsley to
 garnish

Oven temperature: moderate (350°F., mark 4)

Place the rolled-up fillets in a buttered ovenproof dish, dot with 1 oz. of the butter and season. Pour half the wine over, cover and poach for 20 minutes in the centre of the oven. Melt

½ oz. butter in a pan, add the flour and cook without colouring. Gradually add the rest of the wine, with ¼ pint water, and cook until thick. Drain the fillets and keep hot on a serving dish. Add the egg yolks to the sauce, heat gently, remove from the heat and add the remaining butter. Coat the fish with the sauce and garnish with shrimps and parsley.

SOLE IN EGG SAUCE (Chinese)

1½ lb. fillet of sole (or other white fish)
3 eggs
1 level tsp. salt
4 level tbsps. cornflour
4 tbsps. cooking oil
2 scallions or spring onions, finely chopped
2 slices of ginger, finely chopped
1 tbsp. sherry and 2 tbsp. water

Prepare the fish by removing the skin and bones and cutting the flesh into 1½-inch pieces. Beat the eggs lightly and add ½ level tsp. salt. Slowly fold in the cornflour and mix together until smooth. Dip the fish pieces in this batter, covering them well. Heat the oil in a pan and when it is very hot, sauté the fish for about 2 minutes on each side. Add the rest of the ingredients to the egg mixture, blending well; add to the fish and cook for 2–5 minutes, or until the sauce thickens. Serve very hot.

BAKED SOLE IN CHINESE SWEET–SOUR SAUCE

1–2 Dover sole
Salt and pepper
Juice and grated rind of a lemon
2 pickled onions
Sweet-sour sauce (see recipe below)

Oven temperature: fairly hot (400°F., mark 6)

Skin the fish and remove the head and fins, then grease an ovenproof dish and lay the sole on it. Season and sprinkle with a little water, lemon juice and grated rind. Cover with greased greaseproof paper and bake for about 15 minutes in the centre of the oven. Remove from the oven, slice the onions over the fish, pour the heated sauce over and return the dish to the oven for 2–3 minutes. (Serves 2–4.)

SWEET–SOUR SAUCE

2–3 tomatoes, skinned
2 oz. sweet pickle
1 tbsp. oil
¼ pint water
2 tbsps. vinegar
1½ level tbsps. sugar
1 dessertsp. molasses
2 tbsps. soy sauce
1 level tbsp. cornflour blended with 2 tbsps. water

Fry the tomatoes and pickle in the oil for 10 minutes, add all the other ingredients, except the blended cornflour, and simmer for 20 minutes. Thicken with the cornflour.

STURGEON À LA RUSSE

3 sticks of celery
3 leeks
1 carrot
1 onion
10 shallots
10 mushrooms
3 pickled cucumbers
4 lb. sturgeon

Salt and pepper
2 tsps. vinegar
1 oz. butter
1 oz. flour
2 level tbsps. tomato paste
1 tbsp. capers
1 pickled gherkin
5 olives

Wash the celery, cut up 2 of the stalks and dice 1; wash the leeks, cut up 2 of them and dice 1; peel and cut up the carrot; skin and slice the onion; skin and dice the shallots; wash and dice the mushrooms; dice the pickled cucumbers.

Clean and scale the fish, put it into a pan and cover with cold water, adding 1 level tsp. salt, the vinegar, the cut-up celery, leeks and carrot and the sliced onion. Bring slowly to simmering point and cook for about 40 minutes, or until the fish is done. Remove and drain the sturgeon. Strain the stock in which it was cooked, add the diced vegetables and boil for 10 minutes. Melt the butter in a saucepan, add the flour, stir well and add some of the hot stock. Add this mixture to the rest of the stock, with the tomato paste, capers, pickled gherkin and olives and add salt and pepper to taste. Pour over the fish. (Serves 6–8.)

This dish is equally good hot or cold; salmon may be used instead of sturgeon.

GRILLED TROUT

Clean and scale the trout, dry them, brush with olive oil and sprinkle with salt and pepper. Put them on to a hot grill and cook for 5–10 minutes on each side, turning the fish carefully to prevent damaging the skin. Serve at once, garnished with cut lemon and watercress.

Other fresh-water fish which may be served grilled like trout, fried (either whole or cut up) or baked, are barbel, dace, grayling, gudgeon, perch, roach and tench.

TROUT À LA MEUNIÈRE

2 large trout
1 level tbsp. seasoned
   flour
4 oz. butter

Lemon juice
Thinly sliced lemon
   to garnish
Finely chopped parsley

Clean and dry the fish and toss in seasoned flour. Heat half the butter in a frying-pan and fry the fish in it until they are golden-brown on both sides and cooked through; lift them out on to a hot dish. Add the rest of the butter to that already in the pan and heat it until it is golden-brown. Flavour it with lemon juice and pour it over and around the fish. Garnish with the lemon and parsley.

TROUT IN CREAM

4 trout	$\frac{1}{8}$–$\frac{1}{4}$ pint single cream
Juice of 1 lemon	2 tbsps. white bread-crumbs
1 tbsp. chopped chives	A little melted butter
1 tbsp. chopped parsley	

Oven temperature: moderate (350°F., mark 4)
Clean and dry the fish (the heads can be left on or removed). Lay them in a greased shallow ovenproof dish and cover with the lemon juice, herbs and about 1 tbsp. water. Cover with foil and bake in the centre of the oven for 10–15 minutes, or until tender. Heat the cream gently and pour over the fish, sprinkle with the bread-crumbs and melted butter and brown under a hot grill. Serve at once.

TROUT AND ALMONDS

4 trout (about 4–5 oz. each)	2 oz. blanched almonds, cut
Seasoned flour	in slivers
6 oz. butter	Juice of $\frac{1}{2}$ a lemon

Clean and dry the fish, but leave the heads on. Coat with seasoned flour. Melt 4 oz. butter in a large frying-pan and fry the fish two at a time, turning them once, until they are tender and golden on both sides – 12–15 minutes. Drain and keep warm on a serving dish. Clean out the pan and melt the remaining butter; add the almonds and heat until lightly browned, add a squeeze of lemon juice and pour over the fish. Serve at once, with wedges of lemon.

TRUITE AU BLEU

This is suitable only for a freshly killed fish. Clean immediately, leaving the fish whole and the head on; put in a saucepan with 1–2 tbsps. boiling vinegar and cover with boiling court-bouillon (see recipe on p. 10). The fish will curl round, which is quite usual. Reduce the heat and simmer for about 15 minutes, or until tender. Drain and serve with melted butter to which a squeeze of lemon juice has been added.

RIVER TROUT EN PAPILLOTES

8 small trout	Salt and pepper
2 oz. butter	A little chopped parsley
A squeeze of lemon juice	Lemon wedges

Oven temperature: moderate (350°F., mark 4)
Small trout only should be used for this dish. Clean and leave the heads on. Cream the softened butter with the lemon juice and seasoning and add the parsley. Spread the sides of

the fish lightly with this and then wrap each in a piece of
buttered greaseproof paper, twisting the ends to make a bag.
Bake in the centre of the oven for about 20 minutes. Serve in
the bag to retain the flavour and liquor, or dish up if preferred,
after unwrapping the fish. Garnish with lemon wedges.

Good accompaniments are mushrooms poached in milk
and stock and steamed or boiled potatoes.

This is a good way of cooking grayling.

TROUT VIN ROUGE

4 small trout, cleaned	¼ pint dry red wine
2 oz. button mushrooms, sliced	¾ oz. butter
	¾ oz. flour
1 bay leaf	2–3 tbsps. single cream
1 clove	or top of the milk
Salt and pepper	

Oven temperature: moderate (350°F., mark 4)

Wash the fish and cut off the fins. (Leave the heads on or
remove, as preferred.) Place the fish in a shallow ovenproof
dish and add the mushrooms, bay leaf, clove, seasoning and
wine. Cover with foil and bake in the centre of the oven for
about 20 minutes, until tender. Strain off the cooking liquid
(retaining the mushrooms) and keep the fish warm. Make a
roux from the butter and flour and gradually add the cooking
liquid, made up to ½ pint if necessary with stock or water.
When the sauce has thickened, remove it from the heat and
stir in the mushrooms and the cream. Adjust the seasoning if
necessary and pour the sauce over the fish.

TROUT VIN BLANC
(see colour picture No. 9)

4 trout, cleaned	2 oz. mushrooms, finely sliced
Salt and pepper	
1 lemon	1 wineglass white wine
1 oz. butter	(or dry cider)
A little chopped parsley	Lemon wedges to garnish

Oven temperature: moderate (350°F., mark 4)

Grease a shallow ovenproof dish with butter and lay the trout
in this; season inside and out with salt, pepper and lemon
juice. Mix some of the butter with the chopped parsley and
put some inside each fish. Add the mushrooms and pour in
the wine (or cider). Put some small shavings of butter over the
trout, cover, and bake in the centre of the oven for 20 minutes.
Garnish with cut lemon.

TROUT IN ASPIC

Like salmon, trout can be cooked in court-bouillon, left to
cool in the liquid, then skinned, decorated and glazed with

about ½ pint aspic. (see Salmon in Aspic, p. 75.) This is a good dish for a formal buffet.

GRILLED RAINBOW TROUT
Clean and dry the trout, split open and remove the bones, then brush them over with melted butter or olive oil; season and sprinkle with a little lemon juice. Lay the fish on the grill rack and cook for 5–10 minutes on each side. Serve them very hot, garnished with lemon wedges and parsley.

RAINBOW TROUT WITH PIMIENTO SAUCE
(see colour picture No. 11)

2 10½-oz. cans of rainbow trout	2 level tbsps. flour
1 egg, beaten	¼ pint milk
Crushed potato crisps	¼ pint dry white wine
Butter	1 level tbsp. chopped red pimiento

Dip the trout in the egg and coat with crisps; fry gently in a little butter, turning them once, till browned. Put any remaining butter in a saucepan and heat gently; stir in the flour, add the milk gradually, bring to the boil and stir in the wine and pimiento. Serve this sauce with the trout.

BRAISED TURBOT

¾–1 lb. turbot	½ pint Béchamel sauce (see p. 139)
Salt and pepper	
1–2 tbsps. finely chopped onion	2 egg yolks
Chopped parsley	1 tsp. anchovy essence
¼ pint white wine or cider	2 tbsps. capers
	A few gherkins

Oven temperature: fairly hot (375°F., mark 5)
Wash the fish thoroughly and put in an ovenproof dish, dark side uppermost. Sprinkle it with seasoning, chopped onion and 2 tsps. chopped parsley, pour the wine or cider round it, cover with greaseproof paper and bake it near the centre of the oven for 20 minutes. When it is cooked, remove the black skin. Drain off the liquid into a pan, add the Béchamel sauce and the egg yolks and heat gently, without boiling; stir all the time until the sauce is of a coating consistency, then add 2 tbsps. chopped parsley, the anchovy essence and some of the capers. Put the fish in a serving dish, pour the sauce over it and serve garnished with capers and gherkins. (Serves 2–3.)

TURBOT BONNEFOY

4 fillets of turbot	½ lb. mushrooms
Salt and pepper	1 glass of claret
2 medium-sized onions, chopped	1 pint tomato sauce (see Sauces chapter, p. 150)

Oven temperature: moderate (350°F., mark 4)
Put the fish into an ovenproof dish and season. Add the onions, the mushrooms and claret. Cover with buttered greaseproof paper and bake in the centre of the oven for 10–15 minutes. Put the fish on a serving dish. Re-heat the fish liquor with the sauce, boil for 5 minutes and pour over the fish.

TURBOT MARENGO

4 slices of turbot	2 oz. butter
Stock	2 oz. flour
1 onion, skinned and chopped	¼ pint tomato purée
1 oz. dripping	Salt and pepper
1 small carrot, peeled and sliced	Stuffed olives, parsley and sliced lemon to garnish
1 turnip, peeled and sliced	
A bunch of mixed herbs	

Oven temperature: fairly hot (375°F., mark 5)
Put the fish in an ovenproof dish, pour in a little stock, cover with a piece of greased paper and bake near the top of the oven for about 10 minutes, until cooked. Meanwhile fry the onion in the dripping, then fry the carrot and turnip and add the herbs; lastly add ½ pint stock and cook for 15–20 minutes. Melt the butter in a pan, add the flour and cook gently until it is quite brown. Strain the stock into it, add the tomato purée and cook for a further 10 minutes. Season well, then pour this sauce over the fish. Garnish with the sliced olives, etc.

TURBOT WITH CRAB SAUCE

4 pieces of turbot or halibut (about 1½ lb.)	¾ oz. butter
2–3 slices of onion	2 level tbsps. flour
A few sprigs of parsley	¼ pint milk (approx.)
½ a bay leaf	A 3¼-oz. can of crabmeat
Salt and pepper	1–2 oz. Parmesan cheese, grated
¼ pint dry white wine	

Oven temperature: moderate (350°F., mark 4)
Wash and trim the fish, place in a shallow ovenproof dish with the onion, parsley, bay leaf and seasoning and pour in the wine. Cover and bake in the centre of the oven until tender – about 20 minutes, depending on the thickness of the fish. Drain off and retain the cooking liquid and keep the fish warm. Melt the butter, stir in the flour and cook for 2–3 minutes. Remove the pan from the heat and gradually stir in the cooking liquid, made up to ½ pint with milk. Bring to the boil and continue to stir until the sauce thickens. Add the flaked crabmeat and continue cooking for a further 2–3 minutes. Pour over the fish in an ovenproof dish, sprinkle with the cheese and brown under a hot grill.

SUMMER TURBOT

1–1½ lb. cold cooked turbot
Oil and vinegar for
  marinading
Salt and pepper
3 eggs, hard-boiled
¼ level tsp. mustard (dry)

2 tbsps. oil
2 tsps. vinegar
1 tbsp. chopped parsley
A few capers
Watercress to garnish

Remove the bones and skin from the fish, cut in neat slices and marinade for an hour in a mixture of oil, vinegar and salt. Shell and halve the eggs, remove the yolks and fill up the whites with the rest of the ingredients, mixed with the egg yolks and seasoned to taste. Arrange the fish on a dish garnished with the eggs and watercress.

SPANISH WHITING

1 lb. filleted whiting
2 Spanish onions, skinned
  and sliced
1½–2 tbsps. olive oil
2 tsps. vinegar
A few peppercorns

Salt and pepper
1 lb. tomatoes, skinned and
  sliced
2 tbsps. chopped celery
½ pint fish stock or water

Oven temperature: fairly hot (400°F., mark 6)

Wipe the fillets. Boil the onions for about 10 minutes, then drain (reserving the liquor) and put them in an ovenproof dish with the oil, vinegar, whiting and peppercorns. Season well, cover with the tomatoes and celery and pour the stock and 2–3 tbsps. onion water over the fish. Cover the casserole and cook in the centre of the oven for 40 minutes, or until the fish is tender.

RUSSIAN FISH PIE

½ lb. white fish, e.g., cod,
  haddock
1 oz. butter
3 level tbsps. flour
¼ pint milk
2 tbsps. chopped parsley

Salt and pepper
1 hard-boiled egg, chopped
4 oz. ready-made flaky
  pastry
Beaten egg to glaze

Oven temperature: fairly hot (400°F., mark 6)

Cook and flake the fish (see notes on p. 13), retaining ¼ pint of the cooking liquid. Melt the butter, stir in the flour and cook for 2–3 minutes. Remove the pan from the heat and gradually stir in the fish liquid mixed with the milk. Bring to the boil and continue to stir until the sauce thickens. Mix half the sauce with the flaked fish, parsley, seasoning and chopped egg. Roll out the pastry thinly into a fairly large square and place on a baking tray. Put the filling in the centre in a square shape, brush the edges of the pastry with beaten egg and draw them up to the middle to form an envelope shape. Press the edges

89

well together, flake them with the back of a knife and scallop them. Brush the pie with beaten egg and bake towards the top of the oven for about 30 minutes, until golden. Serve with the remaining parsley sauce.

FISH PROVENÇALE

1 onion, skinned and chopped	1 lb. fillet of cod, haddock or whiting, skinned
½–1 green pepper, seeded and chopped	Seasoned flour
	A 15-oz. can of tomatoes
2–3 oz. streaky bacon, rinded and chopped	1 bay leaf
	2 level tsps. sugar
1 oz. butter	Salt and pepper

Fry the onion, pepper and bacon gently in the butter for 5–10 minutes, until soft but not coloured. Wash and dry the fish and cut into 1-inch cubes. Toss the fish in seasoned flour and fry with the vegetables and bacon for a further 2–3 minutes. Stir in the drained tomatoes, bay leaf, sugar and seasoning, bring to the boil, stirring gently, cover with a lid and simmer for 10–15 minutes, until the fish and vegetables are cooked. Serve with boiled rice or potatoes.

MIXED FISH CASSEROLE

1 lb. onions, skinned and chopped	½ lb. cod steaks
	½ lb. filleted mackerel
3 tbsps. olive oil	½ lb. filleted hake
2 cloves of garlic, grated	1 oz. long-grain rice, washed
2 green peppers, cut in strips	Pepper and salt
1 lb. tomatoes, skinned and sliced	2 tsps. lemon juice or wine vinegar

Oven temperature: moderate (350°F., mark 4)

Fry the onions slowly in the hot oil, add the garlic, peppers and tomatoes; cover closely and cook slowly in the centre of the oven or on top of the stove until a thick sauce is obtained – about 1½ hours. Add the prepared fish, cut into neat pieces, and the rice. Season well and continue cooking until fish and rice are tender. Finally, add 2 tsps. lemon juice or wine vinegar and serve hot, or allow to cool and serve with salad.

OCEAN SOUFFLÉ

2 lb. white fish, e.g. cod, skinned	A pinch of pepper
	2 eggs, separated
A 10-oz. can of celery soup	4 oz. cheese, grated
1 bay leaf	3 rashers of bacon
3 peppercorns	Parsley to garnish
½ level tsp. salt	

Oven temperature: fairly hot (400°F., mark 6)

Poach the fish for 15 minutes in the celery soup with the bay leaf, peppercorns and seasonings. When it is cooked, flake it, removing any bones, and return it to the strained liquor. Add the beaten egg yolks and 3 oz. cheese, then fold in the stiffly beaten egg whites. Pour the mixture into a greased ovenproof dish, sprinkle with the remaining cheese and brown towards the top of the oven for 15 minutes. Meanwhile halve the bacon rashers lengthwise, make bacon rolls and grill these. Garnish the soufflé with the bacon rolls and parsley. (6 servings.)

FISH OLIVES

6 fillets of whiting (or other white fish)	½ lb. sausage-meat
	A little butter
Salt and pepper	Parsley
Powdered sage	

For the Mustard Sauce

1 oz. butter	¼ pint water
½ oz. flour	2 tbsps. vinegar
½ level tsp. dry mustard	Pepper and salt

Oven temperature: moderate (350°F., mark 4)

Skin the fillets, season and add some sage. Put a portion of sausage-meat on each fillet, roll up and put in a greased ovenproof dish. Dot with a little butter, cover with greased greaseproof paper and bake in the centre of the oven for 20 minutes. Garnish with parsley and keep hot while preparing the sauce. Melt the butter, add the flour and mustard and fry lightly. Add the water gradually, then the vinegar and seasoning. Stir, boil gently for 3–4 minutes, then pour round the fish.

FISH AND ASPARAGUS MOULD

1 lb. plaice fillets	1 lb. asparagus tips
A small can of crab or prawn paste	2 eggs, hard-boiled, shelled and sliced
Milk	Brown bread and cress sandwiches
Salt and pepper	
1½ pints aspic jelly	Green salad

Skin the fillets and place them on a board, skin side uppermost, spread each fillet with crab or prawn paste and roll it up tightly. Put the rolled fillets on a deep plate, with a little milk and seasoning, and steam for 10 minutes, or until they are quite cooked, then leave them to cool. When the fillets are cold, slice them with a sharp knife. Meanwhile set a little of the aspic jelly in a plain mould and when it is quite firm, decorate with asparagus tips, rounds of hard-boiled egg and slices of stuffed plaice. Cover again with aspic jelly and if desired decorate the sides of the mould in the same way. Build up the mould with layers of egg, fish and asparagus tips, then leave to set firmly. Turn the mould out on to a dish, garnish with asparagus tips and with tiny brown-bread-and-cress sandwiches; serve with green salad.

FISH GALANTINE

1 lb. white fish
A little butter
1 small onion, skinned and chopped
1 small carrot, peeled and chopped
2 tsps. piccalilli

1 tbsp. chopped parsley
1 oz. gelatine
⅛ pint warm water
½ pint fish stock
Salt and pepper
Tomato, cucumber, etc., to garnish

Boil or steam the fish, remove the skin and bones and flake with a fork. Melt the butter and lightly fry the onion, carrot and piccalilli. Remove from the heat and add the parsley and fish. Meanwhile dissolve the gelatine in the water and to it add the fish stock; season very well. Place a little of this mixture at the bottom of a mould and decorate with slices of tomatoes, cucumber, etc. Allow to set. Add the fish mixture to the rest of the jelly and fill up the mould. When set, turn out and serve with salad.

MEDITERRANEAN TUNA RISOTTO

8 oz. long-grain rice
½ level tsp. salt
A 7-oz. can of tuna
A 15-oz. can of mushroom soup

A small pkt. of frozen peas
2 oz. button mushrooms
1 canned pimiento, chopped (optional)

Wash the rice thoroughly, place in fast-boiling salted water and cook for a few minutes. Drain well and rinse in running cold water. Put back in the pan, add the flaked tuna and the soup and bring to the boil. Add the peas, mushrooms and pimiento and simmer till the liquid is absorbed – about 10 minutes. (6 servings.)

INDIAN FISH PELLAO

1¼–1½ lb. cod fillet
2 oz. ghee or butter
1 level tsp. powdered turmeric
½ level tsp. chilli powder
1–2 level tsps. garam masala (see note)

2 tsps. lemon juice
2 onions, skinned and sliced
½ lb. long-grain rice
1¾ pints water
2 bay leaves
Tomatoes to garnish

Skin the fish, wipe it and cut into cubes. Melt half the ghee or butter and add the turmeric, chilli powder and garam masala; fry for 5 minutes and add the lemon juice. Cook the fish in this mixture for 10–15 minutes, then remove and place on a plate. Melt the remaining fat in a second pan and fry the onions until pale golden-brown. Add the washed rice and continue frying for 3–5 minutes. Add the gravy mixture from the first pan, with the water and bay leaves, and cook for 20–30 minutes, by which time the liquid will be absorbed and the rice tender. Add the fish, stir gently and serve garnished with sliced raw tomato.

Note: Garam Masala is a flavouring made by mixing 1 level tsp. each of ground cloves, ground cinnamon, ground black pepper, cumin seeds and ground cardamom seeds.

ORIENTAL FISH STEAKS

2 oz. blanched almonds	Cod steaks
2 oz. seedless raisins	2 level tbsps. flour
5 oz. butter or margarine	

For the Tomato Sauce

1 onion, skinned and chopped	A pinch of pepper
1 oz. butter	A small can of tomato purée
1 lb. tomatoes, quartered	½ pint stock
A bouquet garni (see p. 13)	2 level tbsps. flour
1 level tsp. salt	

Fry the almonds and raisins in 4 oz. butter until light golden-brown; drain carefully on kitchen paper and keep hot. Wash, trim and dry the fish and coat with flour. Melt the remaining butter in a frying-pan, add the fish steaks, cover with a lid and cook them slowly on both sides until done.

Meanwhile make the sauce. Fry the onion in the butter for a few minutes without browning, then add the tomatoes and bouquet garni and cook until reduced. Strain the mixture, and add the seasonings and tomato purée. Mix 2 tbsps. stock with the flour, stir in the rest and add to the sauce. Bring to the boil and boil for 3–4 minutes, until the correct consistency is obtained; stir the sauce continually while cooking.

Put the fish into a dish, pour the sauce over and pile the fried nuts and raisins in the centre, or if preferred, sprinkle them over the fish. Serve at once.

JAPANESE FISH AND VEGETABLE TEMPURA

1½–2 lb. mixed fish, vegetables, etc. (see recipe)	Oil for deep frying

For the Batter

½ level tsp. sugar	4 oz. plain flour
1 egg, beaten	¼ pint milk

Any kind of white fish, prawns or shrimps, carrots, onions, sweet potatoes, French beans, radishes and so on can be used in this dish. Cut the fish into strips about $\frac{1}{4}$–$\frac{3}{4}$ inch thick and of even length; shell prawns and shrimps but leave whole. Wash and prepare the vegetables and cut into strips of about the same size as the fish.

Make the batter by adding the sugar and egg to the flour and beating in the milk; add a little water if the batter is too stiff. Dip the fish pieces and the vegetable strips into the batter and fry in the hot oil.

PRINCE'S CHOWDER (Portuguese)

2 onions, skinned and sliced
$\frac{1}{2}$ a clove of garlic, skinned and crushed
4 oz. butter
4 oz. ham, chopped
1 tomato, skinned and chopped
6 sorrel leaves, chopped (optional)
1 small eel, skinned and sliced
8 shrimps, peeled

1 slice each of 4 varieties of fish
2 dozen mussels
$\frac{1}{4}$ of a bay leaf
$\frac{1}{4}$ level tsp. freshly ground pepper
Salt
8 oysters
2 tbsps. lemon juice

Slowly fry the onions and garlic in the butter in a saucepan, without browning; add the ham and fry it, then add the tomato. Add the sorrel, eel, shrimps and fish and turn them in the mixture, shaking the pan, until they are heated through. Meanwhile, steam the mussels open and remove from the shells. Add sufficient boiling water to the liquid left in the mussel saucepan to make $1\frac{1}{4}$ quarts; drop in the mussels and cook for 15 minutes. Strain the liquid and pour it over the frying fish mixture. Add the bay leaf, pepper and some salt, then place over a low heat and simmer for 10 minutes. Add the oysters, with their liquor, and simmer until they crinkle; add the lemon juice. When serving the chowder put a little of each fish and sea food in each serving; the mussels are discarded. (Serves 8–10.)

BOUILLABAISSE

2 lb. mixed fish: John Dory, red mullet, whiting, mackerel, rock salmon, gurnet, bass, crawfish or lobster, crab, prawns, eel or conger eel
2–3 onions, skinned and sliced
1 stick of celery, scrubbed and chopped
$\frac{1}{4}$ pint olive oil
$\frac{1}{2}$ lb. tomatoes, skinned and sliced

2 cloves of garlic, skinned and crushed
1 bay leaf
A pinch of dried thyme and fennel (if available)
A few sprigs of parsley
Finely shredded rind of $\frac{1}{2}$ an orange
Salt and pepper
A pinch of saffron (if available)
French bread

This is a traditional dish from the South of France. The

authentic version is made from at least 8 different types of fish, many of which are available only along the Mediterranean coasts. However, any variety of white and shellfish can be used to give quite a good imitation.

Have the fish cleaned, skinned and cut in fairly thick pieces; have the shellfish removed from the shells. Lightly fry the onions and celery in the hot oil for about 5 minutes, until soft but not coloured. Stir in the tomatoes, garlic, herbs, orange rind and seasoning. Put all the firmer-fleshed fish in a layer over the vegetables, just cover with water (in which the saffron if used, has been dissolved), bring to the boil and boil for about 8 minutes. Add the softer-fleshed fish and continue cooking for a further 5–8 minutes, until all the ingredients are cooked but still in shape.

The bouillabaisse can be served as a complete dish, or the cooking liquid can be strained off and served in individual bowls containing a slice of French bread – the fish is then served separately.

In some areas sliced potatoes are included in the bed of vegetables; the cooking liquid is sometimes enriched with 2 egg yolks and 3–4 tbsps. cream, blended together and added just before serving.

NORTH SEA BOUILLABAISSE
(see colour picture No. 12)

1 lb. white fish	½ pint cooked peas
2 pints fish stock	4 tomatoes, skinned,
2 oz. butter	seeded and chopped
2 oz. flour	Salt and pepper
1 green pepper, de-seeded and	Yellow food colouring
sliced	3 tbsps. single cream

For the Garlic Bread

1 clove of garlic,	2 oz. butter
skinned	1 French loaf

Cook the fish in the stock for 10 minutes, then remove the skin and bones and roughly flake the fish. Melt the butter, add the flour and stir over a gentle heat. Stir in the stock, bring to the boil and boil for about 5 minutes. Boil the pepper for 15 minutes and add to the sauce, with the peas and the chopped tomato flesh. Season to taste and tint pale yellow. Add the flaked fish and the cream and serve at once, with the garlic bread.

To make garlic bread, chop the garlic clove finely and beat together with the butter; make slits along the loaf at 2-inch intervals and insert a little of the butter in each slit (spread any remaining butter on top of the loaf). Heat in a moderate oven (350°F., mark 4) for a few minutes.

CHAPTER 5

Shellfish

Most of the recipes for shellfish are contained in this chapter, but there are a few in other sections, especially Chapters 2 and 6, pp. 15 and 116, "Starters" and "Savouries and Snacks" where they seem particularly appropriate.

Two points to remember about shellfish:
1. It is important to buy them from a reputable source and to use them as fresh as possible.
2. If you are entertaining, let your guests know before serving them with any dish that contains shellfish in a form that is not immediately recognisable (for instance, a mixed fish soup), in case they are allergic to shellfish.

CRAB SIMPLY DRESSED

Crabs are usually sold ready cooked; in fact, many fish-mongers prepare and dress them as well. If a crab is bought alive, cook it as follows: wash it, place in cold salted water, bring slowly to boiling point and boil fairly quickly for 10–20 minutes, according to size – don't overcook it, or the flesh will become hard and thready. Allow to cool in the water. To give extra flavour, you can add a few parsley stalks, a bay leaf, a few peppercorns and a very little lemon juice or vinegar to the cooking water.

Lay the cooked crab on its back, hold the shell firmly with one hand and the body (to which the claws are attached) in the other hand and pull apart.

Take the shell part and use a spoon to remove the stomach bag (which lies just below the head); discard this. Carefully scrape all the meat from the shell into a basin and reserve it – this is called the soft or dark meat. Wash and if necessary scrub the shell; dry it and rub with a little oil to give a gloss. Knock away the edge of the shell up as far as the dark line round the rim.

Add 1–2 tbsps. fresh bread-crumbs to the brown meat, season with salt, pepper and lemon juice and add a little chopped parsley; pack the mixture into the sides of the prepared shell, leaving a space in the middle for the white meat.

Take the body section and remove from it all the greyish-white frond-like pieces (called the "deadmen's fingers"), which are inedible. Crack all but the very tiny claws with a weight and take out all the flesh or white meat from both claws and body; use the handle of a teaspoon or a skewer to reach into the crevices and take care not to get splinters of shell amongst the meat. Season the flesh with salt, pepper, cayenne and vinegar and pile it into the centre of the shell. Decorate the crab with a little paprika and chopped parsley and lay it on a bed of lettuce, garnished with the small claws.

CURRIED CRAB (Indian)

The meat from a medium-sized crab (or a 7½-oz. can)	1 level tsp. curry powder
	½ pint stock
	Salt
1 oz. butter or lard	½ tsp. curry paste
1 small onion, skinned and finely chopped	2 tsps. chutney
	1 oz. sultanas
1 small apple, peeled, cored and chopped	1 tsp. lemon juice
	2 tbsps. single cream
¾ oz. rice flour	(optional)

Cut the crabmeat up neatly. Melt the butter or lard and fry the onion, then the apple, rice flour and curry powder. Add the stock gradually and stir until boiling. Add salt to taste, the curry paste, chutney, sultanas and lemon juice, cover and simmer for 1 hour, stirring frequently. Add the crabmeat, re-heat and stir in the cream. Serve with rice.

CRAB MORNAY

A 7½-oz. can of crabmeat	Salt and pepper
1 oz. butter	1 oz. cheese, grated
1 oz. flour	1 lb. potatoes, boiled
½ pint milk	

Turn the crabmeat into a basin. Melt the butter, stir in the flour and cook for 2–3 minutes. Stir in the milk, season and bring to the boil; remove from the heat and stir in the cheese (saving a little to be used as topping). Add the crabmeat, mix and keep warm. Mash the potatoes and pipe or fork them round an ovenproof dish. Pour the crab mixture into the centre, sprinkle it with the remainder of the cheese and re-heat under a hot grill until golden. Serve with a green salad.

SUPRÊME OF CRAB

Oven temperature: moderate (350°F., mark 4)
Remove all the meat from 2 cooked crabs and mix it in a basin with 2 oz. fresh white bread-crumbs, a pinch of cayenne pepper, some white pepper and salt, a little lemon juice, a knob of butter and a little top of the milk. Put the mixture back into the crab shells, cover with fine bread-crumbs, add a few shavings of butter and bake till well cooked through – 15–20 minutes. Serve on a napkin.

CRABMEAT SCRAMBLED WITH EGGS

6 eggs, separated	5 level tbsps. flour
1 pint milk	A 3½-oz. can of crabmeat
¼ lb. cooked ham, chopped	Salt and pepper
3 spring onions, chopped	2 tsps. sherry
3 tbsps. oil	

Oven temperature: moderate (350°F., mark 4)
Beat the egg yolks and add ¼ pint milk. Sauté the ham and onions in the oil over a low heat. Add the flour and then the remaining milk, stir over a low heat and then add the crabmeat and seasoning. Stir in the egg yolks and sherry, pouring in the mixture in a thin stream, and allow to thicken. Beat the egg whites with a little salt and fold in. Bake for about 55 minutes in the centre of the oven.

TOMATOES STUFFED WITH CRAB

1 medium-sized onion, skinned and chopped	4 oz. crabmeat
2 oz. celery, chopped	2 eggs
2 rashers of bacon, rinded and chopped	2–3 oz. cheese, grated
2 oz. fresh white bread-crumbs	Salt and pepper
3 oz. butter	6 large tomatoes
	6 small rounds of buttered toast

Oven temperature: moderate (350°F., mark 4)
Mix the onion, celery, bacon and bread-crumbs and fry them in the butter until the onion is tender. Flake the crab, lightly beat the eggs and combine with the onion mixture; add seasoning to taste. Cut the tops off the tomatoes, scoop out the seeds and stuff with the crab mixture; sprinkle with grated cheese. Bake in the centre of the oven for about 20 minutes, then serve the tomatoes on hot buttered toast.

Green peppers may be stuffed in the same way, but should be seeded and cooked in boiling salted water for 5 minutes.

CRAB PILAFF

1 large crab, cooked
Olive oil for frying
1 onion, chopped
4 oz. long-grain rice
¾ pint stock

2 tomatoes, skinned and
  chopped
2 oz. sultanas
Salt and pepper
2 oz. cheese, grated

The countries of the Levant have dozens of versions of the Pilaff or Pilau; this one is well adapted to European tastes.

Remove all the flesh from the crab. Heat the oil in a pan and fry the onion. Wash the rice well and then fry it until quite brown. Gradually add the stock, until it has all been absorbed, then add the tomatoes, sultanas and crabmeat. Season well and cook for a further 10 minutes, to heat the crab thoroughly. Just before serving, add the cheese.

STUFFED CRAB (Caribbean)

2 crabs, cooked
2 slices of crustless
  white bread
Milk
Butter
2–3 rashers of fat bacon,
  rinded and chopped

1 clove of garlic, skinned
  and crushed
1 tbsp. chopped chives
1 red chilli, seeded and
  chopped
Salt
Browned bread-crumbs

Oven temperature: fairly hot (400°F., mark 6)
Prepare the crabs in the usual way, chop the meat and wash and dry the shells. Soak the bread in a little milk for 2–3 minutes, then squeeze out as much moisture as possible. Melt a little butter in a frying pan and fry the bacon; add the bread, crabmeat, garlic, chives and chilli and season with salt. Divide between the crabshells and top with the browned bread-crumbs. Bake in the centre of the oven for 20–30 minutes.

CRAB WITH AVOCADO

1 large avocado pear
Lemon juice
White meat from 1 crab or
  2 3½-oz. cans of crabmeat
2 tbsps. tomato ketchup

1 shallot, skinned and
  chopped
2 tbsps. salad cream
1–2 tbsps. single cream
Salt and pepper to taste

Cut the pear round the centre, twist and separate the two halves and remove the stone; scoop out the flesh, dice it and dip at once in lemon juice to prevent discoloration. If canned crabmeat is used, drain it well. Mix the crab with the remaining ingredients, stir in the drained avocado and adjust the seasoning if necessary.

Serve on a bed of lettuce or watercress, with tomato wedges; if it is to be used as an appetiser, place it in individual glasses on a bed of shredded lettuce. (As this is a rich combination of ingredients, only small servings are needed.)

CRAWFISH TAILS SALAD

Buy the crawfish tails already cooked. Split the shells and take out the flesh carefully, then cut it into rounds. Lay these on beds of lettuce, with pyramids of sliced peeled tomato, diced beetroot and cooked cold potato; add sliced radishes and cucumber and spring onions cut about 3 inches long. Dress with mayonnaise and serve with thinly sliced white or brown bread and butter.

CURRIED CRAWFISH TAILS

2–4 crawfish tails	Chopped parsley
½ pint curry sauce	Lemon slices
(see p. 143)	Boiled rice

Remove the flesh from the tails, cut it up roughly and wash the shells. Prepare the curry sauce and add the crawfish to it; heat the mixture through and place it in the warmed shells. Garnish with chopped parsley and lemon slices and serve at once, with carefully boiled rice. If preferred, the curried fish may be served in a dish, instead of in the shells.

LOBSTER, SIMPLY SERVED

Connoisseurs consider that lobster is best served quite simply with an oil and vinegar dressing or mayonnaise.

A lobster is generally sold ready boiled, but if it has been bought alive, cook it as for crab, allowing 15–25 minutes, according to size, and taking care not to overcook it, as the flesh tends to become hard and thready.

First twist off the large claws and crack them without injuring the flesh. Remove the smaller claws, which are only used for garnishing. Cut off the head. Split the lobster right down the middle of the body from head to tail, using a strong pointed knife. Remove the intestine (which looks like a small vein running through the centre of the tail), the stomach, which lies near the head, and the spongy-looking gills, which are not edible.

Stand the head upright on a dish, arrange the cracked claws and split tail round it and garnish with parsley or salad. Serve the oil and vinegar dressing or mayonnaise separately.

LOBSTER MAYONNAISE

(see colour picture No. 13)

1 medium-sized lobster,	½ pint mayonnaise
cooked	1 hard-boiled egg, sliced
1 lettuce	

Remove the meat from the lobster, retaining the flesh from the claws and any coral for garnishing. Flake the remaining flesh with a fork or divide it into neat pieces. Arrange the

100

shredded outer leaves of the lettuce in a salad bowl. Mix the lobster meat with the mayonnaise and pile lightly on the lettuce leaves in the bowl. Garnish with slices of egg, the lettuce heart, divided into quarters, the claw meat of the lobster and the coral (if present).

Alternatively, split the lobster as described above. Arrange on a dish lined with lettuce leaves and garnish with sliced hard-boiled egg and the lobster coral, which may be piled in cucumber cups. (To make these, cut sections of cucumber and score lengthwise with a fork, so that narrow strips of the skin are removed, to give a striped effect; scoop out some of the centre top of each section to form a shallow cup.)

CARIBBEAN LOBSTER SALAD

3 level tsps. salt	A pinch of cayenne pepper
6 4-oz. frozen rock lobster tails	A few drops of Angostura bitters
4 tbsps. salad dressing (preferably Italian-style, flavoured with garlic)	6 oz. fresh pineapple, diced
3 tbsps. mayonnaise	2 sticks of celery, chopped
½ tsp. soy sauce	Chopped lettuce
A pinch of pepper	6 wedges of fresh lime

Bring 4 pints of water to the boil, add 1½ level tsps. salt and the unthawed lobster tails and bring to the boil once more. Reduce the heat and simmer for 10 minutes, drain and cool. Cut the soft under-shells from the lobster tails, using scissors, and reserve the shells. Remove the lobster meat in one piece, then cut into ¼-inch slices. Toss the lobster with the salad dressing and refrigerate, covered, for at least 30 minutes, stirring occasionally; drain. (The extra dressing may be used later for the lettuce.) Put the mayonnaise into a large bowl and mix with the soy sauce, pepper, cayenne, bitters and remaining salt and blend well. Add the lobster, pineapple and celery and mix lightly. Pile the lobster salad in the shells. Serve on the lettuce and garnish with lime wedges. (Serves 6.)

DEVILLED LOBSTER

½ level tsp. dry mustard	½ pint milk
¾ level tsp. curry powder	½ oz. butter
A pinch of ground mace	½ oz. cornflour
A few grains of cayenne, salt and pepper	An 8-oz. can of lobster (or a fresh lobster tail)

Mix the seasonings with the milk and allow to stand for about ½ hour. Melt the butter, add the cornflour, remove from the heat and add the milk, then return the mixture to the heat and cook until it thickens. Add the lobster meat and stir gently, without breaking up the fish. Serve piping hot.

GRILLED LOBSTER

Split the lobster lengthwise and remove the intestine, stomach and gills. Brush the shell and flesh over with oil and grill the flesh side for 8–10 minutes, then turn the lobster and grill the shell side for 5 minutes. Dot the flesh with small pieces of butter, sprinkle with a little salt and cayenne pepper and serve with melted butter or with shrimp or other suitable sauce.

LOBSTER NEWBURG

2 small cooked lobsters ($\frac{1}{2}$ lb. each)	2 egg yolks
1 oz. butter	$\frac{1}{4}$ pint single cream
White, cayenne and paprika pepper	Buttered toast or boiled rice
Salt	Finely chopped parsley to garnish
4 tbsps. Madeira or sherry	

Cut the lobsters in half, carefully detach the tail meat in one piece (discarding the intestine, etc., – see first recipe) and cut it into fairly thin slices. Crack the claws and remove the meat as unbroken as possible. Melt the butter in a frying-pan, lay the lobster in the pan, season well and heat very gently for about 5 minutes, without colouring. Pour the Madeira or sherry over and continue to cook a little more quickly until the liquid is reduced by half. Beat the egg yolks with a little seasoning and add the cream. Take the lobster off the heat, pour the cream mixture over and mix gently over a slow heat till the sauce reaches the consistency of cream. Adjust the seasoning, pour at once on to hot buttered toast or boiled rice and sprinkle with parsley.

LOBSTER THERMIDOR
(see colour picture No. 14)

2 small cooked lobsters ($\frac{1}{2}$ lb. each)	$\frac{1}{2}$ pint Béchamel sauce (see p. 139)
2 oz. butter	3 level tbsps. grated Parmesan cheese
1 tbsp. chopped shallot	Mustard, salt and paprika pepper
2 tsps. chopped parsley	
1–2 tsps. chopped tarragon	
4 tbsps. white wine	

Remove the lobster meat from the shells (see first lobster recipe, p. 100), chop the claw and head meat roughly and cut the tail meat into thick slices. Melt 1 oz. butter in a saucepan and add the shallot, parsley and tarragon. After a few minutes add the wine and simmer for 5 minutes. Add the Béchamel sauce and simmer until reduced to a creamy consistency. Add the lobster meat to the sauce, with 2 tbsps. of the cheese, the remaining butter, in small pieces, and mustard, salt and paprika to taste. Arrange the mixture in the shells, sprinkle with the remaining cheese and put under the grill to brown the top quickly. Decorate with the claws and serve at once.

LOBSTER CUTLETS

12 oz. cooked lobster	Salt and pepper
1 hard-boiled egg	A squeeze of lemon juice
(optional)	Egg and bread-crumbs
1 oz. butter	Fat for frying
1 oz. flour	Parsley to garnish
¼ pint stock or milk	

Flake or chop the fish and chop the egg, if used. Melt the butter, add the flour and gradually stir in the stock or milk, then boil for 3 minutes. Add the fish, egg, seasoning and lemon juice and put on a plate to cool. Shape the mixture into cutlets and egg-and-crumb them. Heat the fat and fry the cutlets on both sides until golden. Serve garnished with parsley.

Crayfish may be used in the same way.

BAKED LINCOLN LOBSTER

2 medium-sized lobsters	½ tsp. Worcestershire sauce
1 small onion, skinned	1 tsp. made mustard
and chopped	Chopped parsley
1 clove of garlic, skinned	Salt and pepper
and chopped	1 oz. cheese, grated
2½ oz. butter	1 oz. bread-crumbs
2 oz. button mushrooms,	Parsley and lemon to
sliced	garnish
¼ pint double cream	

Oven temperature: moderate (350°F., mark 4)

Remove the flesh from the lobsters (see first lobster recipe, p. 100) and cut it into large pieces. Fry the onion and the garlic in 2 oz. of the butter. Add the mushrooms and cook gently for a few minutes. Stir in the cream, the Worcestershire sauce, mustard and parsley; add the lobster and season to taste. Put the mixture into the shells and sprinkle with grated cheese and bread-crumbs. Dot with the remaining butter and bake in the centre of the oven until golden-brown. Garnish with parsley and lemon.

OYSTER FRITTERS (New Zealand)

4 oz. plain flour	Salt and pepper
1 egg	12 oysters
½ pint milk	Deep fat for frying

Make a batter in the usual way with the flour, egg, milk and seasoning. Mince or chop the oysters, add to the batter and fry spoonfuls of the mixture in the hot deep fat.

OYSTERS AU NATUREL: see p. 18.

PRAWNS NEWBURG

8 oz. prawns, shelled
1 oz. butter
4 tbsps. Madeira or
  sherry
2 egg yolks
A pint single of cream

Salt, pepper and cayenne
  pepper
Boiled rice or toast
Chopped chives or
  parsley

Sauté the prawns very gently in the butter for about 5 minutes. Stir in the Madeira or sherry and cook for a further 2–3 minutes. Mix the egg yolks and cream and pour into the prawn mixture, add seasonings to taste and heat very gently, until a thickened creamy consistency is obtained. Pour at once over boiled rice or toast. Serve sprinkled with chives or parsley and garnished with whole prawns.

Shrimps can of course be used in the same way.

PRAWN CELESTE

A 7½-oz. can of button
  mushrooms
2 oz. butter
2 oz. flour
½ pint milk
A 6-oz. can of cream

Salt and pepper
A 6-oz. can of prawns
1–2 tsps. sherry
Chopped parsley
Cubes of fried bread

Lightly cook the mushrooms in the butter for 2–3 minutes. Stir in the flour, gradually add the milk and cream and bring to the boil, stirring constantly, until the sauce has thickened; season to taste. Rinse the prawns in cold water, then add, with the sherry, and re-heat gently. Sprinkle with the chopped parsley and serve with the fried bread cubes.

CEYLON PRAWN CURRY (MILD)

2 oz. butter
1 onion, skinned and
  chopped
1 clove of garlic, skinned
  and chopped
1 level tbsp. flour
2 level tsps. turmeric
1 level tsp. ground cloves
1 level tsp. ground
  cinnamon

1 level tsp. salt
1 level tsp. sugar
¼ pint coconut milk (see
  below)
½ pint stock
1 pint cooked prawns or
  1 doz. Dublin Bay prawns,
  shelled
1 tsp. lemon juice

Melt the butter and fry the onion and garlic lightly, then add the flour, turmeric, cloves, cinnamon, salt and sugar. Cook gently for 10 minutes and add the coconut milk and most of the stock. Simmer gently for 10 minutes, then put in the prawns (reserving a few for garnish). Add the lemon juice, re-season as necessary and cook for a further 10 minutes. Meanwhile heat the remaining prawns in a little stock. Dish up the curry and garnish with the heated prawns. Serve with boiled rice and a hot chutney.

Shrimps may be used in a similar way.

Coconut Milk: This is traditionally made from fresh coconut, but a good substitute is made by infusing 1–2 tbsps. desiccated coconut in about ¼ pint boiling water, then squeezing out the liquid through a fine tea strainer.

PRAWN OMELETTE (OMELETTE CARDINAL)

4 eggs	6 oz. prawns, shelled
Salt and pepper	1 tbsp. single cream
1 oz. butter	¼ pint white sauce
1 orange	

Mix the eggs with a fork and season. Heat the butter, pour in the eggs and cook the omelette in the usual way. Peel the orange thinly and carefully, in order to obtain only the outer rind, then cut this into very thin Julienne strips. Finish peeling the orange, remove the pith and slice the flesh. Just before folding the omelette, fill it with half the Julienne strips and half the prawns, mixed with the cream. Fold the omelette and slide on to a hot serving dish, make a lengthwise incision and fill with the remaining prawns. Pour the sauce over both ends. Arrange the orange slices around and sprinkle the rest of the Julienne strips on top.

PRAWN FRITTERS

Make a thick coating batter (see recipe given with Deep-frying instructions, p. 12). Shell about ¼ pint of prawns (weight after picking), dip each prawn in the batter and fry in hot fat until crisp and golden brown. Serve hot, piled on a paper doyley and garnished with a few prawn heads.

PRAWN MOUSSE

¼ pint aspic jelly (made as directed on the packet)	1 bay leaf
	3–4 peppercorns
8 oz. prawns, shelled	1½ oz. butter
1 pint milk	1½ oz. flour
1 small onion, skinned and quartered	2 eggs, separated
	Salt and pepper
1 carrot, peeled and quartered	½ oz. gelatine
	¼ pint dry white wine or stock
1–2 cloves	

Make up the aspic jelly and pour a thin layer into a 2-pint jelly mould, add a few prawns for decoration, pour in more jelly, and leave to set. Put the milk, onion, carrot, cloves, bay leaf and peppercorns into a covered pan, bring to the boil,

105

turn out the heat and leave to cool for about 15 minutes, until the milk is well flavoured. Melt the butter, stir in the flour and cook for 2–3 minutes. Remove the pan from the heat and gradually stir in the milk (strained off the vegetables and herbs). Bring to the boil and continue to stir until the sauce thickens. Remove from the heat, cool slightly and stir in the egg yolks and seasoning to taste. Dissolve the gelatine in the wine or stock in a basin over a pan of hot water and stir it into the sauce. Add the remaining prawns, roughly chopped, and leave in a cool place until the mixture begins to set. Whisk the egg whites stiffly, fold them in, turn the mixture into the mould and leave to set. Unmould and serve with salad.

PRAWN AND GRAPEFRUIT SALAD

Lettuce
1 grapefruit
½ a cucumber
2 oz. shelled prawns

French dressing
Prawn heads for garnish
  (if available)

Prepare the lettuce and arrange a neat bed of the heart leaves in a shallow salad bowl. Peel the grapefruit, remove the pith and divide it into sections; cut each section into three and put these pieces and the juice into a basin. Peel and dice most of the cucumber, and then add it with the prawns to the grapefruit. Pour some French dressing on and mix lightly with a spoon and fork. Pile the mixture on the lettuce leaves and garnish with a few of the prawn heads and cucumber slices.

PRAWN AND EGG MOULD

2 pkts. of frozen prawns
1 small pkt. of frozen
  peas
1 pint aspic jelly

3 hard-boiled eggs,
  quartered
Salad

Thaw the prawns and cook the peas in boiling salted water. Melt the aspic and pour a little of it into a mould, then set a few prawns in it. When this is set, mix the remaining prawns, the quartered eggs and the peas with the rest of the aspic and pour into the mould. Turn out when set, chill in the refrigerator and serve with salad.

SCALLOP FRICASSEE

8 scallops, prepared
Milk
1½ oz. butter
1½ oz. flour

Salt and pepper
Lemon wedges and parsley
  to garnish

Cook the scallops gently in a little water for about 10 minutes.

Drain them, reserving the liquor, and make this up to ¾ pint with milk; keep the scallops hot. Melt the butter in a saucepan, stir in the flour and cook for 2–3 minutes. Remove the pan from the heat, gradually stir in the milk, bring to the boil, continue to stir until it thickens and season to taste. Arrange the scallops in a dish, pour the sauce over them and garnish with lemon wedges and parsley.

FRIED SCALLOPS

4 scallops	Fat for frying
Seasoned flour	Cooked peas or spinach
1 egg, beaten	purée
Fresh bread-crumbs	Tartare sauce

Wash and prepare the scallops and dry them well, roll them in seasoned flour and egg-and-crumb them. Heat the fat and fry the scallops until golden-brown. Serve with peas or spinach purée and Tartare sauce.

SCALLOPS IN POTATO BORDER

1½ lb. potatoes	A little milk
4 scallops	1 clove of garlic, skinned
Olive oil	and finely chopped
Salt and pepper	Chopped parsley to garnish
Butter	

Cook the potatoes. Place the scallops on an ovenproof dish, brush with oil and season. Place under a medium grill and grill for 3–4 minutes on each side. Cream the potatoes with some butter and milk and make a border round 4 scallop shells, then place a scallop in the centre of each. Heat 2 tbsps. olive oil with 1 oz. butter and the chopped garlic and pour over the scallops; garnish with parsley.

FRIED SCAMPI (SCAMPI FRITTI)
(see colour picture No. 15)

8 oz. scampi or Dublin Bay	1 tbsp. oil
prawns	1 egg, separated
Seasoned flour	2–3 tbsps. water or milk and
4 oz. plain flour	water
A pinch of salt	Fat for deep frying

If fresh scampi or prawns are used, discard their heads, remove the flesh from the shells and remove the dark veins; if frozen, allow to defrost, then drain well. Dip the prawns in the seasoned flour. Mix the plain flour, salt, oil and egg yolk with sufficient liquid to give a stiff batter which will coat the back of the spoon; beat until smooth. Just before cooking, whisk the egg white stiffly and fold it into the batter. Dip the scampi in the batter. Heat the fat until a cube of bread dropped

107

into it takes 20–30 seconds to brown. Fry the scampi a few at a time until they are golden brown, drain and serve with Tartare or tomato sauce.

Alternatively, the scampi can simply be coated with beaten egg and fresh bread-crumbs and fried until golden-brown.

SCAMPI PROVENÇALE

1 onion, skinned and
   finely chopped
1 clove of garlic, skinned
   and finely chopped
1 oz. butter or 2–3 tbsps.
   cooking oil
4 tbsps. dry white wine

¾–1 lb. tomatoes, peeled and
   chopped (or a 15-oz. can
   of tomatoes, drained)
Salt and pepper
A pinch of sugar
1 tbsp. chopped parsley
8 oz. frozen scampi, thawed

Fry the onion and garlic gently in the butter or oil for about 5 minutes, until soft but not coloured. Add the wine, tomatoes, seasoning, sugar and parsley, stir well and simmer gently for about 10 minutes. Drain the scampi well, add to the sauce and continue simmering for about 5 minutes, or until they are just heated through. Serve with crusty French bread (or with boiled rice, for a more substantial snack).

SHRIMP AND RICE RING

4 oz. long-grain rice
½ green pepper, seeded
   and chopped
1–2 tbsps. cream or top
   of the milk
2 level tbsps. cornflour
   or flour
½ pint milk

A knob of butter
Salt, pepper and paprika
2 oz. mushrooms, chopped
   and sautéed
4 oz. frozen shrimps
1 hard-boiled egg,
   chopped

Cook the rice in boiling salted water for about 15-20 minutes or until tender; drain well. Cook the pepper in boiling salted water for 10 minutes and drain, then add to the rice, with the cream. Turn the mixture into a buttered ring mould or tin and keep in a warm place. Make a sauce by blending the cornflour with 2 tbsps. of the cold milk. Boil the rest with a knob of butter, pour on to the blended mixture, stirring well, then return it to the pan and boil until thickened, stirring all the time. Season well and stir in the mushrooms, shrimps and egg. Turn out the rice ring on to a flat serving dish and pour the sauce into the centre. (If you have no border or ring mould, keep the rice warm in the pan, and just before serving place it in a border on a shallow dish and pour the sauce into the centre.)

Variations
1. Use a can of mushroom soup to make the sauce.

108

2. For extra flavour add 1 tbsp. chopped parsley, a few chopped chives or the grated rind of a lemon to the sauce.

SHRIMP CREOLE
(see colour picture No. 16)

2 small onions, skinned and sliced
2–3 sticks of celery, sliced
2 oz. butter
2 oz. flour
½ level tsp. chilli powder
Salt and pepper
¾ pint water

1½ tbsps. vinegar
1 level tsp. sugar
¾ lb. tomatoes, skinned and finely sliced
1 small pkt. of frozen peas, cooked
6–8 oz. shrimps, prepared
6 oz. long-grain rice

Fry the onions and celery in the butter without browning for 4–5 minutes; stir in the flour, chilli powder and seasoning, add the water and simmer gently for 15 minutes. Stir in the vinegar, sugar, tomatoes, peas and shrimps. Cook gently for a further 5–10 minutes. Meanwhile, wash the rice, cover with cold water, bring to the boil and cook for 16–18 minutes. Strain it and "refresh" it with cold water, then place in a clean tea towel and keep warm. Serve the Créole surrounded or flanked by the rice and garnish as desired – for example with whole shrimps, prawns or sliced pepper.

Prawns may be used in the same way.

CURRIED SHRIMPS

3 oz. butter
1 small onion, skinned and chopped
2 medium-sized sticks of celery, chopped
½ an apple, peeled, cored and chopped

4 level tbsps. flour
2 level tbsps. curry powder
¾ pint milk
6 oz. prepared shrimps
6 oz. almonds, blanched and chopped

Melt the butter, add the onion, celery and apple and cook gently till tender. Add the flour and curry powder, cook for a moment, then add the milk, stirring. When the mixture is thick and smooth, add the shrimps. Brown the almonds under the grill and add to the curry. Serve with rice and chutney.

FRIED RICE WITH SHRIMPS

½ lb. long-grain rice
8 oz. fresh shrimps, shelled
3 eggs

2 spring onions, finely chopped
2 tbsps. oil
½ level tsp. salt

Cook the rice in salted boiling water. Wash and chop the shrimps and set aside. Beat the eggs. Brown the spring onions in 1 tbsp. oil. Add the shrimps and sauté over a high heat for 3

109

minutes, sprinkling with the salt. Pour the beaten eggs over the shrimps and scramble them briefly, removing the mixture from the pan before the egg sets completely; place in a dish and set aside.

Clean and wipe the pan and heat the remaining oil in it; add the drained cooked rice and sauté it quickly, using a folding-in motion for even cooking. When it is thoroughly heated (allow about 3 minutes) add the scrambled eggs and the shrimps, using the edge of a large spoon to cut them into the rice. Serve hot.

SHRIMP RICE MOUSSE

3 oz. long-grain rice
½ oz. gelatine
6–8 oz. fresh or canned shrimps (or thawed frozen shrimps)
¼ pint mayonnaise
A small pkt. of frozen peas, cooked
2 sticks of celery, chopped
Salt and pepper
¼ pint double cream
Sliced cucumber

Cook the rice. Place the gelatine and ½ pint warm water in a bowl in a saucepan of water and heat until the gelatine is dissolved; allow to cool, stirring from time to time. Mix most of the shrimps with the mayonnaise, peas, celery, salt, pepper and gelatine mixture. Whip the cream and fold into the shrimp mixture with the cooked rice. Cool; when nearly set turn out into a wetted mould and chill thoroughly. When set, turn out and decorate with shrimps and sliced cucumber.

SHRIMP AND EGG FLAN

4 oz. shelled prawns or shrimps
¼ pint white sauce
2 eggs
Salt and pepper
Butter
A piece of cucumber
1–2 tomatoes, sliced
1 cooked flan case

Mix the prawns with the white sauce; season the eggs and scramble them in a little butter; peel and slice the cucumber; skin and slice the tomatoes. Divide the flan case into sections and put in alternate portions of shrimps and egg, dividing them with slices of cucumber. Put the tomato in the middle.

SHRIMP AND APPLE SALAD

4 rosy eating apples
4–6 oz. shelled shrimps
Mayonnaise
Lettuce
Small, even-sized tomatoes
Small cress

Polish the apples with a cloth and remove the cores. Mix the shrimps with sufficient mayonnaise to bind, then stuff the apples with this mixture. Arrange on a bed of crisp lettuce and garnish with halved tomatoes and small cress.

SHRIMP AND TOMATO SALAD

4 large tomatoes
2 dozen shrimps, shelled
1 tsp. chopped chives
1 tsp. chopped parsley

¼ of a cucumber, diced
Mayonnaise
Lettuce

Cut the tomatoes in half, scoop out the centres and mix the pulp with the shrimps, chives, parsley, cucumber and mayonnaise. Put this filling back into the tomato cases. Decorate the top of each with a whole shrimp and serve with lettuce.

SEASIDE SALAD

A 1-pint pkt. of lemon jelly
Lemon juice or vinegar
1 small lettuce, shredded
2–3 sticks celery,
  shredded

2 hard-boiled eggs, sliced
2 oz. shrimps or
  prawns, shelled
Watercress

Make up the lemon jelly to 1 pint, replacing 2 tbsps. of the liquid by lemon juice or vinegar. Mix half the jelly with the shredded lettuce and celery and put in the bottom of a bowl or some individual dishes; set in the refrigerator or other cold place. Add the sliced eggs and the shrimps or prawns (or other shellfish as desired). Put the remaining liquid jelly over the egg and shrimp mixture, chill and garnish with shellfish and watercress just before serving.

SHELLFISH RISOTTO

1 onion, skinned and
  finely chopped
3 oz. butter
8 oz. long-grain rice
¼ pint dry white wine
1½ pints boiling chicken
  stock

Salt and pepper
1 clove of garlic, skinned
  and chopped (optional)
8 oz. frozen scampi or
  prawns, thawed
Grated Parmesan cheese

Fry the onion in 2 oz. of the butter for about 5 minutes, until soft. Add the rice and stir until transparent. Add the wine and about ¼ pint of the chicken stock, season and cook over a moderate heat, uncovered, until the stock has been absorbed; continue to cook, adding more stock as required, until the rice is almost soft (about 15 minutes).

Just before the rice becomes tender, gently fry the garlic (if used) and the shellfish in the remaining 1 oz. butter for 5 minutes. Stir into the risotto and serve with the cheese.

A few sliced button mushrooms can be fried with the shellfish or a few frozen peas or strips of canned pimiento can be added to the risotto just before the rice is cooked.

Other shellfish, such as crab or lobster meat (fresh or

canned) may also be used; a mixture of shellfish, with possibly a few mussels (canned or fresh) will give a more unusual touch.

SPANISH PAELLA

8 cooked mussels
1 small cooked lobster
1 pkt. of frozen prawns
½ a small raw chicken, cleaned
3 tbsps. olive oil
3 cups of water
1 small onion, skinned and chopped
1 small clove of garlic, skinned and chopped
2 medium-sized tomatoes, skinned and chopped
1 cup long-grain rice
Salt
½ cup frozen peas
A pinch of saffron
½ a small can of pimientoes

Shell the mussels and lobster and thaw out the prawns. Cut up the chicken. Heat some oil in a frying-pan and fry the chicken until brown; drain the oil into a shallow iron casserole, then add the water to the chicken and stew gently for 20 minutes. Fry the onion and garlic in the oil until half cooked. Add the tomatoes and fry these until cooked. Add the rice and some salt and mix with the oil. Arrange the peas, mussels, lobster, prawns and chicken on the top and add 2 cups of boiling chicken broth. Bring to the boil, add the saffron, blended with a little broth, arrange the pimientos on top and continue to cook very gently until the rice is cooked and the liquid absorbed; serve at once, decorated with the lobster claws.

SEAFOOD SPECIAL

2 oz. butter
An 8-oz. can of lobster or prawns
An 8-oz. can of crab
4 tbsps. sherry
2 level tbsps. flour
1 level tsp. paprika
½ pint milk
A 5-oz. carton of single cream
Salt and pepper
Triangles of fried bread

Melt the butter in a pan and add the fish and the sherry; heat gently. Stir in the flour, paprika, milk and cream, taking care not to break up the fish too much. Cook until thickened, season to taste and serve with the fried bread.

ST. LAWRENCE CLAM CHOWDER (Canada)

2 oz. bacon fat
2 onions, skinned and chopped
4 tbsps. chopped carrot
2 sticks of celery, chopped
2 medium-sized potatoes, peeled and diced
⅝ pint boiling water
A 15-oz. can of tomatoes
2 7½-oz. cans of clams, drained and minced
1 level tsp. salt
¼ level tsp. dried thyme
A pinch of pepper

Melt the bacon fat in a saucepan, add the onions, carrot and celery, cover the pan and cook over a very low heat for 10 minutes. Add the potatoes with the boiling water and cook for 15 minutes, or until the vegetables are nearly tender. Cut the tomatoes into pieces, add and bring to boiling point only. Stir in the clams and seasonings and simmer gently for 10 minutes. Correct the seasoning and serve accompanied by cream crackers.

BOSTON CLAM CHOWDER

3 oz. raw soft-shell clams, peeled
$\frac{3}{4}$ pint cold water
4 oz. salt pork, diced, or 2 level tbsps. butter or margarine
2 medium-sized onions, skinned and sliced
2 level tbsps. plain flour

$\frac{1}{4}$ level tsp. celery salt
$\frac{1}{4}$ level tsp. pepper
2 level tsps. salt
1$\frac{1}{4}$ lb. potatoes, peeled and diced
1$\frac{1}{4}$ pints milk
1 level tbsp. butter or margarine

Snip off the necks of the clams and cut them up finely with scissors; leave the soft parts whole. Place the clams in a saucepan with the strained clam liquid, add the water and bring to the boil. Lift out the clams with a perforated spoon, retaining the liquid. Sauté the salt pork in a large saucepan until golden; add the onions and cook until tender. Stir in the flour, seasoning, the retained clam liquor and the potatoes. Cover and cook for 20 minutes, or until the potatoes are tender. Add the milk, clams and butter and correct the seasoning. Re-heat and ladle into large soup bowls, or into mugs if it is to be served out-of-doors. (8 servings.)
Note: In this country the raw clams would have to be replaced by canned ones; the liquor from the can could be used.

LOBSTER BISQUE

1 cooked hen lobster
2 pints fish stock or water
1 small carrot, peeled and sliced
1 small onion, skinned and sliced
1 bay leaf

A sprig of parsley
Salt and pepper
1 oz. butter
3 level tbsps. flour
A squeeze of lemon juice
A little cream
$\frac{1}{2}$ glass white wine
Lobster butter

Remove the lobster meat from the shell and cut it into neat pieces, reserving the coral. Break up the shell and cook it with the stock, vegetables, herbs and seasoning for $\frac{3}{4}$–1 hour, then strain off the liquid. Melt the butter, stir in the flour and cook for 2–3 minutes. Remove the pan from the heat and gradually stir in the lobster stock, bring to the boil and continue to stir until it thickens; cook for a further 3 minutes. Re-season if necessary and add the lemon juice, cream and wine. Add the pieces of lobster meat and whisk in the lobster butter.

Lobster Butter: Pound ½ oz. lobster coral with 1 oz. butter and sieve the mixture.

LOBSTER CHOWDER

2 rashers of streaky bacon, rinded and chopped
½ a small onion, grated
2 level tbsps. flour
¾ pint water

½ pint evaporated milk
2 medium-sized potatoes, peeled and diced
A 7-oz. can of peas
A 6-oz. can of lobster

Fry the bacon lightly, add the onion and continue cooking for 1–2 minutes, without colouring. Stir in the flour and gradually add the water and evaporated milk, stirring all the time until it thickens. Add the potatoes and simmer for 10 minutes. Add the peas and the lobster (broken up into small pieces) and simmer for 2–3 minutes. Serve in bowls.

MUSSEL SOUP

2 doz. mussels
1 onion, skinned and chopped
2–3 bay leaves
1½ pints water
2 oz. butter

1 large leek (white part only), chopped finely
1 tomato, skinned and sliced
3 oz. vermicelli
Salt and pepper

Wash and scrape the mussels very thoroughly and put them in a pan with the onion, bay leaves and water. Cover and cook until the shells open, then strain the liquid into a basin. Take the mussels from the shells and remove the beard from each. Melt the butter, add the leek and the tomato and cook gently for 5 minutes, then add the liquor in which the mussels were cooked, the vermicelli and the seasoning. Cook until the vegetables and vermicelli are tender and add the mussels just before serving.

PRAWN SOUP

A 1-lb. pkt. of frozen prawns, roughly chopped
1½ pints water
1 onion, skinned and chopped
Grated rind and juice of 1 lemon
A pinch of mixed herbs

1 oz. flour
2 oz. butter
Salt and pepper
Grated nutmeg
3 egg yolks
¼ pint single cream
Sprigs of parsley

Put the prawns into the water, add the onion, lemon rind and herbs and simmer for about 5 minutes, then strain. Make a sauce from this stock with the flour, butter and seasonings. Add the cooked prawns, with the juice of the lemon and a

114

little grated nutmeg and cook for 2–3 minutes. Mix the egg yolks and cream with 2–3 tbsps. of the soup and add to the soup in the pan; re-heat but do not boil. Garnish if desired with parsley sprigs.

SHRIMP SOUP

1 pint shrimps, shelled	1 onion, skinned and chopped
1 oz. butter	¼ pint cream or milk
2 oz. long-grain rice	Salt and cayenne
1 quart stock	pepper
1 carrot, peeled and chopped	

Reserve about 20 shrimps for a garnish; pound the remainder with the butter. Boil the rice in salted water till tender, add it to the shrimps and butter and mix well. Put all into a saucepan and stir over the heat for a few minutes, then add the stock, carrot and onion and simmer for 20 minutes. Pass the soup through a sieve, return it to the pan and add the cream or milk and seasoning. Re-heat without boiling, and before serving add the shelled shrimps.

SHRIMP CHOWDER

1 large onion, skinned and sliced	Salt and pepper
	1 pint shrimps or prawns, shelled
½ oz. butter	
¼ pint boiling water	1 pint milk
3 medium-sized potatoes, peeled and diced	1–2 oz. cheese, grated
	Chopped parsley

Lightly fry the onion in the butter for about 5 minutes, until soft but not coloured. Add the boiling water, potatoes and seasoning. Cover and simmer gently for 15–20 minutes, or until the potatoes are just cooked. Add the shrimps and the milk and re-heat. Stir in the grated cheese and some parsley and serve with crusty bread or toast.

CHAPTER 6

Savouries and snacks

Fish lends itself particularly well to making all kinds of savouries and there is a vast repertoire, from highly flavoured cocktail titbits to light and easily digested dishes suitable for a late supper. In addition to the recipes given here, some of those in chapters 2 and 5, "Starters" and "Shellfish" – pp. 15 and 96 – might equally qualify as savouries.

The first group in this chapter consists of reasonably satisfying savouries, suitable for light meals and snacks, while the second group is composed of the smaller cocktail and after-dinner titbits.

Hearty Savouries

ANCHOVY PIZZA ROLLS

4 soft rolls	4 anchovy fillets
4 tomatoes	2–3 black olives, sliced
2 oz. cheese, grated	

Oven temperature: fairly hot (400°F., mark 6)

Cut a slice off the top of each roll, scoop out the centre and discard. Slice the tomatoes thinly and place a tomato in the centre of each roll. Sprinkle with the cheese and decorate with the anchovies and black olives. Bake in the centre of the oven for 15–20 minutes, until the cheese has melted and the rolls are hot.

ANCHOVY EGG TOASTS

A small can of anchovy fillets	3 tbsps. milk
2 eggs, beaten	1 oz. butter
Pepper	4 slices of toast, buttered

116

Chop most of the anchovy fillets, but keep a few whole for garnishing. Mix the eggs, chopped anchovies, pepper and milk. Melt the butter in a pan, add the mixture and heat very gently, to scramble the eggs. Pile on toast and garnish with the remaining fillets.

BLOATERS
Cover with boiling water, soak for 1–2 minutes and drain well. Remove the head and fins, cut the fish open, remove the roes and backbone and clean the flesh. Place on a greased grill grid, flesh side down, dot with butter and sprinkle with salt and pepper. Cook for about 10 minutes under a gentle heat, turning them once. Serve with butter.

FRIED COD'S ROE
Roe can be bought either cooked or raw. To cook raw roe, tie it in muslin and cook gently in boiling salted water, with a few peppercorns, until tender – ½–1 hour. Lift out and cool. The boiled roe is usually fried; slice it, dip in seasoned flour or fine oatmeal, or coat with egg and browned bread-crumbs, and fry in hot fat until golden-brown. Serve with bacon rolls and parsley or with anchovy sauce.

COD'S ROE FRITTERS
If the roe is raw, first cook it as described in the previous recipe. Skin the roe and with a sharp knife cut it into slices about ½ inch thick. Make about ¼ pint coating batter, dip the slices into it and fry in hot deep fat until crisp and golden-brown. Serve with cut lemon.

SMOKED COD'S ROE AND BACON
Butter 4 rounds of toast and spread them with a good layer of smoked cod's roe. Rind and cut up 1–2 rashers of bacon and sprinkle the pieces over the roe. Put the toast under a hot grill to cook the bacon and serve very hot.

CRAB TOASTS

A little butter
1 oz. fresh white
  bread-crumbs
A small can of crabmeat
  (3½ oz. approx.)

3 tbsps. top of the milk
1 tbsp. sherry
Salt and pepper
4 slices of toast

Melt 1 oz. of butter in a saucepan, add the bread-crumbs and crabmeat, mix well and stir in the top of the milk. Stir for a few minutes over the heat and season well, then stir in the sherry. Cut the toast into fingers, removing all crusts, butter pile high with crabmeat and serve piping hot.

CHEESE CRAB SANDWICH

Put some crab salad on slices of toast, top with processed Cheddar cheese and brown under the grill.

POACHED SMOKED HADDOCK

Cut the fins from the haddock and if the fish is large, cut into serving-size pieces. Place in a frying-pan (or large saucepan), barely cover with milk or milk and water, sprinkle with pepper and simmer gently for 10–15 minutes, or until tender. Garnish with parsley and serve with buttered toast.

Alternatively, cook the fish in the oven in a very little milk or milk and water, with a knob of butter and a little pepper.

The haddock can be served topped with a poached egg on each portion.

GRILLED SMOKED HADDOCK

Trim the fish, put in a basin, cover with boiling water and soak for 5 minutes; drain well. Place the fish on the grill grid, skin side uppermost, and grill under a medium heat for about 3–5 minutes, depending on its thickness. Turn the fish, brush with a little melted butter or oil, sprinkle with pepper and grill for a further 3–5 minutes, until tender. Serve topped with a knob of butter.

CREAMED SMOKED HADDOCK

¾–1 lb. smoked haddock	½ pint milk
1½ oz. butter	4 oz. cheese, grated
1½ oz. flour	Salt and pepper

Wash and trim the fish, put in a pan, cover with water and bring to the boil slowly. Turn out the heat, cover the pan with a lid and leave to stand for 5–10 minutes, until the fish is tender. Drain off the liquid, retaining ¼ pint, and skin and flake the fish. Melt the butter, stir in the flour and cook for 2–3 minutes. Remove from the heat and gradually stir in the fish liquid, made up to ¾ pint with the milk. Bring to the boil and continue to stir until the sauce thickens. Remove from the heat and add the flaked fish, the cheese and seasoning. Re-heat without boiling and serve over hot buttered toast or on boiled rice.

HADDOCK PAPRIKA

1 small Finnan haddock	½ pint milk
2 oz. noodles (weight before cooking)	2 oz. cheese, grated
	Salt and pepper
1 oz. butter	Paprika pepper
1 oz. flour	

Steam the haddock for 10–15 minutes, remove the skin and

bones and flake the flesh. Cook the noodles in boiling salted water until just tender, following the directions given on the packet. Melt the butter, add the flour and cook for 2–3 minutes; gradually add the milk, bring to the boil and cook for 2–3 minutes before adding half of the cheese; season to taste. Arrange the noodles and haddock in alternate layers in a greased pie dish, cover with the cheese sauce and sprinkle with the remaining cheese. Brown under the grill and serve sprinkled with paprika pepper.

HADDOCK IN RICE BORDER

4 oz. long-grain rice
1 lb. smoked or fresh
  haddock
Cheese sauce (see p. 142)

Salt and pepper
1 egg, hard-boiled and sliced
Parsley

Boil the rice, following the instructions given on p. 155. Put the fish in a pan, cover with water and bring to the boil; turn off the heat and leave the fish in the cooking water for 5 minutes. Drain, retaining ¼ pint of the liquid. Skin and bone the fish and chop it roughly. Make the sauce, using half milk and half fish stock; add the fish and season to taste. Place in a shallow ovenproof dish and surround by a border of rice, garnished with hard-boiled egg and parsley.

HADDOCK RISOTTO

4 oz. long-grain rice
1 pint stock or water
1 shallot, skinned
Salt
1 oz. butter

4 oz. smoked haddock, cooked
  and flaked
1 oz. cheese, grated
Paprika

Boil the rice in a saucepan with ½ pint stock or water, the shallot and some salt; when it has absorbed the liquid, add another ½ pint liquid and cook until this too is absorbed. Remove the shallot and add the butter and haddock. When hot, put in an ovenproof dish, sprinkle the grated cheese on top, dust with paprika and brown under the grill. Serve very hot.

HADDOCK AND RICE CROQUETTES

6 oz. smoked haddock, cooked
  and flaked
4 oz. long-grain rice,
  cooked
1 egg, hard-boiled and
  chopped
2 tbsps. white sauce

Salt and pepper
A little chopped parsley
Flour
Egg and browned breadcrumbs
  for coating
Fat for frying

Mix the haddock, rice, egg, sauce, seasonings and parsley.

119

Form into croquettes on a floured board, dip into egg and crumbs and fry until golden-brown.

HADDOCK AND MUSHROOM FLAN

2 lb. smoked haddock	Salt and pepper
½ pint milk	A cooked oblong flan case
¼ lb. mushrooms	(see p. 160)
Butter	2 oz. cheese, finely grated
¾ oz. flour	

Oven temperature: fairly hot (375°F., mark 5)

Poach the haddock gently in the milk until tender, remove the flesh from the bones and flake it. Prepare the mushrooms, leaving the stalks on, slice them and fry until tender in a little melted butter. Make a sauce with ¾ oz. butter, the flour and the milk used for poaching the fish (made up to ½ pint with water). Season the sauce, add most of the flaked fish, reserving some of the best flakes, and half of the mushrooms. Pour the mixture into the pastry case and arrange the large haddock flakes down each side, with the remaining mushrooms down the centre. Pour any fat left from frying over the top, sprinkle with the grated cheese and heat through near the top of the oven for 15 minutes.

HADDOCK (OR GOLDEN FILLET) TOASTS

Flake and bone ½ lb. cooked smoked haddock, removing the skin. Melt 1 oz. butter and add ½ oz. flour. Gradually add ¼ pint milk and water, bring to the boil and cook well. Add the fish, with pepper to taste, and serve piled on buttered toast.

Alternatively, mix the fish with scrambled egg or add 1–2 oz. grated cheese to the mixture, pile on toast as above and heat gently under the grill.

SMOKED HADDOCK SALAD SHELLS
(see colour picture No. 8)

½ lb. smoked fillet of haddock, cooked and flaked	Mayonnaise
	Cucumber to garnish

Divide the fish between 4 scallop shells and cover with mayonnaise. Decorate with cucumber slices or cones.

DEVILLED HERRING ROES

A large can of herring roes	1½ level tsps. curry powder
Flour	2 tsps. chutney
1 small onion, skinned and chopped	Salt and pepper
	4 rounds of buttered toast
2 oz. butter	

Flour the roes. Fry the onion in the butter, add the roes and cook quickly, browning them on both sides. Remove them

120

from the pan and add the curry powder, chutney, salt and pepper. Cook, mixing well, then return the herring roes to the pan. Serve the roes piping hot on the hot buttered toast, after removing the crusts.

HERRING ROES ON TOAST
Wash the roes and dip them in seasoned flour. Brush them over with melted butter and grill on a greased grid, turning them once to ensure even cooking – allow about 8–10 minutes altogether. Serve on hot toast, sprinkled with cayenne pepper if liked, and accompanied by a wedge of lemon.

HERRING ROE FRITTERS
Wash the roes, then dip them in a coating batter (see Chapter 1, p. 12). Fry in deep fat until crisp and golden, drain well and serve with lemon wedges.

KIPPERS
If you suspect that the kippers are very salty, trim, place in a tall jug, pour boiling water over them and leave for 3 minutes; drain and finish by any of the following methods:

Grilling: Dot with butter, sprinkle with pepper and grill gently for 4–5 minutes on each side.

Baking: Place in a greased ovenproof dish, sprinkle with pepper and dot with butter. Cover with foil and bake in a fairly hot oven (400°F., mark 6) for 10–15 minutes.

Poaching: Place in a frying-pan, cover with water and simmer until tender – about 5 minutes. Serve with a knob of butter on each kipper.

Kipper Fillets in Polythene Bags
Cook these in the bag, according to the packer's instructions.

FRITTERED KIPPER FILLETS

8 kipper fillets	4 tbsps. water
2 oz. flour	1 egg white
A pinch of salt	Deep fat for frying
2 tsps. salad oil	

Drain the kipper fillets. Sift the flour and salt and pour the oil and water into a well made in the centre of the flour. Mix to a smooth paste and beat for a few minutes, then cover and leave for 20–30 minutes. Whisk the egg white and fold it into the batter. Dip the kipper fillets into the batter, then lower half of them into smoking hot deep fat. Fry until golden-brown, and drain well; keep warm while the rest of the fillets are fried. Serve very hot.

SAVOURY KIPPER FILLETS

2 kippers
4 fingers of toast

1 oz. cheese, grated
Parsley

Trim the kippers and put them into a jug or basin, pour on some boiling water and leave to stand for 3 minutes. Drain off the water and remove the skin and bones from the kippers. (Alternatively, use packeted kipper fillets.) Place the kipper fillets on the fingers of toast, sprinkle with grated cheese and brown under a hot grill. Serve piping hot, garnished with parsley.

LOBSTER CUSHIONS

¼ pint white sauce (see
   p. 138)
1 oz. mushrooms, chopped
½ oz. butter

3–4 oz. lobster meat (fresh
   or canned), flaked
4 soft rolls
1 oz. cheese, grated

Make the sauce, sauté the mushrooms in the butter and add to the sauce, then add the flaked lobster meat; re-heat the mixture until really hot. Cut off the tops of the rolls and scoop out the insides. Fill with lobster mixture, sprinkle with cheese and place under the grill to melt the cheese.
Note: Starch-reduced rolls may be used if preferred.

SALMON CHEESE FLAN

An 8-inch flan case
1 oz. butter
1 oz. flour
¼ pint milk
4 tbsps. single cream
2 eggs

1 small carton of cottage
   cheese
An 8-oz. can of salmon
1–2 tomatoes to
   garnish

Oven temperature: fairly hot (400°F., mark 6)
Make the flan case in the usual way and bake it "blind" (see directions on p. 160). Make a thick white sauce with the butter, flour and milk. Add the cream, 1 whole egg, 1 egg yolk and the cheese, then the fish, drained and flaked. Beat in the stiffly beaten egg white. Turn the mixture into the pastry case and bake it for about ½ hour towards the top of the oven; 10 minutes before the end of the time, arrange thin tomato slices round the edge. Serve hot.
   Tuna may be used in the same way.

SARDINE ON TOAST

Toast 4 slices of bread, then butter them lightly. Drain an 8-oz. can of sardines and arrange them on the toast. Heat through under a moderate grill for 3–4 minutes.
   Alternatively, sprinkle the sardines with paprika pepper and grated cheese before grilling.

SARDINE AND EGG TOASTS

Drain and mash the contents of a can of sardines. Melt 4 tbsps. butter and add 3 oz. fresh white bread-crumbs; when they are heated through, add 2 chopped hard-boiled eggs, the sardines and seasoning. Pile on to buttered toast, grill till golden-brown and garnish with sliced tomato and parsley sprigs.

SARDINE À LA BARQUE

2½ oz. butter	Salt and pepper
A few button onions, skinned and sliced	4 tomatoes, skinned
	A large can of sardines
2 carrots, peeled and diced	½ oz. cheese, grated
2 oz. French beans, chopped	Parsley sprigs to garnish

Melt the butter in a saucepan and add the onions, carrots and beans. Season, stir well, cover and cook for 5 minutes. Halve the tomatoes, remove the seeds, dice the flesh and add to the mixture. Continue cooking until all the vegetables are tender. Pile on a dish and lay the sardines on top, overlapping each other. Sprinkle with the cheese, brown lightly under the grill and serve garnished with parsley sprigs.

SARDINE-STUFFED EGGS

Cut 4 hard-boiled eggs in half, scoop out the yolks and sieve them. Mix these with 4 mashed sardines and refill the egg-white cups with the mixture. Arrange the eggs on a bed of lettuce and garnish with lettuce, tomato and more sardines.

SHRIMP BAKES

8 oz. cooked long-grain rice (weight before cooking)	1 carton of sour cream
	2 cans of shrimps
2 tomatoes, sliced	½ tsp. Worcestershire sauce

Oven temperature: moderate (350°F., mark 4)

Divide the rice between 4 individual ovenproof dishes. Halve the tomato slices and arrange round the edges of the dishes. Mix the sour cream with the drained shrimps and Worcestershire sauce and pile into the centre of the rice. Bake in the centre of the oven for 20–30 minutes.

SHRIMP CROQUETTES

1 oz. butter	Salt and pepper
1 oz. flour	½ lb. shrimps, shelled
¼ pint milk	Egg and bread-crumbs
1 tbsp. cream	Fat for frying
1 tsp. lemon juice	Parsley to garnish

Make a thick white sauce (see p. 138), using the butter, flour

123

and milk, then add the cream, lemon juice, seasoning and shrimps. Allow the mixture to cool on a plate, divide into 8 portions and shape into croquettes. Coat with egg and breadcrumbs and fry in really hot fat until lightly browned. Serve garnished with parsley.

SHRIMP AND HAM CUPS

12 slices of white bread
1–2 oz. melted butter
½ oz. flour
½ oz. butter
½ pint milk
1 egg, beaten
A pinch of salt
A little pepper

¼ level tsp. curry powder
⅛ level tsp. grated nutmeg
A 2-oz. pkt. of frozen shrimps (thawed)
1 thick slice of ham, diced
Red pepper and parsley to garnish

Oven temperature: moderate (350°F., mark 4)
Cut a round from each slice of bread, using a 2½-inch cutter. Brush one side of each with melted butter and press into deep patty tins, greased side down. Bake towards the top of the oven for 15–20 minutes. Make a sauce with the flour, remaining butter and milk; remove from the heat, add the egg, seasonings and flavourings, then beat until creamy. Stir in the shrimps and ham, pile into the cases and garnish.

FRIED SPRATS

Wash the sprats and dry carefully, then dip them in seasoned flour, coating very lightly. Run a skewer through the heads of about a dozen at a time. Fry in deep fat until crisp and golden, drain and garnish with tomato or lemon and parsley; serve with brown bread and butter.

TUNA SPAGHETTI CRISP

4 oz. short-cut spaghetti
A 7-oz. can of tuna
½ pint white sauce (see note below)

3 oz. cheese, grated
Salt and pepper
A small pkt. of potato crisps

Oven temperature: moderate (350°F., mark 4)
Cook the spaghetti in boiling salted water until tender – 8–12 minutes. Drain well and place in a bowl. Add the drained and flaked fish, white sauce, cheese and seasoning, mix well and transfer to a greased 2-pint ovenproof dish. Slightly crush the crisps and arrange on top. Bake in the centre of the oven for 20–30 minutes and garnish as desired – for example, with cooked sliced mushrooms, if available.
Note: Use plain white sauce or if you wish, flavour it with mushroom stalks. Alternatively, use a canned condensed mushroom soup or a packet soup made up with slightly less water than directed and add a little top of the milk.

124

TUNA FLAN

1 oz. butter
1 oz. flour
¼ pint milk
4 oz. bacon, rinded and
  chopped
1 small onion, skinned and
  chopped

A small pkt. of frozen peas,
  cooked
A 7-oz. can of tuna, flaked
Salt and pepper
A cooked 8-inch flan case
  (see p. 160)

Melt the butter in a pan, stir in the flour and cook for 2–3 minutes. Remove the pan from the heat, stir in the milk, bring to the boil and stir until thickened. Fry the bacon and add to the sauce; fry the onion in the bacon fat and add to the sauce, with the peas (saving some for garnish). Add the tuna, salt and pepper, mix and pour into the flan. Re-heat under the grill and garnish with peas.

TUNA SALAD

A 7-oz. can of tuna, flaked
2 sticks of celery,
  chopped
1 tbsp. horseradish sauce
2 tbsps. mayonnaise
½ level tsp. salt

Lettuce
1 egg, hard-boiled and
  sliced
1 tomato, skinned, seeded
  and sliced

Mix the flaked tuna with the celery and horseradish sauce, bind with mayonnaise and season with salt. Pile on a bed of shredded lettuce and decorate with sliced egg and tomato.

FISH PARCELS

A 14-oz. pkt. of frozen
  fish fillets
Butter
Salt and pepper
2 tomatoes, sliced

1 level tsp. dried onion
  flakes
2 eggs, hard-boiled and
  sliced

Oven temperature: hot (425°F., mark 7)
Cut the fish into 4 portions and put each on a piece of foil measuring about 12 by 10 inches. On each place a knob of butter, some salt and pepper, half a sliced tomato, ¼ tsp. onion and half a sliced egg. Wrap the foil loosely round each portion and put seam side up in a baking dish. Bake for 30 minutes in the centre of the oven; serve in the foil.

Buttered broccoli is delicious with these "parcels".

SCALLOPED FISH

Oven temperature: hot (425°F., mark 7)
This is a favourite way of using up oddments of fish, especially for the small family. Flake and season some cold cooked fish, allowing about 4 oz. per person. Butter the required number

125

of scallop shells, sprinkle each with 1 tbsp. fresh white bread-crumbs and place some of the fish in each shell. Mix a little white sauce with some cream or top of the milk and flavour with a few drops of anchovy sauce. Pour this over the fish in the shells, cover with more breadcrumbs and put a few dabs of butter on each. Heat through near the top of the oven.

For a slightly more elaborate finish, pipe creamed potato round the shells before baking the scallops; before serving, garnish them with baked or grilled tomato slices, small mushrooms and tiny sprigs of parsley.

FISH POTATO PUFFS

$\frac{1}{2}$ lb. potatoes, peeled	Salt and pepper
$\frac{1}{2}$ lb. white fish, e.g., haddock, cod	1 oz. butter, melted
	2 eggs, beaten
$\frac{1}{2}$ a small onion, grated	Deep fat for frying
2 level tsps. curry powder	

Boil and drain the potatoes and mash them. Cook and flake the fish (see p. 13), mix it with the remaining ingredients and beat until smooth. Heat the fat until it will brown a 1-inch cube of bread in 60 seconds. Drop the fish mixture into it with a teaspoon, fry quickly until golden, drain on crumpled kitchen paper and serve with a well-flavoured sauce, e.g. tomato or Tartare.

PIQUANT FISH TURNOVERS

$\frac{1}{2}$ lb. fish, cooked and flaked	1 tbsp. chopped parsley
1 tbsp. chutney	Salt and pepper
1 shallot, skinned and grated	1 large pkt. of frozen flaky pastry
1 oz. cheese, grated	Beaten egg

Oven temperature: hot (425°F., mark 7)

Mix the fish with the flavourings and seasonings. Roll out the pastry thinly and cut into 4 squares. Place some of the fish filling on each, damp the edges with egg and fold over into triangles; flake the edges with the back of a knife, scallop and brush the pastry with egg. Cook on a baking sheet at the top of the oven for about $\frac{1}{4}$ hour, till golden-brown.

FISH FRITTERS

4 oz. fish, cooked and flaked	Salt and pepper
1 oz. self-raising flour	1 egg
1 tsp. chopped parsley	A little milk
	Fat for shallow frying

Mix the fish with the other ingredients, adding sufficient milk to allow the mixture to drop easily from a spoon. Fry in spoonfuls in the hot fat until golden on each side.

126

FISH CROQUETTES

1 lb. white fish (cod or
   haddock), cooked and
   flaked
2 eggs, hard-boiled and finely
   chopped
1 tsp. chopped parsley

Salt and pepper
1½–2 tbsps. salad cream
Beaten egg and bread-crumbs
   for coating
Deep fat for frying

Mix the fish, egg, parsley and seasoning and add enough salad cream to bind. Put on a flat plate, leave until cold, then divide into 6–8 portions and shape into rolls. Coat with egg and bread-crumbs twice, then fry in deep fat for 3–4 minutes, until golden-brown. Serve with tomato sauce.

FISH PASTRY SCALLOPS

12 oz. shortcrust pastry
1 oz. butter
1 oz. flour
½ pint milk and stock
8 oz. uncooked white fish,
   cut up

1 tsp. chopped parsley
A little lemon juice
Salt and pepper
Beaten egg to glaze
Green salad

Oven temperature: fairly hot (400°F., mark 6)

Grease 6 scallop shells and line with pastry, saving some for the "lids". Make a sauce with the butter, flour and liquid and add the fish, flavourings and seasoning. Put some filling in each shell and cover with pastry, sealing the edges firmly. Glaze the scallops with egg and bake near the top of the oven until the tops are brown. Turn out on to a baking sheet, glaze the reverse sides and bake for a further 10–15 minutes, till golden. Serve hot or cold, accompanied by a green salad.

FISH SOUFFLÉ SANDWICHES

8 oz. white fish, cooked
   and flaked
Juice of ½ a lemon

3 large slices of bread
2 tbsps. mayonnaise
1 egg white, beaten stiffly

Blend the fish and lemon juice. Toast the bread on one side, halve each slice and remove the crusts. Spread the fish on the untoasted side and top with mayonnaise mixed with egg white. Grill to a delicate brown.

SURPRISE SANDWICH LOAF

½ lb. cream cheese
¼ pint prawns, shelled
A little butter
Anchovy essence
Salt and pepper
Pink colouring
Milk

4 oz. watercress
Green colouring
1 small loaf
Radish "concertinas"
   (see note below)
Cucumber skin
Lettuce leaves

Divide the cheese into three portions and leave one portion

127

plain. Cream one-third of the cheese with the chopped prawns, some butter, a few drops of anchovy essence, seasoning to taste, a little pink colouring and a little milk. Reserve 1–2 sprigs of watercress for garnish and chop the rest finely; mix with another one-third of the cheese, then colour this a pale green. Cream the remaining portion of cheese with a little seasoning and milk until fairly soft. Remove the crusts from the loaf and cut lengthwise into ½-inch slices. Spread one slice of bread thickly with the prawn filling; spread the watercress filling on a second slice and place on top of the prawn-covered slice. Place another slice of bread on top. Repeat until all the slices are used, press lightly and leave in a cool place until firm. Cover the whole loaf with the plain cream cheese, as though icing a cake. Pipe with small stars of cream cheese and decorate with radish concertinas and diamonds of cucumber skin. Garnish the serving dish with some small lettuce leaves and the remaining sprigs of watercress. To serve the loaf, cut it downwards into slices.

Any other savoury fillings may be used instead of those given, provided they contrast well with each other.

Note: To make a radish concertina, wash and trim the radish, then using a sharp knife, make parallel cuts close together, but not right through,so that the radish is held together at one side by the skin and the slices fall slightly apart, like the "folds" of a concertina.

Cocktail Savouries

ANCHOVY OLIVES
Drain some anchovy fillets. Wrap each fillet round a stuffed olive. Tint some cream cheese with a few drops of yellow and pink colouring and pipe a little on to each. Garnish with parsley.

SALMON AND GRAPE ROLLS
Sprinkle a little lemon juice on thin slices of smoked salmon, place half a peeled green grape on each, roll up and serve on sticks.

SCAMPI DUNK
8 oz. frozen scampi   Deep fat for frying
Beaten egg and bread-crumbs

Thaw out the scampi and dry well, then coat with beaten egg and the bread-crumbs. Heat the fat until it will brown a 1-inch

(Cont'd page 129)

cube of bread in 60 seconds and fry the scampi until they are a light golden brown. Drain them on crumpled kitchen paper and serve hot, on cocktail sticks, with a suitable sauce for dunking – for example, Spicy Tomato Sauce (see p. 149).

SEAFOOD COCKTAIL DIP
Begin by making the Tangy Curry Sauce (see recipe below). Prepare some peeled prawns, shrimps and scampi and cut some lobster flesh into small chunks. Place a bowl of sauce on a large platter and arrange the shellfish around it. Garnish with parsley and put ready a good supply of cocktail sticks for spearing the pieces of fish and dipping them into the sauce.

Tangy Curry Sauce

¼ pint mayonnaise	1 tbsp. lemon juice
1 level tsp. curry powder	2 tbsps. chopped
1 tbsp. minced onion	chutney

Mix all the ingredients and chill for 1½–2 hours before serving.

SALMON DIP

A 3½-oz. can of salmon	2 gherkins, chopped
¼ lb. cottage cheese	Salt and pepper
2 rashers of streaky bacon, rinded	1–2 tbsps. mayonnaise
	Parsley
A 3-oz. carton of dairy sour cream	Potato crisps

Drain the excess liquid from the salmon; flake the fish into a basin and add the cottage cheese. Fry the bacon till crisp, crush and fold into the salmon mixture, then add the sour cream and the gherkins. Check the seasoning and finally fold in the mayonnaise. Garnish with a sprig of parsley and serve with potato crisps for dunking.

TUNA CHEESE DIP

A 3½-oz. can of tuna, flaked	¼ cup well-drained sweet pickle
3 3-oz. pkts. of cream cheese	1 tbsp. grated onion
¼ cup dry white wine	A dash of Tabasco sauce
1 tbsp. mayonnaise	¼ level tsp. salt
2 tbsps. chopped parsley	¼ level tsp. garlic salt

Drain the tuna, blend with the cream cheese, then with the remaining ingredients. Serve with potato crisps for dunking.

CROUSTADES OF HADDOCK

8 oz. smoked haddock	Fat for deep frying
Bread	1 oz. cheese, grated
Egg and bread-crumbs	Parsley to garnish

Illustrations

13. Lobster Mayonnaise
14. Lobster Thermidor

15. Fried Scampi
16. Shrimp Créole

Poach and flake the haddock. Cut slices of bread 1½ inches thick and stamp out 6 rounds. Egg-and-crumb them and mark out the centres with small round cutters. Fry in very hot fat, then remove the centre of each, leaving the shells of fried bread to form the croustades or cases. Heat the smoked haddock in a little fat, with the cheese. Pile the filling into the croustades and garnish with parsley.

ANGELS ON HORSEBACK

4 rounds of bread, about 2 inches in diameter	4 oysters
1 oz. butter	A little cayenne pepper
2 rashers of streaky bacon, rinded	Lemon juice
	Watercress or parsley

Oven temperature: fairly hot (400°F., mark 6)

Fry the bread until golden in the butter. Flatten out the rashers with a knife blade and cut in half. Put an oyster in the middle of each piece of bacon, sprinkle with cayenne pepper and a squeeze of lemon juice and roll the bacon round the oyster; secure each with a cocktail stick or small wooden skewer to keep it rolled. Place one roll on top of each croûte of bread and bake towards the top of the oven for about 15 minutes, or until the bacon is lightly cooked. Serve at once, garnished with a little watercress or parsley.

SCALLOPS AND BACON

8 scallops, prepared	8 rashers of streaky bacon, rinded
Salt and pepper	Tartare sauce
Lemon juice	

Sprinkle the scallops with salt, pepper and lemon juice. Wrap a rasher round each scallop and secure with a cocktail stick. Grill under a moderate heat until cooked through – about 5 minutes on each side. Serve with Tartare sauce.

When served on toast, these are sometimes known as "Pigs in Blankets".

TINY CURRIED FISH CAKES

¼ lb. cold fish	Lemon juice
2 oz. cold potato, sieved	¼ oz. butter
Salt and pepper	Egg and bread-crumbs to coat
½ level tsp. curry powder	Fat for frying
½ tbsp. beaten egg	

Put all the ingredients except the egg, bread-crumbs and fat into a pan and beat well over a gentle heat. Cool and shape on a floured board into small sausages. Coat with egg and bread-crumbs and fry in deep fat. Serve on sticks.

130

ANCHOVY PIN-WHEELS

A small can of anchovy
 fillets
2 oz. butter
Pepper

Red colouring
A sandwich loaf
Stuffed olives

Chop the anchovy fillets and mix with the butter; add some pepper and tint pink with a few drops of colouring. Cut the bread into slices lengthwise and spread generously with the filling; place the stuffed olives down one edge of the slice, roll it like a Swiss roll and cover completely with a damp cloth. Leave for several hours and cut into thin slices.

Other savoury fillings may, of course, be used in this way.

CURRIED ANCHOVY TOASTS

5–6 fillets of anchovy
A little curry powder
Cayenne pepper
A little very finely chopped
 chives or parsley

A knob of butter
1 egg, hard-boiled
4–6 fingers of toast
Butter

Pound the anchovy fillets with a little curry powder and cayenne pepper and the chopped chives or parsley. Heat the butter in a small pan and add the anchovy mixture; make very hot and stir in the sieved egg yolk. Spread on to the buttered toast fingers and garnish with the chopped egg white.

DEVILLED SHRIMPS ON TOAST

½ pint shrimps, shelled
1 oz. butter, melted
2 tsps. chutney
1 level tsp. curry powder

1 level tsp. dry mustard
Cayenne pepper
Fingers of toast

Toss the shrimps in the melted butter. Chop the chutney and mix it with the seasonings. Place the shrimps on the toast and spread with the chutney mixture, place under a grill for a few minutes to heat through and serve piping hot.

ANCHOVY CANAPÉS

2 slices of bread
½ oz. butter
Lemon juice
5 fillets of anchovy,
 chopped

A little pepper
A pinch each of ground
 nutmeg and ground mace
Parsley

Toast the bread and cut it into fingers. Melt the butter, add a squeeze of lemon juice, the anchovies, pepper, nutmeg and mace, beat well and rub through a sieve. Spread this mixture on the fingers of toast and decorate with sprigs of parsley.

Similar savouries can be made with sardines or herrings.

DUTCH CANAPÉS

1 egg, scrambled
2 oz. cooked smoked
  haddock, flaked

Salt and pepper
Small rounds of toast
Capers to garnish

Mix together the egg and haddock and season to taste. Pile on to the toast and decorate each round with capers.

INDIAN CROÛTES

2 oz. smoked haddock
  or lobster, cooked
1 shallot
½ oz. butter
1 level tsp. curry powder
Salt and pepper

1 tbsp. cream
1 tomato, sliced
6 rounds of toast,
  buttered
Chopped parsley to
  garnish

Chop the haddock and shallot. Melt the butter in a pan, fry the shallot and add the curry powder and seasoning. Stir over the heat for a few seconds and add the haddock. Mix well and stir in the cream. Place a slice of tomato on each piece of toast, pile the mixture on top, put in the oven to make really hot and serve sprinkled with some finely chopped parsley.

DEVILLED CRAB CANAPÉS

1 tbsp. finely chopped onion
½ oz. butter
A 3½-oz. can of crabmeat
1 tsp. Worcestershire sauce
  or a good dash of
  Tabasco sauce

A pinch of dry mustard
2 tbsps. white sauce or
  double cream
24 fried bread croûtes
Parsley or paprika

Fry the onion in the butter lightly for 5 minutes, until golden-brown. Drain and add to the crabmeat; stir in the seasonings and sauce or cream. Use as a topping for the croûtes. Decorate each with a sprig of parsley or sprinkle with paprika.

LOBSTER CANAPÉS

1 tbsp. chopped onion
Butter
2 tbsps. chopped
  watercress
1 level tbsp. flour
A pinch of curry powder
1 teacupful cream or
  milk

1 cupful lobster meat
  (canned or fresh)
Salt and pepper
Rounds of fried bread
Paprika
Parsley and lemon to
  garnish

Fry the onion in 1 tbsp. butter until golden brown. Add the watercress, flour, curry powder and cream or milk. Stir until boiling, then add the lobster meat, season to taste and heat the mixture well. Heap on to the rounds of fried bread. Sprinkle with paprika and heat through under the grill or in the oven. Garnish with parsley and cut lemon.

132

SMOKED SALMON CANAPÉS
Spread neatly-shaped pieces of toast with a savoury butter (see below) and lay an evenly cut piece of smoked salmon on each. Pipe the edges of each canapé with green butter (below); when this is quite firm, pour some cold but still liquid aspic jelly over them; leave to set.

SAVOURY BUTTERS FOR CANAPÉS
With 4 oz. butter use one of the following flavourings:

Anchovy Butter - 6 anchovy fillets, mashed with a fork
Green Butter – 2 oz. finely chopped watercress
Tomato Butter – 2 tbsps. tomato ketchup (or 2 tsps. tomato paste and 1 level tsp. sugar)
Lobster Butter – 2 oz. lobster coral
Golden Butter – The sieved yolks of 2 hard-boiled eggs
Curry Butter – 2 level tsps. curry powder
Sardine Butter – 4 canned sardines, mashed with a fork
Onion Butter – 2 level tbsps. finely grated raw onion
Pimiento Butter – 2 level tbsps. sieved canned pimiento
Horseradish Butter – 2 tbsps. horseradish sauce
Maître d'Hôtel Butter – see recipe page 146

After-Dinner Savouries
SOFT ROE SAVOURY

12 herring roes	Salt and pepper
Butter for frying	A squeeze of lemon juice
4 fingers of bread	Parsley

Wash the roes, dry them well and fry gently in some butter for 8–10 minutes, until golden. Remove them from the pan and drain on crumpled kitchen paper. Add more butter to the pan and fry the bread fingers for 2–3 minutes, until golden. Place the roe mixture on the fried bread, season, add a squeeze of lemon juice and garnish with a sprig of parsley.

SHELLFISH TARTLETS

¼ lb. flaky pastry	1½ oz. cheese, grated
¼ pint white sauce	2 oz. almonds, blanched and
3–4 oz. shelled shrimps or	chopped
canned crabmeat	Salt and pepper

Oven temperature: hot (425°F., mark 7)
Roll the pastry out thinly and line patty tins with it. Mix all the other ingredients, reserving half the cheese and the nuts. Fill the cases with this and sprinkle the remaining cheese and nuts on top. Bake towards the top of the oven for 15 minutes.

133

SARDINE AND BACON ROLY-POLYS

8 small pieces of streaky
  bacon, rinded
8 sardines

Fingers of fried bread
Parsley to garnish

Roll a piece of bacon round each sardine and cook under the grill until the bacon is crisp. Serve on pieces of fried bread and garnish with parsley.

SHELLFISH BOUCHÉES

8 oz. flaky pastry (see p. 158)
3–4 oz. flaked lobster,
  the flesh of 1 fresh crab,
  a small can of crabmeat
  or other shellfish

$\frac{1}{4}$ pint thick white sauce (see
  p. 138)
Salt and pepper
1 tsp. vinegar

Oven temperature: hot (425°F., mark 7)

Make the pastry, then mix the filling – fold the lobster into the sauce and add salt and pepper to taste, with the vinegar. If the bouchées are to be served hot, the filling should be hot when added to the pastry; otherwise, add the cold filling to cold cases. Roll out the pastry about $\frac{1}{2}$ inch thick and cut in 2-inch circles. Using a smaller cutter (1-inch diameter) mark a circle in the middle of each pastry case, pressing only half-way through the pastry. Bake towards the top of the oven till well risen, pale brown and crisp. Take off the lids, fill up with the lobster filling and replace the lids.

A variety of other fish fillings may be used (see below).

RISOTTO TARTLETS

4 oz. shortcrust pastry
5 oz. cream cheese
Salt and pepper
1 egg, beaten

$1\frac{1}{2}$ oz. smoked salmon
$1\frac{1}{2}$ oz. ham
1 oz. Gruyère cheese

Oven temperature: hot (425°F., mark 7)

Roll out the pastry and line small tartlet tins with it. Beat the cream cheese, season and gradually stir in the egg. Cut the salmon and the ham into shreds and mix in carefully. Fill the tartlet cases with this mixture, cut the Gruyère in thin slices and lay these over the top of the tartlets. Bake towards the top of the oven till golden brown and crisp – about 15 minutes.

SALMON BOATS

4 oz. cheese pastry
4 oz. canned salmon

1 tbsp. cream cheese
Cooked peas to garnish

Oven temperature: hot (425°F., mark 7)

Roll out the pastry, line some boat-shaped patty tins with it and bake "blind" towards the top of the oven for 7–10 min-

134

utes. Mash the salmon and mix with the cream cheese. When the pastry boats are cold, fill with this mixture and decorate with peas.

FISH FILLINGS FOR BOUCHÉES, TARTLETS, ETC.
Any flaked cooked fish, mixed with a little white sauce and mayonnaise.
Chopped anchovies, olives and gherkins, with anchovy sauce.
Chopped shrimps, pineapple and celery, with mayonnaise.
Chopped hard-boiled egg and flaked salmon, moistened with mayonnaise.
Canned oysters, mixed with white sauce.
Chopped shrimps mixed with whipped cream or cream cheese.
(This filling is good in cheese pastry tartlet cases.)

ANCHOVY DARTOIS

4 oz. flaky pastry	1 egg, beaten
A 2-oz. can of anchovies, drained	Pepper
1 oz. butter, melted	Beaten egg to glaze

Oven temperature: fairly hot (400°F., mark 6)
Roll out the pastry into a square, cut it in half and place one half on a greased baking tray. Mash the anchovies with a fork, blend to a smooth cream with the butter and egg and season with pepper. Spread this mixture over the pastry to within $\frac{1}{4}$ inch of each edge. Damp the edges with water and cover with the remaining pastry. Glaze with the beaten egg and mark the pastry into fingers. Bake towards the top of the oven for about 10–15 minutes, until well-risen and golden brown. Cut into fingers before serving.

ANCHOVY TWISTS

Trimmings of flaky pastry	1 egg, beaten
A 2-oz. can of anchovies	

Oven temperature: hot (425°F., mark 7)
Roll out the pastry and cut it into thin finger lengths 4 inches by $\frac{1}{4}$ inch. Rinse the anchovies in cold water, dry and cut in half lengthwise. Place a half on each piece of pastry and twist the fillet and pastry together. Put on to a greased baking tray, brush the pastry with egg and bake towards the top of the oven for about 10 minutes, until golden brown.

HADDOCK TALMOUSE

$\frac{1}{2}$ oz. butter	1 egg, beaten
2 oz. cooked haddock	Cayenne pepper
1 oz. cheese, grated	4 oz. cheese pastry

Oven temperature: fairly hot (400°F., mark 6)

Melt the butter in a pan and stir in the fish, cheese, most of the beaten egg and some pepper. Roll out the pastry thinly and cut into small rounds. Put a little of the mixture in the centre of each round, wet the edges and fold to the centre to form a triangle. Seal the edges firmly, brush with egg and bake towards the top of the oven for 10–15 minutes.

HERRING PUFFS

A small can of herrings	4 oz. flaky pastry
Lemon juice	Beaten egg to glaze
Salt and pepper	

Oven temperature: hot (425°F., mark 7)

Bone the herrings and mix with some lemon juice and seasoning to taste. Roll out the pastry, cut into 2½-inch squares and place a little mixture on each. Moisten two of the edges and fold into a triangle. Flake the joined edges, brush the top with egg and bake towards the top of the oven for about 15 minutes.

KIPPER FINGERS

4 oz. shortcrust pastry	Pepper
2 kippers, cooked	Chopped parsley to
A little thick white sauce	garnish

Oven temperature: hot (425°F., mark 7)

Cut the pastry into fingers and bake towards the top of the oven until lightly browned – about 10 minutes. Bone and pound the kippers and mix with a little sauce to bind and some pepper. Sandwich the pastry fingers together with this filling and decorate with parsley round the join.

SALMON FINGERS

½ lb. shortcrust pastry	Salt and pepper
¼ lb. cooked salmon, flaked	Cucumber to garnish
Mayonnaise	

Oven temperature: hot (425°F., mark 7)

Roll out the pastry, cut into fingers and bake towards the top of the oven for about 10 minutes, until golden-brown. Mix the salmon with a little mayonnaise, season and spread on the pastry fingers. Decorate with small pieces of cucumber.

SARDINE TRICORNES

4 oz. cheese pastry	¼ pint thick cheese
4 oz. sardines (or cooked	sauce (see p. 142)
smoked haddock)	Egg or milk

Oven temperature: fairly hot (400°F., mark 6)

Roll out the pastry thinly; cut into rounds 3½–4 inches in dia-

136

meter with a plain cutter. Mix the sardines, or flaked and boned haddock, with the cheese sauce and place 1 tsp. of this filling in the centre of each round. Brush the outside edge with a little egg or milk, draw the pastry up over the filling, and pinch to form a three-cornered shape. Brush with a little egg or milk and bake just above the centre of the oven for about 15 minutes, until golden brown.

YARMOUTH STRAWS
Oven temperature: hot (425°F., mark 7)
Make about 4 oz. shortcrust pastry, but before adding the liquid mix in half a bloater, uncooked but skinned and boned. Mix to a stiff dough with water, roll out, cut in strips and bake towards the top of the oven for 10–15 minutes.

Fish Pastes

COD'S ROE PASTE
Pound some cooked cod's roe with an equal quantity of softened butter, season to taste and put into small jars. Pour a little warm clarified butter on top. Serve on toast or as a sandwich spread.

BLOATER PASTE
Poach 2 bloaters gently for about 4–5 minutes, then remove the skin and bones. Rub the fish through a sieve, weigh it and add an equal weight of butter. Mash thoroughly together, season to taste and use for canapés, small savouries and sandwiches.

Note: Kippered herrings may be used in the same way.

TUNA FISH PATE
A 3½-oz can of tuna fish   Lemon juice
3 oz. butter   Pepper

Pound the tuna fish, work in the butter and season with a little lemon juice and pepper. Use for canapés, sandwiches, etc.

CHAPTER 7

Sauces, stuffings, accompaniments, garnishes

In addition to the more obvious recipes, we also give here the various kinds of pastry needed for fish main-meal dishes and savouries.

When dealing with garnishes, we include directions for skinning tomatoes, which figure in so many made-up fish recipes, casseroles and so on – this little detail makes so much difference to the enjoyment of the finished dish.

Sauces for Fish

We begin with the basic white and brown sauces and then give, in alphabetical order, a wide range of interesting and often unusual sauces and "butters" for various kinds of fish. The section ends with French Dressing, Mayonnaise, Aspic Jelly and Aspic Dressing.

SIMPLE WHITE SAUCE – ROUX METHOD
1 – Pouring Consistency

¾ oz. butter
¾ oz. (approx. 2 level tbsps.) flour

½ pint milk or milk and stock
Salt and pepper

Melt the butter, without allowing it to brown, add the flour and stir with a wooden spoon until smooth. Cook over a gentle heat for 2–3 minutes, stirring until the mixture (called a roux) begins to bubble. Remove from the heat and add the liquid gradually, stirring after each addition to prevent lumps forming. Bring the sauce to the boil, stirring continuously, and when it has thickened, cook for a further 1–2 minutes. Add seasoning to taste.

II – Coating Consistency

1 oz. butter	½ pint milk or milk and
1 oz. (3 level tbsps.)	stock
flour	Salt and pepper

Make the sauce as above.

For a thick coating sauce increase the quantities to 1½ oz. each of butter and flour.

III – Binding Consistency (Panada)

2 oz. butter	½ pint milk or milk and
2 oz. (6 level tbsps.)	stock
flour	Salt and pepper

Melt the butter, add the flour and stir well. Cook gently for 2–3 minutes, stirring, until the roux begins to bubble and leave the sides of the pan. Add the liquid gradually, bring to the boil, stirring all the time, and cook for 1–2 minutes after it has thickened; add salt and pepper to taste.

This very thick sauce is used for binding mixtures such as croquettes.

SIMPLE WHITE SAUCE – BLENDING METHOD
I – Pouring Consistency

½ oz. (1½ level tbsps.)	A knob of butter
cornflour	Salt and pepper
½ pint milk	

Put the cornflour in a basin and blend with 1–2 tbsps. of the milk to a smooth cream. Heat the remaining milk with the butter until boiling; pour on to the blended mixture, stirring all the time to prevent lumps forming. Return the mixture to the pan and bring to the boil, stirring continuously with a wooden spoon. Cook for 1–2 minutes after the mixture has thickened, to make a white, glossy sauce. Season to taste before serving.

II – Coating Consistency

Increase the quantity of cornflour to 2 level tbsps.

BÉCHAMEL (RICH WHITE) SAUCE

½ pint milk	½ a bay leaf
1 shallot, skinned and sliced	3 peppercorns
(or a piece of onion)	1 oz. butter
A small piece of carrot	1 oz. (3 level tbsps.)
peeled and cut up	flour
½ a stick of celery,	Salt and pepper
chopped	

Put the milk, vegetables and flavourings in a saucepan and bring slowly to the boil. Remove from the heat, cover and

139

leave to infuse for about 15 minutes. Strain the liquid and use this with the butter and flour to make a roux sauce (see earlier recipe). Season to taste before serving.

This classic sauce may be used with almost any white fish, and also forms the basis of many other sauces.

FISH SAUCE

Make a white sauce using half milk and half the liquid in which the fish was cooked – this gives a well-flavoured sauce that can be used instead of plain white sauce for any fish dish. Any additional flavouring can then be added, for instance, parsley or shrimps – see the separate entries for exact quantities.

ESPAGNOLE (RICH BROWN) SAUCE

1 oz. streaky bacon, rinded and chopped	1 small carrot, peeled and chopped
1 oz. butter	$\frac{3}{4}$–1 oz. (2–3 level tbsps.) flour
1 shallot, skinned and chopped (or a small piece of onion, chopped)	$\frac{1}{2}$ pint beef stock
	A bouquet garni (see p. 13)
1 oz. mushroom stalks, washed and chopped	2 level tbsps. tomato paste
	Salt and pepper

This classic sauce is used as a basis for many other savoury sauces. Fry the bacon in the butter for 2–3 minutes, add the vegetables and fry for a further 3–5 minutes, or until lightly browned. Stir in the flour, mix well and continue frying until it turns brown. Remove from the heat and gradually add the stock (which if necessary can be made from a stock cube), stirring after each addition. Return the pan to the heat and stir until the sauce thickens; add the bouquet garni, tomato paste and salt and pepper. Reduce the heat and allow to simmer very gently for 1 hour, stirring from time to time to prevent it sticking; alternatively, cook in the centre of a warm oven (325°F., mark 3) for $1\frac{1}{2}$–2 hours. Strain the sauce, re-heat and skim off any fat, using a metal spoon. Re-season if necessary.
Note: 1 tbsp. sherry may be added just before the sauce is served.

ANCHOVY SAUCE

$\frac{1}{2}$ pint white sauce (made with half milk and half fish stock)	A squeeze of lemon juice
	A few drops of red colouring (optional)
1–2 tsps. anchovy essence	

Make the sauce and when it has thickened, remove it from the heat and stir in anchovy essence to taste, then the lemon juice

140

and enough colouring (if used) to tint the sauce a dull pink.

Serve with almost any white fish, especially cod and haddock, and with pike. It is particularly good with steamed fish.

AURORE SAUCE

½ pint Béchamel sauce   1 oz. butter
1–2 level tbsps. tomato   Salt and pepper
  paste

Make the sauce and when it has thickened stir in the tomato paste. Add the butter a little at a time and season to taste.

Serve with lobster or with cold fish dishes; especially good with plaice, sole, halibut and turbot.

BÉARNAISE SAUCE

Make this in the same way as Hollandaise sauce (see recipe, p. 144), except that 1 oz. finely chopped shallot is first boiled with the wine or vinegar (it is a good plan to use tarragon vinegar for this sauce). When the sauce is cooked, sieve it, re-season if necessary and add 1 tbsp. chopped chervil and tarragon.

Béarnaise sauce is delicious with many kinds of fish, especially with scampi, prawns, salmon and salmon trout.

BERCY SAUCE

Add 1 tbsp. finely chopped shallot to 4 tbsps. white wine and cook until the wine is reduced by half. Add ½ pint Béchamel or Velouté sauce made with fish stock and bring to the boil. Stir in 1 oz. butter in small pieces and at the last minute add 2 tsps. chopped parsley.

Serve with baked and grilled hake, halibut, turbot, sole and plaice.

BEURRE ROUGE

Cook a finely chopped shallot with salt, pepper and a pinch of sugar in a glass of red wine until the wine is reduced. Gradually add about 5 oz. butter, beating all the time and keeping it warm.

Serve with plain baked or steamed cod, hake or trout.

BLACK BUTTER SAUCE

2 oz. unsalted butter   Salt and pepper
1½ tbsps. vinegar   2 tsps. finely chopped
  (tarragon-flavoured   parsley
  if possible)

Cut the butter into small pieces and put in a small strong pan. Heat until it is a golden-brown colour, then remove from the heat and cool. Meanwhile put the vinegar in another small pan and reduce to about half the original quantity. Stir in the butter and re-heat. Season and add the parsley.

Serve with plaice, sole and skate.

CAPER SAUCE

½ pint white sauce   1–2 tsps. vinegar from
1 tbsp. capers   the capers (or 1–2 tsps.
Salt and pepper   lemon juice)

Make the sauce, using all milk or – to give a better flavour – half milk and half liquid in which the fish was cooked. When the sauce has thickened stir in the capers and vinegar or lemon juice. Season well and re-heat for 1–2 minutes.

Good with boiled fish, especially cod, or with hake and plaice, cooked by any method.

CARDINAL (LOBSTER) SAUCE

Make up ½ pint Velouté sauce (see p. 150). Pound some lobster coral and a little lobster flesh with an equal quantity of butter and sieve the mixture, then add 2 oz. of this lobster butter to the sauce, stirring it in well.

Serve the sauce with fried or baked sole, plaice or lobster.

CHAUDFROID SAUCE (WHITE)

½ an envelope of aspic   ½ pint Béchamel sauce
  jelly powder   ⅛–¼ pint single cream
¼ pint hot water   Salt and pepper
¼ oz. gelatine

Put the aspic jelly powder in a small basin and dissolve it in the hot water. Stand the basin in a pan of hot water, sprinkle in the gelatine and stir until it has dissolved, taking care not to over-heat the mixture. Stir into the warm Béchamel sauce, beat well and add the cream, with extra salt and pepper if necessary. Strain the sauce and leave to cool, stirring frequently so that it remains smooth and glossy. Use when at the consistency of thick cream, for coating whole fish or cutlets – especially salmon, turbot and sole.

Note: A simpler Chaudfroid Sauce can be made by adding ¼ pint melted aspic jelly to ½ pint warm Béchamel sauce; beat well, strain, cool and use as above.

CHEESE SAUCE

½ pint white sauce   A pinch of Cayenne
2–4 oz. strong cheese,   pepper (optional)
  grated   Salt and pepper
A pinch of dry mustard

Make the sauce and when it has thickened, remove it from the

142

heat and stir in the cheese and seasonings. Don't re-boil, or the cheese will be over-cooked – there is sufficient heat in the sauce to melt the cheese.

Serve with steamed fish such as cod, haddock or plaice, also with hake, halibut, turbot, pike and lobster.

CIDER SAUCE

Measure out ½ pint cider. Cream 1 oz. butter and 1 oz. flour together and blend with a little of the cider; bring the rest to the boil, pour it on to the blended flour, stirring well to prevent lumps, then return the mixture to the pan. Cook for about 5–7 minutes, until the sauce thickens, and season to taste.

Serve with white fish such as cod, hake, plaice or turbot, or with herring or mackerel.

CUCUMBER SAUCE

Peel and steam a cucumber (the outdoor variety serves admirably for this purpose), sieve it and add this purée to some Béchamel sauce.

Serve with fish, particularly salmon and salmon trout.

CURRY SAUCE

1 oz. dripping or butter	A clove of garlic, skinned
2 medium-sized onions,	and chopped
skinned and chopped	⅓ pint stock or coconut milk
1 level tbsp. curry powder	(see p. 105)
1 level tsp. curry paste	Salt and Cayenne pepper
1 level tbsp. rice flour or	2 level tbsps. chutney
ordinary flour (optional)	

Melt the fat, fry the onions golden-brown and add the curry powder, paste and rice (or ordinary) flour. Cook for 5 minutes, then add the garlic, pour in the stock or coconut milk and bring to the boil. Add salt, a little Cayenne pepper and the chutney, then simmer for 30–40 minutes. This sauce is much improved by the addition of 1 tbsp. cream immediately before use, and less curry powder may be used for those who prefer a "mild" dish.

Use for fish curries, based on cod, haddock or plaice, etc.

Note: The rice flour and ordinary flour can be omitted, since a curry is thickened by reduction of the liquid and by long, slow simmering.

EGG SAUCE

½ pint white sauce	1–2 tsps. chopped chives
1–2 eggs, hard-boiled and	(optional)
chopped	Salt and pepper

In making the white sauce, use all milk or (if possible), half

GOLDEN CUTLETS (Sometimes called Fillets)
Small haddocks, similar to Finnan haddocks, but boned.
Cook in the same way.

HAKE
In season all the year, but at its best from June to January.

Hake is somewhat like cod in shape, but has a closer tex-
tured white flesh and a better flavour; it may be cooked by
any method, and is particularly tasty when baked, either whole
or in steaks, with or without stuffing.

Scotch hake, which has rather dark-coloured flesh, is less
expensive than Devonshire hake, but equally flavoursome.

HALIBUT
In season all the year, but best from August to April.

Halibut is a very large flat fish with an excellent taste, and
like turbot is regarded as one of the "good-class" fish, though
perhaps its flavour is a little less delicate than that of turbot,
and it is a little less expensive. It is usually baked or grilled,
but may also be cooked by any recipe suitable for turbot or
cod. It is especially good when steamed or grilled and served
with Hollandaise or another well-flavoured sauce, and is also
excellent cold, with salad.

HERRING
In season all the year, but best from June to December.

Fairly small, round-bodied, oily fish with creamy-coloured
flesh of distinctive flavour. Though they are generally sold
whole, the fishmonger will fillet them for you on request.

The herring, like the mackerel, the sprat and the pilchard
(all members of the same family), though of the lowliest is the
most valuable of all fish. Rich in oils and vitamins, it can be
cooked and served in many delicious ways. It is, however,
never better than when simply grilled, or coated with oatmeal
and fried in the Scottish style. Herring is good cold, and many
piquant-flavoured herbs and spices can be combined with it in
such dishes as soused herring, without masking the rich flavour
of the fish.

Herrings are also sold prepared in various special ways, the
chief ones being as follows:

Kippers: Herrings that have been split open, soaked in brine,
then smoked over wood chips and sawdust to give them their
unique smoky flavour. Some of them are now dyed. They are
usually poached or grilled.

Bloaters: Herrings that have been soaked in brine, smoked and
cured: cured whole and for a shorter period than kippers.

Buckling: Herrings, smoked whole and mild-flavoured; used
for hors d'oeuvres.

fish stock and half milk. Add the egg with the chives. Season well and re-heat for 1–2 minutes.

Serve with kedgeree or with poached or steamed fish such as cod, haddock, plaice, sole or turbot.

As a variation, replace the chives by parsley.

FENNEL SAUCE

Boil some fennel for 3 minutes in salted water, chop it finely and add in the proportion of 3 tbsps. fennel to ½ pint white sauce.

Serve with cod, plaice, hake, turbot, haddock or halibut.

GENOESE SAUCE

½ pint Espagnole sauce	2 tsps. anchovy essence
1 shallot, skinned	A pinch of caster sugar
2 tsps. mushroom	2 tsps. chopped parsley
ketchup	1½ oz. butter
2–3 tbsps. claret	

Boil together all the ingredients, except the parsley and butter, for 10 minutes. Strain the sauce and add the parsley, then gradually beat in the butter, in small pieces.

Serve with sole, plaice, halibut or turbot.

GOOSEBERRY SAUCE

½ lb. gooseberries, topped	1 oz. butter
and tailed	1–2 oz. sugar (optional)

Stew the fruit in as little water as possible, or until soft and pulped. Beat well, then sieve or put in a blender. Add the butter and a little sugar if the fruit is very sour.

Serve with mackerel and herrings.

HOLLANDAISE SAUCE

2 tbsps. wine or	2 egg yolks
tarragon vinegar	3–4 oz. butter
1 tbsp. water	Salt and pepper

Put the vinegar and water in a small pan and boil until reduced to about 1 tbsp. Cool slightly. Put the egg yolks in a basin and stir in the vinegar. Put over a pan of hot water and heat gently, stirring all the time, until the egg mixture thickens (never let the water go above simmering point). Divide the butter into small pieces and gradually whisk into the sauce; add seasoning to taste. If the sauce is too sharp add a little more butter – it should be slightly piquant, almost thick enough to hold its shape and warm rather than hot when served.

Serve with salmon and other fish and shellfish, e.g. sole, plaice, turbot, scampi or shrimps.

144

Notes: The vinegar can be replaced by lemon juice – this tends to give a slightly blander sauce.

Since this sauce sometimes curdles during the making, you may find it easier to make the version which follows.

MOCK HOLLANDAISE SAUCE (SAUCE BÂTARDE)

Make ½ pint white sauce and add 1 egg yolk, then stir in 2 oz. butter, in small pieces, and when this is well blended, add 1 tsp. lemon juice.

Serve with such fish as sole, salmon, plaice, halibut, turbot, prawns and scampi.

HORSERADISH SAUCE

To ½ pint hot Béchamel sauce add 1 tbsp. or more cream or evaporated milk and 1 small teacupful grated horseradish mixed with 1 tsp. vinegar. Season to taste and blend well, simmering for only a few moments after adding the horseradish and cream.

Serve with fresh-water fish and smoked trout.

HORSERADISH CREAM

Wash and scrape some horseradish and grate finely sufficient to make 2 oz. Partly whip ¼ pint double cream or thick top of the milk, stir in seasoning to taste and lastly add 2 tsps. lemon juice and the horseradish. Blend thoroughly and chill before serving.

Serve with smoked trout.

LEMON MUSTARD BUTTER

1 oz. butter	½ tsp. mustard prepared
1 tsp. lemon juice	with 1 tsp. lemon juice
A pinch of cayenne pepper	and water

Soften the butter on a plate with a flat-bladed knife, add the other ingredients and mix well. Roll the mixture into a long finger shape, wrap it in greaseproof paper and chill in the refrigerator.

Place a slice of the lemon butter on each piece of fried or grilled fish; especially good with herrings and mackerel.

LEMON SAUCE

Rind and juice of 1 lemon	¾ oz. flour
½ pint milk and fish stock	1–2 level tsps. sugar
mixed	Salt and pepper
¾ oz. butter	

Simmer the lemon rind in the milk and stock for 5 minutes; strain and use the liquid to make a white sauce in the usual way. When it has thickened, stir in the lemon juice and sugar and season to taste.

Serve with plaice, sole, turbot and halibut.

Note: This sauce is quite sharp; if preferred, reduce the lemon juice or counteract it by stirring in 1–2 tbsps. single cream just before serving.

LOBSTER SAUCE
See Cardinal Sauce.

MAÎTRE D'HÔTEL BUTTER

1 oz. butter	1 tsp. lemon juice
1 tsp. chopped parsley	Salt and pepper

Mix all the ingredients to a creamy paste, using a fork, then form into pats or balls and chill. (Failing parsley, use very finely chopped watercress.)

Serve with most white fish, e.g. sole, plaice, hake, halibut or turbot.

MELTED BUTTER SAUCE
With fine-flavoured fish, such as salmon and sole, plain melted butter is delicious.

MORNAY SAUCE

½ pint Béchamel sauce	Paprika pepper, salt and
2 oz. Parmesan or Gruyère cheese, grated	pepper to taste

Make the sauce and when it has thickened remove from the heat and stir in the cheese and seasonings. Don't re-heat or the cheese will become over-cooked and stringy.

Serve with plaice, hake, turbot, halibut or haddock.

MUSHROOM SAUCE

½ pint white sauce	½–1 oz. butter
2–3 oz. button mushrooms, washed and sliced	Salt and pepper

Make up the sauce. Lightly fry the mushrooms in the butter until soft but not coloured. Fold into the sauce and season to taste.

Serve with carp, turbot, halibut, plaice or sole.

MUSSEL SAUCE (SAUCE MARINIÈRE)
To ½ pint white wine sauce add ½ pint poached and shelled mussels, together with the reduced liquor in which they were cooked.

Serve with sole, turbot and other fish.

MUSTARD SAUCE

½ pint white sauce
1 level tbsp. dry mustard

2 level tsps. sugar
1 tbsp. vinegar

Make the white sauce, using all milk or half milk and half stock from the fish (or a chicken bouillon cube). Blend the mustard, sugar and vinegar to a smooth cream and stir in.

Serve with herrings or mackerel.

MOUSSELINE MUSTARD SAUCE

2 egg yolks
Salt and pepper
Cold water

2 tbsps. vinegar
4 oz. butter
½ tsp. made mustard

This is a rich version of the mustard sauce served with mackerel and herrings. Put the egg yolks in a saucepan with the seasoning, a very little cold water, the vinegar and the butter, cut in small pieces. Put the pan in a bain marie and cook the sauce, whipping it well; it should become frothy almost at once. Add about ½ tsp. made mustard (English or French), the exact amount depending on your personal taste. If the sauce is too thick, add a little more butter and re-season.

Serve with herrings or mackerel.

NORMANDY SAUCE

½ pint white sauce
  made with fish liquor
1 egg yolk

½ oz. butter
Lemon juice

Make the white sauce in the usual way, but using fish liquor; cook and beat well. Cool slightly, beat in the egg yolk and re-heat carefully without boiling. Stir in the butter a little at a time and add lemon juice to taste.

Serve with cod, hake, sole, turbot or haddock.

OYSTER SAUCE

Scald 6–12 canned oysters and cut in two. Use the strained oyster liquor to make the sauce; add the oysters before serving.

Serve with sole, plaice, turbot or halibut.

PARSLEY SAUCE

½ pint white sauce
1–2 tbsps. chopped parsley
Salt and pepper

A squeeze of lemon juice
  (optional)

Make the white sauce using half milk and half fish stock (if available). When it has thickened, stir in the parsley and seasonings. Don't re-boil or the sauce may turn green.

Serve with fried, grilled or steamed fish, fish cakes, etc; especially good with cod, hake, plaice, sole, turbot, halibut or salmon.

147

PIQUANT SAUCE

A blade of mace
A few peppercorns
½ pint milk, or milk
  and stock

1 oz. butter
1 oz. flour
1 tsp. vinegar
1 tsp. chopped parsley

Infuse the mace and peppercorns in the milk for 10 minutes over a low heat. Melt the butter and add the flour to make a roux; strain the milk and gradually add to the roux. Bring to the boil and add the vinegar and parsley.

Serve with steamed cod, hake, plaice, turbot or halibut.

PORTUGAISE SAUCE

Peel and cut up 1 lb. ripe tomatoes, add 1 clove of garlic and cook until tender with 1 tsp. olive oil and seasoning to taste. Add ¼ pint Espagnole sauce and bring back to the boil.

This sauce goes well with white fish such as cod or hake, and with fish cakes.

POULETTE SAUCE

Heat ½ pint Béchamel sauce and remove it from the stove. Beat in 1 tbsp. cream or top of the milk and 1 egg yolk, the juice of 1 lemon and seasoning to taste. Re-heat without boiling.

Serve with mussels, plaice, sole, haddock or hake.

SHARP EGG SAUCE

1 egg, hard-boiled
1 raw egg yolk
1 level tsp. dry mustard
¼ level tsp. salt

Pepper
2 level tsps. sugar
1 tbsp. wine vinegar
About ¼ pint double cream

Cut the hard-boiled egg in half, take out the yolk and sieve it. Mix the sieved egg yolk and the raw egg yolk with the seasonings, sugar and vinegar. Whip the cream and gradually fold it into the sauce.

This is good with plaice, sole, herrings or mackerel.

SHRIMP SAUCE

Rind of 1 lemon
1 small bay leaf
½ pint white sauce

2 oz. frozen, canned or
  potted shrimps
Salt and pepper

Simmer the lemon rind and bay leaf for 5 minutes in the liquid from which the sauce is to be made (this can be milk or milk and stock, if available). Strain and use to make the white sauce. When it has thickened stir in the shrimps, season to taste and re-heat for 1–2 minutes.

Serve with any white fish, e.g. sole or plaice.

Prawn sauce is made in the same way.

SHRIMP WINE SAUCE

Make ½ pint white wine sauce and add 1 oz. small shelled shrimps and 2 oz. shrimp butter. (To make this, pound together and sieve equal quantities of shelled shrimps and butter.) The sauce should be of a fresh, very pale pink colour and if necessary a few drops of colouring should be added.

This is suitable with any white fish, such as sole, plaice, halibut or turbot.

SOUBISE (ONION) SAUCE

Cook some finely sliced onions in butter in a saucepan without allowing them to brown. When they are transparent, softened and yellow, add an equal amount of Béchamel sauce and simmer for 15 minutes, until the onions are completely cooked. Rub the sauce through a sieve and adjust the seasoning as required.

Soubise sauce may be served with various fish, and is very good with cod, haddock and skate.

TARTARE SAUCE – COLD

¼ pint mayonnaise or salad cream	2 tsps. chopped gherkins
1 tsp. chopped tarragon or chives	2 tsps. chopped parsley
	1 tbsp. lemon juice or tarragon vinegar
2 tsps. chopped capers	

Mix all the ingredients well, then leave the sauce to stand for at least 1 hour before serving, to allow the flavours to blend.

Serve with fried plaice, sole, prawns, shrimps or scampi.

TARTARE SAUCE – HOT

¼ pint Béchamel sauce	1 tsp. chopped parsley
2 egg yolks	A little lemon juice
2 tsps. chopped gherkins	Cayenne and salt

Heat the Béchamel sauce until hot but not boiling and add the egg yolks; mix well and heat gently without boiling. Add the gherkins and parsley, also the lemon juice, and season to taste.

Serve with fried and grilled plaice, sole or scampi.

SPICY TOMATO SAUCE

A 10-oz. can of tomato soup	A pinch of pepper
½ a soup can of milk	A dash of Worcestershire sauce
1 small onion, skinned and finely chopped	A squeeze of lemon juice
1 tsp. horseradish sauce	1 clove of garlic (optional)
¼ level tsp. salt	1 tsp. vinegar

Combine all the ingredients in a saucepan except the garlic.

Squeeze out the garlic juice in a garlic press and add; bring the sauce to boiling point and then simmer for 20 minutes.

Very good with fish cakes and fish fingers, and also with cod or hake.

TOMATO SAUCE
(Made from fresh tomatoes)

1 small onion, skinned and chopped	½ pint chicken stock (made from a cube)
1 small carrot, peeled and chopped	½ a bay leaf
1 oz. butter	1 clove
½ oz. flour	1 level tsp. sugar
1 lb. tomatoes, quartered	Salt and pepper

Lightly fry the onion and carrot in the butter for 5 minutes. Stir in the flour and add the tomatoes, the stock, flavourings, etc. Bring to the boil and simmer for 30–45 minutes, or until the vegetables are cooked. Sieve, re-heat and re-season if necessary.

Serve with fish cakes and other made-up dishes, or with steamed or fried fish.

Note: You can add 2 level tsps. tomato paste to give a full flavour and better colour; 1–4 tbsps. white wine or sherry can also be added just before serving.

VELOUTÉ SAUCE

¾ oz. butter	2–3 tbsps. single cream
¾ oz. (2 level tbsps. approx.) flour	A few drops of lemon juice
¾ pint light or fish stock	Salt and pepper

Melt the butter, stir in the flour and cook gently, stirring well, until the mixture is a pale fawn colour. Stir in the stock gradually, bring to the boil, stirring all the time, and simmer until slightly reduced and syrupy. Remove from the heat and add the cream, lemon juice and seasoning.

Serve with turbot, halibut, plaice or sole.

WHITE WINE SAUCE
Poach the fish (e.g., rolled sole fillets) in the oven with some Graves wine. When the fish is cooked, strain off the liquor and add it to ½ pint Velouté sauce made with fish stock. Bind with 1 egg yolk, if desired – otherwise cook the sauce in an un-covered pan for a few minutes, stirring constantly, until it has reduced sufficiently. Add 1 tbsp. cream or top of the milk and ½ oz. butter, in small pieces, and stir these in well.

This creamy sauce is often used with sole and also with plaice and halibut.

150

RED WINE SAUCE

1 shallot, skinned and finely chopped	¼ pint red wine
2 oz. butter	½ level tsp. caster sugar
1 tsp. anchovy essence	1 tsp. chopped parsley

Fry the shallot in the butter until it is golden-brown, then add the anchovy essence, red wine and sugar. Boil together until the mixture is reduced by half, then add the parsley.

Serve with trout, halibut or turbot.

Dressings for Fish Salads

FRENCH SALAD DRESSING

¼ level tsp. salt	A pinch of sugar
⅛ level tsp. pepper	1 tbsp. vinegar
¼ level tsp. dry mustard	2 tbsps. olive or salad oil

Put the salt, pepper, mustard and sugar in a bowl, add the vinegar and mix well. Beat in the oil with a fork and when the mixture thickens, use it at once. The oil separates out on standing, so if necessary whisk immediately before use. A good plan is to mix the dressing in a salad-cream bottle, then shake up vigorously just before serving.

A little tarragon vinegar is sometimes added. The proportion of oil to vinegar varies with individual taste, but use vinegar sparingly.

VINAIGRETTE DRESSING

Add a little chopped parsley, chopped gherkin or capers and chives to a French dressing.

MAYONNAISE

2 egg yolks	2 tsps. white vinegar or strained lemon juice
½ tsp. made mustard	
Pepper and salt	
¼ pint (approx.) olive oil	1 tsp. tarragon vinegar
	1 tsp. chilli vinegar

Put the egg yolks into a basin with the mustard and pepper and salt to taste. Mix thoroughly, then add the oil drop by drop, stirring hard with a wooden spoon or a whisk the whole time, until the sauce is thick and smooth. Add the vinegars gradually and mix thoroughly.

If liked, lemon juice may be used instead of the vinegars or it may replace white vinegar only.

Note: To keep the basin firmly in position, twist a damp cloth tightly round the base – this prevents it from slipping. In order that the oil may be added 1 drop at a time, put into the bottle-neck a cork from which a small wedge has been cut. Should the sauce curdle during the process of making, put another egg yolk into a basin and add the curdled sauce very gradually in the same way as the oil is added to the original egg yolks.

ASPIC JELLY

1 small onion, 1 carrot,	1½ pints water
1 stick of celery	¼ pint sherry
8 white peppercorns	¼ pint vinegar
½ level tsp. salt	White and shells of
Rind and juice of 1	2 eggs
lemon	1½–2 oz. gelatine

Scald the onion and cut the carrot and celery into large pieces. Put all the ingredients into a pan which has been rinsed with cold water. Heat, stir to dissolve gelatine and whisk briskly till a good froth forms. Remove the whisk and let the jelly boil up vigorously; draw the pan aside and leave for 10 minutes; strain through the cloth till clear.

Use to coat cooked salmon or salmon trout, or other fish as desired.

If more convenient, use packet aspic jelly.

ASPIC DRESSING

Make up ¼ pint aspic jelly and when it is on the point of setting, stir it into ½ pint mayonnaise (see recipe in this chapter).

Use at once to coat cold fish when making a chaudfroid.

Stuffings for Fish
FISH FORCEMEAT

3 oz. fresh white	Grated rind of ½ a lemon
bread-crumbs	2 tsps. chopped parsley
1 oz. suet, chopped or	Salt and pepper
butter, melted	Egg or milk to bind
½ level tsp. dried herbs	

Mix all the ingredients together, adding sufficient beaten egg or milk to bind.

Use with cod or hake cutlets.

CHEESE AND TOMATO STUFFING

2 large tomatoes, skinned	1 level tsp. dried mixed
and chopped	herbs or sage
3 oz. cheese, grated	Salt and pepper
2 oz. fresh white	Milk to bind
bread-crumbs	

Mix all the ingredients together.

Use for cod, haddock or hake.

152

CRABMEAT STUFFING

4 oz. butter
2 rashers of bacon, rinded and chopped small
1 oz. finely chopped onion
A few chopped celery leaves

5½ oz. fresh white bread-crumbs
3 eggs, beaten
Salt, pepper, Cayenne
Grated nutmeg
A 3½-oz. can of crabmeat, flaked

Melt the fat and fry the bacon. Add the onion and celery leaves and cook for 5 minutes, stirring frequently. Mix in the bread-crumbs thoroughly, then stir in the well-beaten eggs and season to taste. Remove from the heat, add the crabmeat and leave to cool slightly before using.

May be used to stuff turbot, halibut, plaice or sole.

MUSHROOM STUFFING

3–4 oz. mushrooms, finely chopped or minced
1–2 shallots, skinned and finely chopped or minced
2 tbsps. chopped parsley

Salt and pepper
2 oz. fresh white bread-crumbs
Sauce, cream or beaten egg to bind

Fry the mushrooms and shallots in the hot butter for a few minutes. Add the parsley, seasoning and bread-crumbs and mix well, then moisten the mixture with a little sauce, cream or beaten egg.

Use to stuff plaice, halibut or turbot.

MUSSEL STUFFING

1 doz. mussels (fresh or canned)
4 oz. fresh white bread-crumbs
1 oz. butter, melted

1 tsp. grated lemon rind
Salt and pepper
1 tsp. chopped parsley
1 egg, beaten

Beard the mussels (this may already have been done with canned ones) and cut them into small pieces. Mix with the bread-crumbs, butter, lemon rind, seasoning, parsley and enough beaten egg to bind.

Use to stuff plaice or sole.

OYSTER STUFFING

1½ doz. canned oysters
6 oz. fresh white bread-crumbs
2 oz. suet or 1½ oz. butter

Grated rind of ½ a lemon
1 tbsp. chopped parsley
A pinch of mace
Salt and cayenne
1 egg, beaten

Beard the oysters and cut them in pieces. Simmer the beards in the oyster liquor to extract the flavour, then strain. Mix all the dry ingredients in a basin, add the oysters, the lightly beaten egg and enough oyster liquor to moisten.

Use with plaice or sole.

RICE STUFFING

2 oz. long-grain rice, cooked
1 small onion, skinned
and chopped
2 oz. raisins
2 oz. almonds, blanched
and chopped

2 level tbsps chopped
parsley
1 oz. butter, melted
Salt and pepper
1 egg, beaten (optional)

Combine all the ingredients, season and bind them well together with egg.

Use with plaice.

SOFT ROE STUFFING

6 soft herring roes
Milk
2 oz. fresh white
bread-crumbs
Salt and pepper

2 level tsps. grated lemon
rind
A little lemon juice
1 tsp. anchovy essence

Simmer the roes in a little milk, then drain, beat up and add to the bread-crumbs. Mix well and season. Add the grated lemon rind and juice and the anchovy essence. Moisten if necessary with a little of the fish milk.

Use with cod or hake.

SHRIMP STUFFING

Make in the same way as Oyster Stuffing, substituting $\frac{1}{2}$ pint peeled shrimps for the oysters and adding a little milk to the beaten egg for moistening.

Use for stuffing plaice, sole, hake, haddock or cod.

VEAL FORCEMEAT

2 oz. suet
1–2 oz. ham or bacon
4 oz. fresh white
bread-crumbs
1 tbsp. chopped parsley

$\frac{1}{2}$ level tsp. mixed herbs
Rind of $\frac{1}{2}$ a lemon
Salt and pepper
Beaten egg

Chop the suet and the ham or bacon finely and mix with the bread-crumbs. Add the chopped parsley, mixed herbs and grated lemon rind. Season well with salt and pepper and add enough beaten egg (or egg and milk) to bind.

Use to stuff cod, hake cutlets, plaice or sole. Alternatively, roll the stuffing into small balls, using a little flour for coating, then fry or bake until brown and serve with the fish as a garnish or separately.

154

Accompaniments and Garnishes for Fish

CREAMY MASHED POTATOES

Boil some potatoes in the ordinary way and mash them with a knob of butter, salt and pepper to taste and a little milk. Beat them well over a gentle heat with a wooden spoon until fluffy. Use as an accompaniment for fish pies and similar dishes.

CHIPPED OR FRENCH-FRIED POTATOES

Cut peeled old potatoes into $\frac{1}{4}$–$\frac{1}{2}$ inch slices and then into strips $\frac{1}{4}$–$\frac{1}{2}$ inch wide. (For speed, several slices can be put on top of one another and cut together.) Place in cold water and leave for at least $\frac{1}{2}$ hour; drain well and dry with a cloth.

Heat a deep fat fryer of oil until when one chip is dropped into the fat, it rises to the surface straight away, surrounded by bubbles. Fill the basket about a quarter full of chips and lower carefully into the fat. Cook for about 6–7 minutes. Remove the chips and drain on absorbent paper. Follow the same procedure until all the chips have been cooked. Just before serving, re-heat the fat, test to make sure it is hot enough and fry the chips rapidly for about 3 minutes, until crisp and brown. Drain well on kitchen paper and serve uncovered, with salt.

STRAWS OR MATCHSTICK POTATOES

Cut potatoes into very small chips of matchstick size. Cook like chips, but as they are very much smaller, allow a shorter cooking time – about 3 minutes at the first cooking.

BOILED RICE

Work to the proportion of 1 cup raw rice to 2 cups liquid and 1 level tsp. salt. (This is called the 1–2–1 method; these amounts will be enough for 3–4 people.)

Place the rice, liquid and salt in a saucepan and bring to the boil. Cover with a closely fitting lid or a piece of aluminium foil and simmer for 14–16 minutes without stirring. After this time remove the lid and test the rice – if it is not tender replace the lid and cook for a further 2–5 minutes. Fluff the rice with a fork.

To obtain a still drier result, leave the rice in a covered pan for 10 minutes after cooking, to steam dry. Fluff the rice before serving as required.

CROÛTONS

Fried: Cut bread into $\frac{1}{4}$–$\frac{1}{2}$-inch cubes and fry quickly in lard or oil until crisp and golden.

Toasted: Cut slices of toast into $\frac{1}{4}$–$\frac{1}{2}$-inch dice.

Serve with creamed fish, fricassees, etc., and with fish soups, in a separate dish, or sprinkled over the surface of soups.

CUCUMBER CONES
Use thin slices of cucumber. Make a cut in each slice from the centre to the outer edge, then wrap one cut edge over the other to form a cone.

CRIMPED CUCUMBER
Run a fork down the sides of the cucumber to remove strips of peel and slice the cucumber thinly in the usual way – this gives the slices an attractive deckled edge.

GHERKIN FANS
Use whole gherkins, choosing long, thin ones. Cut each length-wise into thin slices, but leave these joined at one end. Fan out the strips of gherkins so that they overlap each other.

HARD-BOILED EGGS
Put the eggs into boiling water, bring back to the boil and cook for 10–12 minutes.

Hard-boiled eggs should be placed at once under running cold water and left until they are cold; this prevents a dis-coloured rim forming round the outside of the yolk and enables the shell to be easily removed. Crack the shell all round by tapping on a firm surface, then peel it off. Slice, cut into wedges or halves, or use as required. The yolk is some-times sieved for use as garnish, and the white may be chopped.

LEMON FANS OR BUTTERFLIES
Cut $\frac{1}{8}$-inch slices; now halve each, making semi-circles. Cut the rind again in half, leaving centre membranes attached, then open each piece out to form a "fan" or "butterfly".

LEMON BASKETS
Remove the peel from the top half of a lemon in two pieces, leaving a strip about $\frac{1}{4}$ inch wide between them. Cut away the underlying flesh, leaving only the strip of peel for a "handle". Serrate the top edge of the basket with a knife or a pair of kitchen scissors.

FRIED PARSLEY
Choose good-sized pieces of well-curled parsley. If it is necessary to wash them, shake well to remove the water, then dry thoroughly in a cloth.

After frying the fish to be garnished, draw the pan of fat from the heat and allow it to cool for 2–3 minutes. Then put in the parsley carefully and a little at a time, as the fat tends to spit, especially if the parsley is at all wet. Cook for a minute or so, until the parsley is crisp, then remove with a frying spoon, drain well and use at once.

RADISH ROSES
Trim the radishes. Make 4 or 8 small, deep cuts, crossing in the centre at the root end. Leave the radishes in cold or iced water for 1–2 hours, till the cuts open to form "petals".

TOMATO LILIES
Choose firm, even-sized tomatoes. Using a small sharp-pointed knife, make a series of V-shaped cuts round the middle of each, cutting right through to the centre. Carefully pull the halves apart.

TOMATO TWISTS
Slice a firm tomato crosswise. Slit each piece up to the core, leaving a piece at the top holding the halves together; turn the halves in opposite directions to make the twist.

Use beetroot, lemon or cucumber similarly.

SKINNING TOMATOES
To remove the skins from tomatoes, plunge them for a minute into boiling water, then lift them out and put them immediately into cold water; when they are cool, the skins will peel off easily with a knife. Alternatively, spear a tomato on the prongs of a fork and turn it gently over a gas jet until the skin bursts, then peel it off with a knife.

Pastry for Fish Dishes

SHORTCRUST PASTRY

8 oz. plain flour	Cold water to
½ level tsp. salt	mix
4 oz. lard	

Try to keep the pastry as cool as you can while you are mixing and rolling it. Put the flour and salt in a bowl. Cut up the fat roughly, then rub it into the flour, using the fingertips only (the coolest part of your hand) until the mixture is free from lumps and resembles fine bread-crumbs. Add the cold water a little at a time, mixing with a round-bladed knife until the mixture just begins to stick together. Using one hand, collect together to form a firm dough and knead lightly until free from cracks. Roll out and use as required. Do not stretch the pastry as you roll it out, because it will go back to its former shape when it is cooked.

The usual oven temperature is hot (425°F., mark 7).

If preferred, use 2 oz. lard and 2 oz. margarine.

SUETCRUST PASTRY

8 oz. self-raising flour	4 oz. shredded suet
½ level tsp. salt	Cold water to mix

Mix the flour, salt and suet. Add cold water gradually and mix with a round-bladed knife until a soft elastic dough is obtained. Knead lightly and use as required.

This pastry is usually steamed or boiled, but is occasionally baked, when it is usually cooked in a fairly hot oven (400°F., mark 6).

FLAKY PASTRY

8 oz. plain flour	8 tbsps. cold water to mix
A pinch of salt	(approx.)
6 oz. butter or a mixture	A squeeze of lemon juice
of butter and lard	Beaten egg to glaze

Mix together the flour and salt. Soften the fat by "working" it with a knife on a plate; divide it into 4 equal portions. Rub one quarter of the softened fat into the flour and mix to a soft, elastic dough with the water and lemon juice. On a floured board, roll pastry into an oblong 3 times as long as it is wide. Put another quarter of the fat over the top two-thirds of the pastry in flakes, so that it looks like buttons on a card. Fold the bottom third up and the top third of the pastry down and give it half a turn, so that the folds are now at the sides. Seal the edges of the pastry by pressing with the rolling pin. Re-roll as before and continue until all the fat is used up.

Wrap the pastry loosely in greaseproof paper and leave it to "rest" in a refrigerator or cool place for at least ½ hour before using. This makes the handling and shaping of the pastry easier and gives a more evenly flaked texture.

Sprinkle a board or table with a very little flour. Roll out the pastry ⅛ inch thick and use as required. Brush with beaten egg before baking, to give the characteristic glaze.

The usual oven for flaky pastry is hot (425°F., mark 7).

PUFF PASTRY

8 oz. plain flour	8 tbsps. cold water to mix
A pinch of salt	(approx.)
8 oz. butter (preferably	A squeeze of lemon juice
unsalted)	Beaten egg to glaze

Mix the flour and salt. "Work" the butter with a knife on a plate until it is soft, then rub about ½ oz. of it into the flour. Mix to a fairly soft, elastic dough with the water and lemon juice and knead lightly on a floured board until smooth. Form the rest of the butter into an oblong and roll the pastry out into a square. Place the fat on one half of the pastry and enclose it by folding the remaining pastry over and sealing the edges with a rolling pin. Turn the pastry so that the fold is to the side, then roll out into a strip 3 times as long as it is wide. Fold the bottom third up and the top third down and seal the edges by pressing lightly with the rolling pin. Cover the pastry with waxed or greaseproof paper and leave to "rest" in a cool place or in the refrigerator for about 20 minutes. Turn the pastry so that the folds are to the sides, and continue rolling, folding and resting until the sequence has been completed 6 times altogether.

After the final resting, shape the pastry as required. Always brush the top surfaces with beaten egg before cooking, to give the characteristic glaze of puff pastry.

The usual oven for puff pastry is very hot (450°F., mark 8).

ROUGH PUFF PASTRY

8 oz. plain flour
A pinch of salt
6 oz. fat (butter or margarine and lard mixed)

8 tbsps. cold water to mix (approx.)
A squeeze of lemon juice
Beaten egg to glaze

Mix the flour and salt; cut the fat (which should be quite firm) into cubes about ¾ inch across. Stir the fat into the flour without breaking up the pieces and mix to a fairly stiff dough with the water and lemon juice. Turn on to a floured board and roll into a strip 3 times as long as it is wide. Fold the bottom third up and the top third down, then give the pastry half a turn so that the folds are at the sides. Seal the edges of the pastry by pressing lightly with a rolling pin. Continue to roll and fold in this way 4 times altogether. Wrap in greaseproof paper and leave to "rest" in a cool place or in the refrigerator for about ½ hour before using. Use as for flaky pastry.

Rough puff gives a similar result to flaky pastry, but the flakes are not usually as even, so where even rising and appearance are particularly important, e.g., with patties and vol-au-vents, it is better to use flaky pastry. On the other hand, rough puff has the advantage of being quicker to make.

The usual oven for rough puff is hot (425°F., mark 7).

CHEESE PASTRY

4 oz. plain flour
A pinch of salt
2 oz. butter or margarine and lard

2 oz. Cheddar cheese, finely grated
A little beaten egg or water

Mix the flour and salt together and rub in the fat, as for shortcrust pastry, until the mixture resembles fine bread-crumbs in

159

texture. Mix in the cheese. Add the egg or water, stirring until the ingredients begin to stick together, then with one hand collect the dough together and knead very lightly to give a smooth dough. Roll out as for shortcrust pastry. Use as required.

The usual temperature for cooking cheese pastry is fairly hot (400°F., mark 6).

MAKING A FLAN CASE

Use shortcrust or ordinary (not rich) cheese pastry. The pastry is shaped by being baked in a special ring or circle of tin, which is placed on a baking sheet; alternatively, a sandwich tin may be used. Occasionally a Swiss Roll tin is used to give an oblong flan case. Roll the pastry out into a round $\frac{1}{8}$–$\frac{1}{4}$ inch thick and about 1 inch larger all round than the flan ring. Place the round inside the flan ring and press it into position, taking care not to stretch or pull the pastry. Press the pastry well on to the ring and on to the baking tray, to make a neat case, then trim the edges with a knife or by pressing the rolling pin sharply over the edge of the rim to cut the pastry clearly. Prick the bottom of the pastry lightly. If the flan is to be baked "blind", place a piece of greased greaseproof paper inside the case and half-fill it with dried beans, bread crusts or something similar. If possible, leave the flan in a cool place to "recover" for $\frac{1}{2}$ hour before baking.

Bake in a hot oven (425°F., mark 7) until the pastry is almost cooked (about 15 minutes), then remove the paper and filling and return the case to the oven to dry off and complete cooking.

If the flan case is filled before baking, follow the particular recipe for cooking time and temperature.

MAKING BOUCHÉE CASES: see Shellfish Bouchées, p. 134

MAKING VOL-AU-VENTS

Oven temperature: very hot (450°F., mark 8)

Roll out $\frac{1}{2}$ lb. puff or flaky pastry about 1 inch thick. Put on to a greased baking sheet and cut into an oval. (Try not to cut nearer than $\frac{1}{2}$ inch to the edge of the slab of pastry.) With a small knife mark an oval $\frac{1}{2}$–$\frac{3}{4}$ inch inside the larger one, to form a lid, cutting about halfway through the pastry. Brush the top with beaten egg. Bake towards the top of the oven for 30–35 minutes, covering the pastry with greaseproof paper when it is sufficiently brown. Remove the lid, scoop out any soft pastry inside and dry out in the oven for a further 5–10 minutes.

Serve hot or cold, filled with a savoury sauce as suggested for Bouchées, p. 134.

160

Supplement

A Dictionary of Fish

This list has been prepared to show the times of year at which different types of fish are available, when they are at their best and the methods of cooking most suited to the fish.

Fishing is still an unpredictable business, however, dependent on tides, weather and many other factors, so do not always expect supplies of a fish when it is said to be in season, or be surprised if you see it out of season. Your fishmonger will know the day-to-day market position and what is in best condition – let him advise you on the best buy of the day. Broadly speaking, fish are usually less seasonable during and immediately after spawning. However, the immense developments in quick-freezing have filled many of the gaps in the fishmonger's calendar with excellent supplies of frozen fish. Prices also fluctuate considerably and even the so-called cheap fish such as herring and whiting can be relatively dear when supplies become scarce: here again, it pays to consult the fishmonger.

Many of the recipes in this book require special preparation of the fish. Any reputable fishmonger will be happy to prepare the fish for you if you do not wish to do it yourself, but try to give him a little notice, or at any rate to avoid asking him at a very busy time.

Note: A common way of grouping fish is into sea and fresh-water types. Another classification, which cuts across these two groups, is into white and oily fish. White fish have a low fat content and characteristic white flesh; familiar examples are cod, haddock, hake, sole, plaice and turbot. Oily fish have quite a high fat content and their flesh is usually darker; the best-known are herring, mackerel, sprat, eel and salmon.

Shellfish – lobster, scampi, shrimps and so on – always make a separate group.

The entries here are arranged alphabetically under the headings "Sea Fish", "Fresh-water Fish" and "Shellfish".

Sea Fish

ANCHOVIES

Small fish, which are filleted and cured, then packed either in bottles or cans, in brine or olive oil; they are thus available all the year round. Anchovies are used – in small amounts only, for they are very salty – in appetisers and cocktail nibblers and in such Mediterranean dishes as Pizza and Salade Niçoise. They also make anchovy butter for use in savouries and sandwiches and as a spread for toast.

BASS

In season May to August.

Bass are not unlike salmon in shape, but the flesh is very white. Large bass, which have a good flavour, are usually poached or baked; small ones can be grilled or fried.

BLOATER: See Herring.

BREAM (SEA)

At its best from June to December; supplies often erratic.

A round-bodied, coarse-skinned fish with white flesh and a rather delicate flavour. Bream is often stuffed and baked, but may also be poached, fried or grilled.

BRILL

In season all the year (though available only in small quantities), but at its best from April to August.

A flat fish with a good flavour and texture resembling those of turbot. It may be poached, served cold with mayonnaise, or cooked like turbot.

COALFISH, COLEY, SAITHE (also occasionally called Rock Salmon)

Available all the year round; best September to February.

A member of the cod family, with rather coarse flesh, greyish when raw, although it turns white when cooked. It can be used in the same ways as cod or haddock.

COD, CODLING

In season all the year, but at its best from October to May.

A large round-bodied fish with close, white flesh, somewhat lacking in flavour, but improved if cooked with herbs, vegetables or a stuffing; it needs a well-flavoured sauce as accompaniment. Cod can be grilled, baked, steamed or fried in batter and may also be used in made-up dishes. If skilfully prepared, with imagination and care, this staple fish is palatable and indeed enjoyable to eat.

SMOKED COD FILLETS
Cook as for smoked haddock fillets, which they resemble, though the flavour is not so good.

SMOKED COD'S ROE
On sale at delicatessen shops. It is sliced and served on lettuce, with lemon wedges and fingers of toast, as an appetiser.

CONGER EEL
In season all the year, at its best March to October.
  Cook as for Eels.

DAB
In season all the year.
  Small, white-fleshed fish of the plaice family – they have an excellent flavour and are delicious either fried or baked.

FLAKE (Sometimes called Dog fish)
Available all the year; best from October to June.
  Suitable for frying, poaching, steaming, made-up dishes.

FLOUNDER
In season from February to September; supplies rather small.
  Flounders resemble plaice, but have not such a good texture and flavour; cook in the same ways.

GURNET, GURNARD
In season from July to April.
  A small fish with a large, bony head and firm, white flesh, of good flavour. Cook as for haddock. Excellent cold, with salad.

HADDOCK
At its best from September to February.
  A round-bodied fish, distinguished from cod by the dark streak which runs down the back and the two black "thumb marks" above the gills. Haddock has firm white flesh and may be cooked by any method suitable for white fish; it is useful for made-up dishes.
  See the notes on Cod, above, regarding flavourings, etc.

SMOKED OR FINNAN HADDOCK
Whole haddock, split open and smoked. Usually poached or grilled; also good for use in kedgeree, fish pie and haddock soufflé.

SMOKED HADDOCK FILLETS
Fillets taken from large haddocks and smoked. Use as above.

Salt Herrings: The fish are gutted and preserved between layers of salt in barrels.

Rollmops: The herrings are filleted, packed in barrels with brine and vinegar, then later rolled up and packed in jars with spices, onions or other flavourings, according to the manufacturer's particular recipe.

Bismarck Herrings: Are pickled and spiced like rollmops but left whole.

Herring Roes: The roes can be left in the fish or removed and served by themselves. They may also be bought separately.

HUSS: See Rock Salmon.

JOHN DORY
In season from October to December, but supplies erratic.

An ugly fish, with very large jaws and a body that is nearly oval in shape, John Dory is used less often than it deserves, for it has firm white flesh with a good flavour. After the head and fins have been removed the fish can be poached or baked whole, but it is more usually filleted and cooked according to any recipe for sole. It may also be served cold with salad.

LEMON SOLE: See Sole.

MACKEREL
In season from October to July, but at its best during April, May and June.

A fairly small, round-bodied, oily fish, rather bigger than a herring, with characteristic blue-black markings on the back, creamy-coloured flesh and a distinctive flavour. It can be left whole or filleted and cooked by any method suitable for herrings; it is particularly good simply grilled or fried. Mackerel must be eaten very fresh; and if possible, should be taken straight from the sea to the kitchen; take care if you are buying it in an inland town.

MULLET (Red and Grey)
At its best from April to October.

Red mullet is a round-bodied fish, similar in size to a herring and with firm white flesh which may be poached, baked, grilled or fried. Good cold, with salad.

Grey mullet is larger and coarser; cook it in any way suitable for white fish.

PLAICE
In season all the year round, but best towards the end of May.

The most plentiful flat fish, plaice is distinguished by its red spots on a dark ground. It has soft white flesh and a very deli-

165

cate flavour. You can cook it whole or filleted, by most methods, including steaming, frying, grilling and baking. It is perhaps most widely popular when filleted, egg-and-crumbed and fried. Although not quite so tasty or firm-textured as sole, it may be cooked in many of the same ways, though a little more care must be taken with the flavouring and accompaniments.

ROCK SALMON (or Huss)
These names are given by fishmongers to several similar kinds of fish such as the common catfish, rock eel or nurse (dogfish). The fish is sold skinned and has firm, pinkish-tinged flesh. Considerable quantities are bought for the fried fish trade and it can also be used in fish stews and so on.

ROCKFISH (sometimes called Catfish)
Available all the year, best from February to July.
Suitable for frying, steaming, poaching and for made-up dishes. Usually sold skinned.

SALMON TROUT
In season from March to August.
This resembles salmon, but is much smaller and when cooked has slightly pinker flesh; it has not quite such a good flavour, so is cheaper. Salmon trout is cooked whole and is usually poached in court-bouillon or baked. It may be served hot or cold, and is ideal for coating with aspic and serving at a formal buffet.

SARDINE
Sardines are strictly speaking young pilchards, but the name is also applied to the young of other fish (e.g., sprats and herrings) which are canned in olive oil or tomato sauce. Fresh sardines – usually available at the seaside only – can be grilled or fried as for sprats. The canned types are very useful for hors d'oeuvre and snack dishes.

SKATE
In season from September to April.
A large, coarse white fish with a high percentage of bone. Only the "wings" or side parts are eaten. Cook by poaching or frying, or eat cold with salad.

SMELT
In season from September to April.
A small, round-bodied, silvery fish with a delicate flavour. They should be cooked as soon as possible after being caught. To prepare smelts, make a small cut with scissors just below the gills and gently press out the entrails, then wash the fish well.

166

Smelts are usually fried, but larger ones may be baked. Serve with fried parsley and a good sauce.

SOLE
In season all the year round.

One of the finest flat fish. Its flesh is firm and delicate, with a delicious flavour, and it tends to be expensive. The true or "Dover" sole is easily distinguished by its dark brownish-grey back skin from the lemon, witch and Torbay soles, which are not considered to have quite such a fine flavour.

Sole can be cooked by most methods, especially grilling, frying, baking and steaming, and is the basis of many classic fish dishes. Gourmets have evolved more recipes for the sole than for almost any other fish; but few dishes are more delicious than a Dover sole simply grilled and eaten with sliced lemon. Sole is also ideal for children and invalids, being very easily digested.

SPRAT
In season from November to March; supplies are affected by the weather.

A fairly small, round-bodied fish of the same family as the herring. To prepare sprats, wash them and draw them through the gills, as for smelts. Deep-fry or grill.

STURGEON
In season from August to March, although not usually available in this country.

The hard roe of various members of the sturgeon family is known as caviare when it is salted.

TORBAY SOLE: See Sole.

TURBOT
In season all the year, but at its best from March to August.

Turbot has creamy-white flesh with a very delicious flavour and is considered to be the finest of the flat fish. It is usually cut in steaks and grilled or baked – very often with wine – but may be cooked by almost any method; excellent served cold.

WHITEBAIT
At their best in May, June and July.

Very small silvery fish (the fry of various kinds, chiefly herring and sprat). They are deep-fried whole and served as the first course of a meal. When well prepared they become a gourmet's delight.

Whitebait must be perfectly fresh – the uncooked fish should look very silvery in colour.

WHITING
In season all the year, but at its best from December to March.

A round-bodied fish with a pleasant but not very distinctive flavour. Cook it whole or in fillets, by any of the usual methods, or use it for made-up dishes. A savoury stuffing helps to give it flavour. Whiting is light and easy to digest.

WITCH: See Sole.

Fresh-water Fish

BREAM
In season July to February.

Cook as for Sea Bream.

CARP
In season October to February.

A round-bodied fish. If small, it may be grilled or fried, but when larger, it is better stuffed and baked.

To counteract the somewhat muddy flavour which the flesh tends to have, soak the fish in salted water for 3–4 hours and rinse well before cooking.

EEL (Fresh-water)
Best during the autumn and winter.

In this country eels are one of the very few fish seen alive in the fishmonger's shop. The Severn river is one of the most noted centres for eels in these islands; thousands of young elvers are caught each spring, and are locally popular when fried like whitebait. Larger eels are usually served fried or grilled, or cooked in a court-bouillon, which may be flavoured with wine. However, in this country more eels are probably cooked and sold in jellied form than in any other way. Eel pie, a dish mentioned in bills of fare of the past, is rarely found now; the cut-up and partly cooked eels were baked with sliced hard-boiled eggs, herbs, onion, forcemeat balls and stock under a pastry crust.

Smoked eels are also sold, chiefly for use as an hors d'oeuvre.

The Conger eel, which is often of immense size, is surprisingly good to eat, particularly when stewed.

PERCH
In season from the beginning of June to the end of February.

Perch, though seldom on sale in the fishmonger's shop, is one of the commonest fresh-water fish. It is very difficult to scale, but the job is easier if you first plunge the fish into boil-

168

ing water for 2 minutes. The fish is scored on both sides and grilled or fried, baked or sometimes stewed.

PIKE
No special season.

A large fish, which tends to have dry, rather coarse flesh and a lot of sharp bones. Soak it in salted water, as for carp. Pike is best stuffed and baked.

ROACH, SHAD, TENCH
These are all found in our rivers and waterways, but town housewives will not often encounter them unless their husbands are keen anglers. When available, however, these fish are worth trying, although the flesh of some of them may have a muddy flavour, which can only be overcome by soaking them for some hours in slightly acidulated water. Serve au gratin, fried, baked or in made-up dishes.

SALMON
In season in England and Scotland February to August, but imported the year round. Also available as canned and smoked salmon.

A round-bodied fish, highly regarded and expensive, salmon has bright red flesh which turns pink on cooking and is very close in texture, with a delicate and distinctive flavour.

Salmon is reckoned king among fish and is most prized of all the kinds found in our lakes and rivers. Its delicately tinted flesh has a succulence and richness of its own not found in any of its rivals. Salmon is at its best simply poached, steamed or baked and is equally good either hot or cold. Small cuts and steaks are excellent grilled and served hot. Small and medium-sized salmon are to be preferred to the larger fish.

Smoked salmon is a delicacy used chiefly for hors d'oeuvre – see Fish Starters chapter, p. 15.

TROUT (River)
In season from February to early September, but at its best from April to August.

Trout are much prized for their firm flesh and excellent though delicate flavour, which is best appreciated if they are cooked very simply; they may be fried, grilled or baked. Some people consider that to savour trout at their best, they should be cleaned and cooked immediately after being caught – preferably over the glowing embers of a picnic fire – to be eaten with just butter, salt and pepper. They may be baked in wine or lemon juice and a little stock to which have been added a few capers, a knob of butter and some seasoning, and can then be served hot or cold.

Smoked trout is also available and is used mainly as an hors d'oeuvre. (See Fish Starters chapter, p. 15.

Shellfish

COCKLES
Available all the year.
   Normally sold cooked.
   Serve cold with vinegar or hot in sauces, pies, etc.

CRAB
At its best from May to August. Can also be bought canned.
   Crabs are usually sold ready boiled and many fishmongers will also prepare and dress them.
   Choose a crab that is heavy for its size and which does not rattle with water when you shake it. If you are in any doubt as to the wisdom of your choice, ask the fishmonger if he will open the crab, so that you can see for yourself. Hen crabs are the more esteemed.
   The edible portion of the crab consists of two parts – the white flesh of the claws and the "brown" meat or liver, a soft, rich, yellow substance which nearly fills the interior of the shell. Although crabs are somewhat overshadowed by the more glamorous lobsters, they have a succulence and sweetness which lobsters sometimes lack and at the height of the season they are not expensive.
   Plain dressed crab and crab salad are excellent, and many of the less familiar hot crab savouries are equally good. Crab flesh also combines well with the flavour and texture of cooked rice, as in risottos and pilaus.

CRAWFISH
Seasonable all the year round.
   Often called the spiny lobster, it resembles a lobster without the big claws, and is prepared and cooked like that fish. Also obtainable canned.

CRAYFISH
In season from September to April.
   Crayfish resemble miniature lobsters. They have a delicate flavour and the smaller ones can be used for soups and garnishes, while the larger ones can be served hot in a cream sauce or cold with salad and brown bread and butter.
   To prepare crayfish, wash them well and remove the intestinal tube under the tail, using a pointed knife. Place the fish in salted water and cook for about 10 minutes after the liquid has reached boiling point.

170

DUBLIN BAY PRAWNS

Obtainable most of the year, but at their best during the summer. Frozen ones are also available.

These large prawns can be substituted for scampi, which they closely resemble – in fact, most of the so-called scampi sold in this country are really Dublin Bay prawns. Their flavour, colour and appearance are all good.

They can be served fried (after egg-and-crumbing or coating with batter), au gratin, in risottos or in any way suitable for prawns. Some people appreciate them best when they are served *au naturel*, with Tartare sauce.

LOBSTER

In season all the year round, but at their best in the summer months; lobsters are sometimes difficult to obtain from December to April. Lobster meat may be bought ready prepared in cans.

Like crabs, lobsters are usually sold ready boiled.

They can be served hot, grilled or in such classic dishes as Lobster Newburg or Thermidor. The remains can be curried, scalloped or served up in the form of patties or omelettes, but there is really nothing to equal plainly dressed lobster, or Lobster Mayonnaise. The exotic appearance of a dressed lobster makes it the cold buffet dish *par excellence*.

MUSSELS

In season from September to March.

When buying these fish, see that they are alive – the shells should either be tightly closed up, or they should close when touched; any that do not pass this test should be rejected.

They are most frequently served as Moules Marinière, but mussel sauce and mussels baked with bacon and cheese, are among the many delicious ways in which these piquant but inexpensive small fish may be enjoyed. Canned or commercially bottled mussels may be used in many of these dishes.

OYSTERS

In season from September to April.

The renowned Colchester and Whitstable oysters are among the best, but those from the Helford river beds in Cornwall, though small, have an excellent flavour and are less expensive.

When oysters are bought, the shells should be firmly closed. Open them as near as possible to the time of eating.

First-quality oysters are served raw and cold, in their own shells. A suspicion of lemon juice to give an edge to the appetite, or a little Tabasco sauce, is all that the connoisseur will have added. But the less choice varieties, and even canned oysters, may be used very successfully in patties and many hot after-dinner savouries. Remember that oysters should be cooked only very lightly, otherwise they become tough.

PRAWNS
Obtainable all the year round, but at their best from February to October. Also sold canned, bottled and frozen.

Fresh prawns are usually sold ready boiled – in the shell or picked.

They can be served hot or cold in fish cocktails, salads and moulds, curried and in rice dishes. Prawns also make a good garnish for cold fish dishes.

SCALLOPS
In season from October to March and at their best in January and February. Frozen scallops are obtainable at any time of the year.

Scallops should be used very fresh; the roe should be a bright orange colour and the flesh white. They are delicate in flavour and are delicious fried with bacon, served in a cheese sauce, fricasseed, etc.

SCAMPI
Strictly speaking, these giant prawns are found only in the Mediterranean and Adriatic. In this country they are usually replaced by Dublin Bay prawns – see separate entry.

SHRIMPS
Fresh shrimps are available all the year round; they may also be bought frozen, potted in butter and canned. The fresh ones are usually sold ready boiled.

Shrimps may be served in the same ways as prawns, but being cheaper, they are also used in fish chowders, casseroles, sauces, savoury butters and so on, and they often serve as a garnish. Potted shrimps are served as a "starter" and can be used in sandwiches.

Fish Recipes for Invalids
Many of the simpler dishes given elsewhere in this book are of course suitable for invalids, but here, to save time and trouble, are gathered together some particularly useful recipes that can be used for a convalescent, an elderly person or someone on a "light" diet; a number of them (especially those where the bones and skin are removed) are very suitable for young children's meals.

To begin with, here is a reminder of the fish that can safely

be given to an invalid (unless the doctor specifies otherwise):
The white fish, such as plaice, sole, fresh haddock, cod, turbot, hake and halibut; trout; soft herring roes; a little smoked haddock.

As a general rule, avoid the following:
Fatty fish such as salmon, herrings (also bloaters and kippers), sardines, pilchards and eels; shellfish, especially lobster, crab, prawns and shrimps; fried fish.

The best methods of cooking are steaming, poaching, baking and grilling.

CREAMED HADDOCK

1 oz. butter	Salt and pepper
1 small onion, skinned and chopped (optional)	¾ lb. fresh haddock
	2 tomatoes, skinned and quartered
1 oz. flour	2 oz. mushrooms, sliced
½ pint milk	(optional)

Melt the butter in a frying-pan and gently fry the onion (if used) till tender. Stir in the flour and cook for 1–2 minutes. Remove from the heat and gradually stir in the milk. Cook until the sauce thickens and add the seasoning. Skin the fish and cut into 2 portions; add all these ingredients and the tomatoes to the sauce in the pan, cover and cook gently for 25–30 minutes. (2 servings.)

SCALLOPED HADDOCK WITH CELERY

4 oz. smoked haddock, cooked	Browned bread-crumbs
	1 oz. butter
½ pint white sauce (coating)	4 or 5 sticks of celery
	Salt
4 oz. cooked potatoes, diced	1 tbsp. chopped parsley

Mash the fish finely and add the sauce, beating well. Fold in the diced potatoes and turn the mixture into greased scallop shells. Sprinkle with bread-crumbs and dot with butter. Place in a moderate oven to heat through and brown the top.

Meanwhile wash the celery and cut into ½–1 inch lengths. Cook in a very little boiling salted water till tender, drain and add a small knob of butter and the parsley to the celery; shake the pan, to coat the celery evenly with fat and parsley, and use this celery to garnish the scallops. (1 serving.)

SMOKED HADDOCK SAVOURY

A small piece of smoked haddock	Salt and pepper
	1 hard-boiled egg
1 oz. butter	

Place the haddock in a greased tin or dish, pour a little water

173

round and cook in the oven for about 10 minutes. Remove the skin and bones and flake the fish. Heat in a small saucepan with the butter and seasoning and add the shredded or chopped white of the egg. Serve in a small dish, sprinkled with the sieved egg yolk. (1 serving.)

SMOKED HADDOCK WITH TOMATOES

1 teacupful cooked smoked haddock
½ oz. butter
1 tsp. finely chopped onion (optional)

1 tomato, skinned and sliced
Salt and pepper
2 tsps. cream

Flake the haddock and remove all bones and skin. Melt the butter in a small pan, add the onion and cook for 1–2 minutes, then add the tomato, fish and seasoning. Stir over the heat for a few minutes longer and add the cream just before serving. Serve with toasted brown bread. (1 serving.)

SCALLOPED SMOKED HADDOCK

½ lb. smoked haddock
½ pint milk
1 tbsp. chopped onion
1 blade of mace
1 oz. butter
1 oz. flour

Salt and pepper
Browned bread-crumbs
Creamed potato
Watercress or parsley to garnish

Wash the fish and simmer gently in the milk with the onion and mace. Remove the fish and flake it, then divide between 4 scallop shells. Melt the butter, add the flour, then gradually add the milk, stirring all the time. Bring to the boil, season well, and pour the sauce over the fish; sprinkle with bread-crumbs. Pipe the potato all round the edge of the shells, or just across the straight edge. Put under the grill to heat through and brown the potato. Garnish and serve.
Notes: If preferred, omit the onion and/or mace. See also the recipes in Chapter 6, p. 116.

CREAMED HAKE

1 hake steak
2 cloves (optional)
1 small onion (optional)
Parsley

Milk
A little cornflour
Lemon juice
1 egg, beaten

Put the hake into a pan with the cloves, onion, some parsley and a little milk and cook slowly until the fish is tender. Remove the skin and bones and put the fish into a hot dish. Strain the liquor, thicken with cornflour and add a squeeze of lemon juice and the beaten egg. Stir the sauce until it thickens, but don't let it boil. Pour it over the fish and decorate with sprigs of parsley.

174

CREAMED HERRING ROES

½ lb. soft herring roes
¼ pint milk or milk and
  water
Salt and pepper

¾ oz. butter
½ oz. flour
A little chopped
  parsley

Simmer the roes in the liquid, then drain (reserving the liquor), mash and season. Melt the butter, stir in the flour and cook for a few minutes. Gradually add the liquor, stirring, add the roes and parsley, and serve with fingers of bread and butter or on buttered toast. (2 servings.)

Alternatively, add the roes to ¼ pint white sauce, simmer for 10–15 minutes, and serve on toast, garnished with parsley.

STEAMED PLAICE

1 plaice
1 oz. butter
¾ oz. flour
½ pint fish stock
Pepper

Lemon juice
2 tsps. anchovy
  essence (optional)
Parsley and lemon
  to garnish

Clean and wash the plaice, lay it spotted side downwards in a steamer over boiling water, cover with greaseproof paper and steam for about 20 minutes, according to thickness. Make a sauce with the butter, flour and stock, and flavour with pepper, lemon juice and anchovy essence (if used). Serve the fish with the sauce, garnished with chopped parsley and cut lemon.

PLAICE OR SOLE STEAMED IN MILK

1 small filleted plaice or
  sole
Salt
1 teacupful milk

1 tbsp. bread-crumbs
A small piece of butter
A pinch of nutmeg (optional)
Parsley to garnish

Wipe the fillets, season lightly with salt and make into little rolls. Put them into a basin with the milk, bread-crumbs, butter and nutmeg, if used. Cover with a saucer or a piece of foil and steam for ½ hour. Serve very hot, garnished with parsley. (1–2 servings.)

PLAICE AU GRATIN

2 small fillets of plaice
1–2 tbsps. milk
1–2 tbsps. fresh white
  bread-crumbs
Finely chopped parsley

Pepper and salt
2 tsps. browned
  bread-crumbs
A little butter

Oven temperature: fairly hot (400°F., mark 6)

Dip the fillets in milk, then in a mixture of fine bread-crumbs, a

175

little parsley, pepper and salt; coat each piece rather thickly. Place the fish in a small greased ovenproof dish, pour the milk round, put a cover or a piece of greaseproof paper on the top and bake near the top of the oven for 10–15 minutes. Remove the cover, sprinkle some dry bread-crumbs over the fish, put a few small pieces of butter on the top and brown lightly. (1 serving.)

SOLE FOR AN INVALID

1 small sole, filleted	1 egg yolk
Salt and pepper	Sliced lemon and
4 tbsps. water	parsley to garnish

Sprinkle the sole with salt and pepper, place in a saucepan with the water and simmer until the fish is cooked – 20 minutes. Remove any scum, then lift out the fish on to a warm serving dish. Stir the beaten egg yolk into the liquor in the pan and whisk until it thickens. Strain it over the fish and garnish with sliced lemon and parsley. (1–2 servings.)

FILLETS OF SOLE ON TOAST

1 sole, filleted	½ oz. butter
A pinch of salt	A slice of toast
A little lemon juice	1 level tsp. cornflour
⅛ pint water	1 tsp. chopped parsley

Wipe the sole fillets lightly with a cloth, season with salt and a few drops of lemon juice and roll up skin side inside. Place these rolls in a small saucepan with the water and butter and cook slowly for 10–15 minutes, then lift out carefully. Arrange them on a piece of toast and keep warm while making the sauce. Blend the cornflour with a little cold water, add it to the liquid in the saucepan and stir until boiling; add the parsley, cook for 2–3 minutes longer and pour over and round the fish. The yolk of an egg may be added to the sauce at the last moment, to make it richer. (1–2 servings.)

STUFFED FILLETS OF SOLE

2 sole fillets	Salt
2 large cubes of bread	A little lemon juice or
A little milk	salad cream
A little butter	A little tomato paste
1 egg, hard-boiled	2–3 oz. cooked macaroni
½ pint white sauce	or diced cooked potato

Oven temperature: moderate (350°F., mark 4)

Prepare and skin the fillets, wrap each round a cube of bread and place in a greased ovenproof dish with a little milk. Dot with butter, cover with greaseproof paper and bake for 10–15 minutes in the centre of the oven until almost cooked. Remove the bread carefully and keep the fillets hot. Chop the egg

roughly, add to about half of the hot white sauce and season
with a little salt and the lemon juice or salad cream. Mix the
remaining sauce with a little tomato paste and heat up the
macaroni or potato in it. Dish up the macaroni and arrange
the fish on top. Fill the fillets with the egg mixture and re-heat
in the oven, covered with greaseproof paper, for a few minutes.
(1–2 servings.)

GRILLED SOLE
Cook in the usual way, but serve very simply, with creamed
potato or thin bread and butter. (1–2 servings.)

SOLE AU GRATIN
1 small sole, filleted	Fresh white
Salt and pepper	bread–crumbs
⅛ pint milk	Butter

Oven temperature: fairly hot (375°F., mark 5)
Lay the pieces of fish in a greased ovenproof dish, season well
and pour the milk round. Sprinkle with bread-crumbs, dot
with pieces of butter and bake in the centre of the oven for
about 20 minutes. (1–2 servings.)

PARMESAN SOLE
Place a small filleted sole in a well-greased ovenproof dish,
sprinkle with seasoning and put a little butter on the top.
Cook under the grill and when nearly ready, sprinkle with
grated Parmesan cheese, brown and serve at once. (1–2 servings.)

STEWED SMELTS
Behead and clean 2–3 smelts, place in an ovenproof dish with a
little chicken stock (or some white wine, if allowed). Cover
the dish and cook in a moderate oven (350°F., mark 4) until
tender. Serve in the dish, garnished with sliced lemon. (1 serving.)

STEAMED FISH
This is one of the simplest methods of cooking fish for an
invalid and all the flavour and goodness are retained. Take a
small filleted sole, whiting, haddock, or a fish cutlet, remove
all skin and bone and wipe lightly with a damp cloth. Season
(omitting pepper if this is not allowed) and sprinkle with
lemon juice; then either roll up the fillets or cut them in
several pieces. Place on a buttered plate, cover with greased
paper and another plate or a saucepan lid and put over a pan
of fast-boiling water; cook until the fish loses its transparent
appearance and looks white and creamy (keep the water boiling

177

all the time) – 15–20 minutes. Make a sauce, using the fish liquid and some milk, coat the fish with it and garnish with parsley and lemon. Serve with creamed potatoes and carrot matches or creamed spinach, etc., or with dry toast. (1 serving.)

BAKED FILLETS
Oven temperature: hot (425°F., mark 7)
Arrange 2 pieces of filleted white fish in an ovenproof dish and brush with melted butter. Pipe some mashed potato round the edge and arrange 1–2 sliced tomatoes on the fish. Brush the potato with beaten egg and bake towards the top of the oven for 15–20 minutes. Garnish with lemon or parsley. (1–2 servings.)

CREAMED FISH AND TOMATOES

½ lb. white fish	A little butter
2 tomatoes	½ pint white sauce (scant
Salt	measure)
Pepper (optional)	Fresh white bread-crumbs

Cook the fish and divide it into large flakes. Slice the tomatoes thinly, lay them on an ovenproof dish and place under the grill to cook. Lay the fish over the tomatoes, season and coat with a well-flavoured sauce made from the fish liquor and milk. Sprinkle with bread-crumbs and a few shavings of butter, then brown under the grill. (1–2 servings.)

FRICASSEE OF WHITE FISH

½ lb. any white fish, filleted	A little white sauce
	1 egg, hard-boiled
Salt and pepper	Lemon and parsley to
Lemon juice	garnish

Season the fish and sprinkle with lemon juice. If the fillets are thick, cut them into convenient portions; thin fillets may be rolled neatly. Make a well-seasoned white sauce, then add the fish to the pan. Cover and cook very gently for about 15–20 minutes, until the fish is cooked but unbroken; remove it carefully on to a hot dish. Add the chopped white of egg and half the yolk to the sauce, reduce to a coating consistency again if the fish juices have thinned it down, and pour over the fish. Sieve the rest of the egg yolk and use this as a garnish, together with some lemon and parsley. (2 servings.)

SCALLOPED FISH

4 oz. cooked fish	Fresh white bread-crumbs
Salt and pepper	Butter
A little white sauce	Parsley to garnish

Flake the fish and lay it in a greased scallop shell or small ovenproof dish. Season, cover with the white sauce, sprinkle with bread-crumbs and dot with small pieces of butter. Brown under the grill or in a hot oven (425°F., mark 7). Garnish with parsley. (1 serving.)

FISH AND EGG PIE

¼ lb. white fish, cooked	Salt
1 oz. butter	A little grated cheese
1 level tbsp. flour	1 egg, lightly beaten
¼ pint milk or fish stock	Creamy mashed potatoes

Lay the fish in an ovenproof dish. Melt the butter, stir in the flour, gradually add the liquid and cook for 2–3 minutes, stirring. Add the salt and cheese. Stir in the egg, beat well and pour over the fish. Cover with potato and rough up with a fork. Put into the centre of the oven to heat through and brown the top – about ½ hour. (2 servings.)

FISH CUSTARD

4 oz. white fish, cooked	1 egg
¼ pint milk	Salt and pepper

Oven temperature: warm (325°F., mark 3)

Flake the fish. Make an egg custard, seasoning it with salt and pepper. Lay the fish in a greased pie dish, pour the custard mixture over and bake in the centre of the oven for 45 minutes. (1 serving.)

Here is another version, made with sole and steamed:
Skin 2 fillets of sole and roll them up with the skinned side inside, starting from the tail. Add a beaten egg to ¼ pint milk and a little salt and pepper. Pour this custard mixture into a small greased basin and put the fillets in it. Cover with grease-proof paper, stand the basin in a pan of simmering water and steam for about 20 minutes. (1–2 servings.)

HOT FISH CREAMS

½ oz. butter	Salt and pepper
½ oz. fresh white bread-crumbs	2–3 tbsps. cream
2–3 tbsps. milk	1 egg, separated
4 oz. filleted fish, skinned	Sauce, if desired

Melt the butter in a pan, add the crumbs and milk, cook till thick, add the finely shredded fish and mix. Season to taste and add the cream and the egg yolk. Beat up the egg white stiffly and fold it into the mixture. Turn this into 2 small greased moulds or a basin, cover with greased paper and steam gently for 30–40 minutes. When firm, leave for a minute or two, then turn out on to a hot dish. Serve with the sauce.

179

INDIVIDUAL FISH PUDDINGS

½ lb. cod fillet
1–2 tbsps. fresh white
   bread-crumbs
1 tbsp. melted butter

1 tsp. chopped parsley
1 egg yolk
2 tbsps. milk
Parsley sauce

Skin the fish, then shred it. Mix it with the dry ingredients, add the butter, egg yolk and milk and put into 4 small well-greased moulds. Cover with greased paper and steam for 1 hour. Turn out and serve very hot, with parsley sauce.

SIMPLE FISH SOUFFLÉ

¼ pint white coating sauce
3 oz. fish, cooked

Salt and pepper
1 egg, separated

Oven temperature: moderate (350°F., mark 4)

Mix the sauce, flaked fish and seasonings together, stir in the egg yolk and fold in the stiffly beaten white. Place in a small greased soufflé dish and cook in the centre of the oven for 25 minutes. (1–2 servings.)

FISH OMELETTE

Whisk 2 eggs lightly, season with salt and pepper and add 1 tbsp. water. Place the frying pan over a gentle heat and when it is hot add a knob of butter to grease it lightly. Pour the beaten eggs into the hot fat. Stir gently with the back of the prongs of a fork, drawing the mixture from the sides to the centre as it sets and letting the liquid egg from the centre run to the sides. When the egg has set, stop stirring and cook for another minute until it is golden underneath. Place 3 oz. flaked cooked fish in the centre of the omelette. Tilt the pan away from you slightly and use a palette knife to fold over a third of the omelette to the centre, then fold over the opposite third. Turn the omelette out on to the warmed plate, with the folded sides underneath, and serve at once. Don't overcook or the omelette will be tough. (1 serving.)

Alternatively, mix the fish with the eggs before cooking the omelette.

SOUFFLÉ FISH OMELETTE

2 eggs, separated
Salt and pepper to taste
2 tbsps. water

½ oz. butter
3 oz. flaked cooked fish
to fill (hot)

Whisk the egg yolks until creamy. Add the seasoning and the water and beat again. Whisk the egg whites as stiffly as possible. At this point place the frying pan containing the butter over a low heat and let the butter melt without browning. Turn the egg whites into the yolk mixture and fold in carefully, using a spoon, but don't overmix. Grease the sides of

180

the pan with the butter by tilting it in all directions and then pour in the egg mixture. Cook over a moderate heat until the omelette is golden-brown on the underside. Now place the pan under the grill or in a moderate oven (350°F., mark 4) until the omelette is browned on the top. Remove at once when it is ready, as over-cooking tends to make it tough. Run a spatula gently round the edge and underneath the omelette to loosen it, make a mark across the middle at right angles to the pan handle, add the fish filling and double the omelette over. Turn it gently on to a hot plate and serve at once. (1 serving.)

FISH CREAM MOULD

¾ lb. cooked and flaked
  white fish
½ pint white sauce
1 oz. gelatine
¼ pint fish stock

Salt and pepper
¼ pint evaporated milk
1 egg white
Cress to garnish

Mix the fish with the sauce. Dissolve the gelatine in the warm fish stock, add to the fish mixture and season well. Whip the evaporated milk until it is light and frothy and fold it into the fish. Lastly, fold in the stiffly beaten egg white, and pour the mixture into a wetted mould, leave to set and serve cold garnished with cress. (2–3 servings.)

FISH IN RICE BORDER

3 oz. rice (weight before
  cooking)
½ lb. fish (fresh haddock,
  cod, plaice, sole), skinned
A little milk
Salt
1 bay leaf

¼ pint sauce made with
  fish stock and milk
1 tsp. tomato paste
½–1 oz. melted butter
2 tomatoes, skinned, de-seeded
  and sliced

Cook the rice in boiling salted water. Poach the fish in a little milk, adding some salt and a small bay leaf, then strain off the liquor and flake the fish. Make a good white sauce, then add the tomato paste and mix this sauce with the flaked fish. Strain the rice, add the butter and the tomatoes and arrange as a border in a small au gratin dish. Fill the centre with fish and serve very hot. (2 servings.)

TIMBALE OF FISH AND RICE

4 oz. rice (weight before
  cooking)
½ pint fish stock
½ lb. fish, cooked
1 oz. butter

Salt and pepper
2 eggs, beaten
1 tbsp. finely chopped parsley
Tomato or anchovy sauce
  (see pp. 150, 140)

Put the washed rice into a saucepan with the fish stock and allow it to cook slowly, adding a little extra liquid if necessary. When the rice is cooked add the flaked cooked fish, butter, salt and pepper, eggs and the parsley. Put the mixture into a plain greased mould, cover it closely and steam for about 1 hour, or until it is firm. Turn the timbale out and serve with a well-flavoured tomato or anchovy sauce. (2–3 servings.)

FISH AND TOMATO CASSEROLE

1 oz. butter	$\frac{1}{4}$ pint stock or water
1 onion, sliced (optional)	$\frac{1}{4}$ lb. tomatoes (or tomato
$\frac{1}{2}$ lb. white fish	pulp)
Salt and pepper	1 tbsp. chopped parsley

Oven temperature: moderate (350°F., mark 4)
Heat the butter in a flameproof dish and sauté the onion until slightly browned. Wipe the fish, cut into neat portions and add, with the seasoning and liquid, to the casserole. Cover and cook gently in the centre of the oven for about 20 minutes. Add the tomatoes (sliced if fresh) and cook for a further 10 minutes, until the fish and vegetables are all cooked. Sprinkle the parsley over the surface and serve hot. (2 servings.)

FISH QUENELLES

$\frac{1}{2}$ lb. cod or any similar	$\frac{1}{8}$ pint milk
white fish	1 egg, beaten
1 oz. butter	1 tbsp. cream
3 level tbsps. flour	Salt and pepper

Poach the fish and mash it thoroughly or put it in an electric blender. Melt the butter, stir in the flour and cook for 2–3 minutes; remove the pan from the heat and gradually stir in the milk. Return the pan to the heat and stir until the sauce thickens. Remove from the heat and stir in the fish, egg, cream and a generous amount of salt and pepper. Grease a large frying-pan, three-quarters fill it with water and heat to simmering point. Using 2 wetted tablespoons, make the fish mixture into egg-shaped or oval pieces, put into the pan and simmer for about 10 minutes, basting well, until the quenelles are swollen and just set. Remove them from the pan with a slotted spoon and serve coated with a sauce. (2 servings.)

Index

190